The American History Series

SERIES EDITORS
John Hope Franklin, *Duke University*
A. S. Eisenstadt, *Brooklyn College*

Brooks D. Simpson
ARIZONA STATE UNIVERSITY

America's Civil War

HARLAN DAVIDSON, INC.
WHEELING, ILLINOIS 60090-6000

Visit us on the World Wide Web at www.harlandavidson.com.

Library of Congress Cataloging-in-Publication Data

Simpson, Brooks D.
　　America's Civil War / Brooks D. Simpson
　　　p.　cm.—(The American history series)
　　Includes bibliographical references and index.
　　ISBN 0-88295-929-8
　　1. United States—History—Civil War, 1861–1865. I. Title. II. Series :
(American history series—Wheeling, Ill.)
E468.S57　　　　1996
973.7–dc20
　　　　　　　　　　　　　　　　　　　　　95-26687
　　　　　　　　　　　　　　　　　　　　　CIP

Cover: Detail of painting by Paul Phillipateaux. General Grant looking over
the battlefield at Fort Donelson, ca. 1863. *Courtesy of the Chicago Historical
Society.*

Manufactured in the United States of America
04 03 02 3 4 5 VP

For Jean, Rebecca, and Emily

FOREWORD

Every generation writes its own history for the reason that it sees the past in the foreshortened perspective of its own experience. This has surely been true of the writing of American history. The practical aim of our historiography is to give us a more informed sense of where we are going by helping us understand the road we took in getting where we are. As the nature and dimensions of American life are changing, so too are the themes of our historical writing. Today's scholars are hard at work reconsidering every major aspect of the nation's past: its politics, diplomacy, economy, society, recreation, mores and values, as well as status, ethnic, race, sexual, and family relations. The lists of series titles that appear at the back of this book will show at once that our historians are ever broadening the range of their studies.

The aim of this series is to offer our readers a survey of what today's historians are saying about the central themes and aspects of the American past. To do this, we have invited to write for the series only scholars who have made notable contributions to the respective fields in which they are working. Drawing on primary and secondary materials, each volume presents a factual and narrative account of its particular subject, one that affords readers a basis for perceiving its larger dimensions and importance. Conscious that readers respond to the closeness and immediacy of a subject, each of our authors seeks to restore the past as an actual present, to revive it as a living reality. The individuals and groups who figure in the pages of our books appear as real people who once were looking for survival and fulfillment. Aware that historical subjects are often matters of controversy, our authors present their own findings and conclusions. Each volume closes with an extensive critical essay on the writings of the major authorities on its particular theme.

The books in this series are designed for use in both basic and advanced courses in American history, on the undergraduate and graduate levels. Such a series has a particular value these days, when the format of American history courses is being altered to accommodate a greater diversity of reading materials. The series offers a number of distinct advantages. It extends the dimensions of regular course work. Going well beyond the confines of the textbook, it makes clear that the study of our past is, more than the student might otherwise understand, at once complex, profound, and absorbing. It presents that past as a subject of continuing interest and fresh investigation. The work of experts in their respective fields, the series, moreover, puts at the disposal of the reader the rich findings of historical inquiry. It invites the reader to join, in major fields of research, those who are pondering anew the central themes and aspects of our past. And it reminds the reader that in each successive generation of the ever-changing American adventure, men and women and children were attempting, as we are now, to live their lives and to make their way.

John Hope Franklin
A. S. Eisenstadt

CONTENTS

PREFACE AND ACKNOWLEDGMENTS

The Civil War is the central event of American history. It continues to fascinate Americans and engage their passions. Over the last fifteen years, it has also enjoyed something of a renaissance in scholarly circles. Historians have challenged long-accepted notions about the military history of the war, offering reassessments of strategy, tactics, military leadership, and campaigns and battles—traditional concerns for students of war. At the same time, other scholars, influenced by recent interpretive trends in historical studies, have brought new perspectives to bear on the war. The dimensions of race, gender, and class are now part of the study of the Civil War, and this has added much to our understanding of home front, battlefront, and the interplay between them. Indeed, it may not be too much to claim that as of this writing, the Civil War is one of the most exciting areas of study for American historians, rich with possibilities for future research.

To cover these myriad themes in the compass of a concise volume has proven a challenge. To write is to choose: inevitably one must emphasize some subjects at the expense of others. Recent work on the social history of the war and its impact has broadened our understanding of the conflict, but it should not displace political and military themes, which remain essential to a complete understanding of the war. This volume highlights the interplay of war and politics to suggest how the Union and Confederacy waged war, and it reaffirms the pivotal role of military operations in shaping the contours and outcome of the conflict. Too often military history is relegated to the status of "popular history" (as opposed to "scholarship," which in some cases means monographs written by historians for historians—and no one else). We would do well to remember that the outcome of Civil War battles and campaigns shaped American history in decisive fashion, and it was the war itself that created the circumstances in which the greatest revolutionary act in American history— emancipation—took place.

Nevertheless, this book is not a traditional military history of the war. The topics of slavery and emancipation and the war aims of the rival governments are integral to a complete comprehension of the American Civil War, but so is a fuller treatment of the interplay of the home front and the battlefield in shaping the course of events—a major contribution of the new scholarship—and of how the experience of war changed the lives of Americans, white and black, male and female, across the land. The findings of recent scholarship enrich this account in many ways: in an extended examination of the war, many themes of the new research would receive far more elaborate treatment.

To thank all the people who have in various ways contributed to the writing of this study might result in doubling the number of pages in the volume. Nevertheless, several individuals should be singled out for the quality and quantity of their encouragement. My parents encouraged and cultivated my interest in the American Civil War from an early age in many ways. Robert Brugger, Michael Holt, Richard Sewell, Allan Bogue, and James Mohr had much to do with transforming my advocation into a vocation; in turn, my students at the University of Wisconsin–Madison, Wofford College, and Arizona State University have pushed me to ponder how best to share with others my evolving understanding of the war. So, in a somewhat different fashion, have members of various USENET discussion groups.

In many ways the person most responsible for this book is Andrew Davidson: it has been a real pleasure to work with him on this project from inception through copyediting and publication. Along with Maureen Hewitt, Andrew brought my name to the attention of John Hope Franklin and A. S. Eisenstadt for possible inclusion as a contributor to the American History Series; in turn they have guided me in turning a proposal into a book, as have James McPherson and Michael Perman, who read the manuscript at the series editors' request. Steven Woodworth and Mark Grimsley took time off from their own labors to do a friend a favor by looking over what I had written.

I owe the most, however, to three women who have been giving in so many ways that I was able to see this project through—my wife Jean and my daughters Rebecca and Emily. That all three share to some degree my interest in the Civil War has been a welcome bonus—and certainly unexpected in the cases of Rebecca, who turned four on the 135th anniversary of the secession of South Carolina, and Emily, whose second birthday marks the 131th anniversary of the fall of Petersburg. As a Yankee sympathizer, I am less happy to report that my wife was born on the centennial of the battle of Fredericksburg, but one can ask for only so much. I dedicate this book to them.

INTRODUCTION

On Understanding the Civil War

Although the American Civil War is the central event in the history of the United States, Americans (including historians) do not always agree on the nature of that event. This is immediately evident when one looks at the various ways the conflict is described, from the "War of the Rebellion" to the "Slaveholders' Rebellion" to the "War Between the States" to the "War of Yankee Aggression." Each of these labels reflects a point of view and a partial understanding of the conflict, but none truly defines it—in this book I have settled upon the "Civil War" simply as a matter of convention. Of equal interest are the efforts of students of that conflict to categorize it. While such discussions have yielded valuable insights about the conduct and significance of the war, the resulting classifications suffer their own shortcomings. Perhaps one can start to understand what the Civil War *was* by first suggesting what it *was not*.

Historians have long debated whether what happened during the Civil War warrants calling it "the Second American Revolution." These discussions frequently become entangled in disputes over what constitutes a "revolutionary" change. Nevertheless, one can point to two major transformations due to the war. The end of slavery and the emancipation of over four million people promised radical changes in politics, economics, and society both in the South and in the nation; this was certainly sudden and significant enough to deserve the label "revolutionary." Somewhat less dramatic but with important long-range consequences were the remaking of American institutions and the reshaping of federal policy in several fields, changes rendered possible by the absence during the conflict of Southern delegations in Congress. Though American politics was once dominated in crucial respects by white Southerners, the war offered Republicans the opportunity to establish their new party as a major and lasting force in American politics, transcending as they did the party's antislavery, anti-Democratic, and anti-Southern origins. In both instances Reconstruction would mark the extent and limits of these transformations, but they would have been difficult if not impossible without the war.

In other ways, the war had an impact upon American society—in many cases a deep and lasting one—although the nature and extent of that impact would not be completely evident until later. The brute fact of death, injury, and destruction marked the lives of those who survived the war, leaving a gash in many souls that would never completely heal. Some veterans would agree with Oliver Wendell Holmes, Jr., who later reflected, "Through our great good fortune, in our youth our hearts were touched with fire"; others were simply seared by the experience. The conflict brought forth new leaders—of the six men elected president between 1868 and 1900, five served in the Union army—and offered others opportunities to gain experience that would be of great value to them in the postwar world. The interrelationship of the war and industrialization makes it difficult to attribute direct responsibility for certain changes to either phenomenon, and in any case the two would ever more be associated to some extent in the minds of most Americans. While it is difficult to deny that the Civil War shaped the course of American history, the changes it wrought were not always readily apparent or revolutionary. In many cases the continuities in pre– and post–Civil War American society were as striking as the differences. This should not surprise us. After all, the people who went to war in 1861 on both sides fought to preserve their world, not to change it. There were limits to the scope, extent, and duration of the war's influence on Americans.

Another way of approaching the Civil War is to place it in the context of the other wars of national independence and unification of the mid to late nineteenth century. Bracketed by the wars of Italian unification and the wars leading to the formation of the German empire, the American Civil War was in a sense a war of national unification, in that a new nation-state emerged from it. However, unlike Italy and Germany, the United States had existed as a political entity prior to its civil war. Confederates argued that they were waging a war of national independence akin to the American Revolution—although they stressed the conservative nature of that struggle. Scholars today who argue that the strength of Confederate nationalism proved insufficient to the task at hand inevitably find themselves trapped in a circular argument, for the single most important variable in making that assessment is a foregone conclusion. Had the Confederacy succeeded in securing its independence, we probably would not hear of any lack of Confederate nationalism—although the two are analytically distinct.

If it seems rather unremarkable to term the Civil War as a struggle for independence from the Confederate perspective, it is a bit more difficult to classify it as a war of national unification from the Union point of view. It is more accurate to suggest that what began as a war of national preservation was transformed during the conflict into something approaching a second American founding, or, as Lincoln put it, "a new birth of freedom." One need not accept in its entirety the argument, presented by Garry Wills in *Lincoln at Gettysburg* (1992), that Lincoln used his remarks at Gettysburg to remake America to see that those remarks did describe the logical result of what was happening and thus gave voice to the intellectual revolution wrought by the war. Essential to that refounding of the nation was the end of slavery. It would be left to Ulysses S. Grant to explain that fact to one of the great masters of national unification, Otto von Bismarck. When Bismarck commented that Grant "had to save the Union just as we had to save Germany," Grant replied that there was more to it than that—one had to destroy slavery in order to ensure a lasting peace, for in the persistence of slavery were "the germs of new rebellion." If principles of federalism remained intact, the triumph of the Union nevertheless put an end to the viability of secession, silencing one of the major disruptive themes in American political discourse. As so much in the American polity depends on the definition of terms and the meaning of words such as "freedom," "equality," and "liberty," this was no small feat.

Our understanding of the Civil War as a military conflict is also evolving. Certainly some military historians have gone too far in declaring the struggle the first modern war, for the term "modern" is a relative one. Many of the innovations used during the conflict actually appeared first in the Crimean War. And certainly the Franco-Prussian War and other late nineteenth-century conflicts proved better tests of the impact of industrial technology and railroads upon warfare. It would perhaps be better to view the American Civil War as one of several conflicts in the industrializing world during the middle third of the nineteenth century that anticipated future military developments, one case in a period of transition in the history of warfare. For if there is much about the conduct and technology of the Civil War that seems modern, there is also a great deal that beckons back to the age of Napoleon and earlier. In likening George McClellan to Napoleon and Robert E. Lee to George Washington, Americans of the period revealed the contexts in which they viewed the conflict, though Grant and William T. Sherman did point the way to new conceptions of leadership and war. Grant best understood the place of the conflict in the evolution of warfare: "War is progressive, because all the instruments and elements of war are progressive."

If the status of the American Civil War as a modern war must be qualified, even more suspect is the statement that it was a total war. In recent years historians have cast much doubt upon this once-accepted notion, although it must be said that these new scholars rest much of their case upon extreme characterizations of "total war" as defined by twentieth-century military theorists. Of far more importance is to explain why both sides were willing to place limits on the war they sought to wage. These decisions are most easily understood if one recalls why each side went to war in the first place.

At the heart of the Confederate experiment in nationhood was a determination to protect a political, economic, and social order grounded in the institution of slavery. The centrality of slavery to the Southern way of life shaped the war waged to preserve it, as did, to a lesser extent, the concept of states rights, itself a key means used to protect the peculiar institution in the years leading to secession. To wage a war that did not expressly serve these ends would (and did) result in the rapid erosion of popular support for the conflict; few shared Jefferson Davis's willingness (once defeat was imminent) to transform the war into a guerrilla conflict, arguing that such a war would only complete the destruction of the rationale for Confederate independence.

The vast majority of white Northerners went to war in 1861 to preserve the United States and the experiment in representative political institutions it represented. For Northerners the goal of reunion remained the primary goal of the war effort: what changed, sometimes drastically, were the means they were willing to employ to achieve that end. Lincoln and others justified emancipation as a means to the end of reunion, and only a few of the most radical abolitionists would have accepted Confederate independence in exchange for the end of slavery. Traditional impressions of the unidirectional escalation of the Union war effort from a limited conflict fought with an eye to conciliating recalcitrant rebels to a total war bent upon complete conquest blur and sometimes erode under closer examination, for throughout the struggle Union leaders used both olive branch and sword to erode the ability and the will of Confederates to continue their struggle for independence—as a glance at Lincoln's Second In-augural Address and the terms Grant offered Lee at Appomattox Court House suggest.

We might do better to forego efforts to categorize or define the American Civil War in favor of gaining a better understanding of the conflict on its own terms. The writings of the Prussian military theorist Karl von Clausewitz (1780–1831) prove instructive in this endeavor. In *On War* (1832), Clausewitz offered some observations on war that are as brilliant and insightful as they are deceptively simple. Among the most famous of these is the statement that war is an act of policy, a continuation of politics by other means, and has to be understood and assessed as such. The political dimensions of warfare form a central theme of the American experience during the Civil War, as does the interplay between means and ends in waging war.

Of equal importance is the interrelationship between battle-front and home front, civil and military leadership, and public support and the course of the conflict. Clausewitz specified that the destruction of the enemy's will as well as his ability to resist was essential to victory, and that the former was far easier to effect than the latter. Certainly how to go about building and maintaining support at home for the war while eroding the enemy's will to keep fighting remained a fundamental challenge for both sides engaged in what Lincoln called "a people's contest." Allied to this is Clausewitz's notion that how a society wages war reflects that society's values and structure.

Therefore, a keener understanding of military history rescues it from narrow presumptions that it is a field confined merely to a recounting of battles, leaders, and campaigns. When joined to an examination of how the experience of war in turn shapes society, it can tell us much about the all-encompassing nature of such a struggle as America's civil war. By exploring the course of military operations in light of this broader context, one can clearly see why battles and campaigns matter.

CHAPTER ONE

Secession
and the First Shot

On a clear, cool Tuesday morning in November 1860, lawyer George Templeton Strong left his home on New York's Twenty-first Street intending to vote in the day's presidential election. Slowed in his purpose by the block-long line in front of the polls, he waited until the afternoon to cast his ballot. The large turn-out was somewhat surprising, for most voters were already fairly sure of the result. The outcome of state contests in Indiana and Pennsylvania in October had forecasted the election of Republican Abraham Lincoln of Illinois as the nation's next chief executive. Nevertheless, Strong believed that the day would prove a memorable one: "We do not know yet for what. Perhaps for the disintegration of the country, perhaps for another proof that the North is timid and mercenary, perhaps for demonstration that Southern bluster is worthless."

That night of November 6 found most Americans waiting for election returns, although they were far more anxious about what might happen after the winner was declared. Before long telegraph-borne messages confirmed Lincoln's triumph—the first for a Republican presidential nominee. Running against three candidates, he had secured 180 electoral votes and just under 40 percent of the popular vote. But these statistics masked the true message of the results, for Lincoln won all but three of the electoral votes of states in which slavery was extinct (or virtually so, in the case of New Jersey), while his opposition overwhelmed him in the fifteen slave states. Much was made of the fact that the Democratic party itself, unable to agree upon a single candidate, had divided along sectional lines: Senator Stephen A. Douglas of Illinois, a long-time foe of Lincoln, represented primarily the interests of Northern Democrats, while Vice President John C. Breckinridge of Kentucky ran on behalf of Southerners who wanted increased federal protection for slavery. Another coalition of conservatives, mostly former Whigs, styled itself the Constitutional Union party and put forward Tennessee's John Bell as their candidate to preserve the Constitution and the Union, presumably through a negotiated compromise to settle sectional disputes. Although the divided opposition may have eased Lincoln's path to the White House, it had not delivered him there, for even against a united opposition he would have polled enough votes in Northern states to secure a majority of the electoral vote.

Lincoln's victory was a triumph for the Republican North alone. It signified the extent of sectional division in the nation, and it promised to exacerbate that division still more. Although the Republican platform of 1860 included planks calling for a government-supported and national economic development—in the form of protective tariffs, a western homestead program, river and harbor improvements, and the completion of a transcontinental railroad—its opposition to the expansion of slavery into federal territory made it a threat to continued national unity. For years American politicians had struggled with slavery and its future. Several times politicians had crafted compromises in an effort to resolve the debate, only to discover that such arrangements merely postponed conflict. Southern whites, in a spirited defense of their "peculiar institution," increasingly sought not only guaranteed access for slaveholders to new territory but also special federal legislation protecting slavery. That such safeguards infringed on the civil rights of free Northerners (white and black), negated previous agreements, and increasingly challenged the ability of free labor to expand was of little concern to them. By 1860, enough Northern whites had grown unhappy enough with the behavior of this so-called "slave power" to support a candidate who would stand firm against the South, evidence that politics had indeed become polarized on sectional lines over the issue of slavery and its place in America's future.

Lincoln's election capped the emergence of the Republican party as a power in national politics. In 1856, John C. Frémont, the first Republican presidential candidate, had lost to Democrat James Buchanan in a three-way race with Know-Nothing nominee Millard Fillmore. In the next four years, the Republican party expanded from its antislavery base in the upper North to carry the critical swing states of Illinois, Indiana, and Pennsylvania, thus securing an electoral victory for Lincoln. Yet this first victory might well have proven the new party's last. For many Southern whites, most of whom had cast their ballots for Breckinridge, had made it clear that they were prepared to break away from the Union should the Republican candidate triumph. "Equality and safety in the Union are at an end," Georgia's Howell Cobb, a prominent political leader, declared after the election. "The Union formed by our fathers was one of equality, justice, and fraternity. On the 4th of March it will be supplanted by a union of sectionalism and hatred." Others agreed. "The tea has been thrown overboard," proclaimed the Charleston (South Carolina) *Mercury*. "The revolution of 1860 has been initiated."

In 1820 Thomas Jefferson spoke of the debate over slavery as "a firebell in the night," sounding the death knell of the Union. Now, as news of Lincoln's election spread throughout the nation, bells rang long into the night. Before long their peals would give way to the roar of cannon and rifle fire.

Secession

It did not take the Deep South long to react to Lincoln's election. Indeed, the citizens of South Carolina, whose precipitate political behavior in the past had justified the snide comment that their state was too small to be an independent republic and too large to be an insane asylum, had anticipated it. Governor William H. Gist had called the state legislature into session just prior to election day for the express purpose of arranging for the election of delegates to a convention empowered to dissolve the state's ties to the Union. The state's secessionists had waited a long time for this moment. In fact, they had helped it along, working with like-minded Deep South Democrats to break up the Democratic party by walking out of the party's presidential convention in Charleston the previous April. Lincoln's election provided the best opportunity to secure what they had so long desired. On December 20, 1860, they triumphed at last when the special convention unanimously passed an ordinance of secession. The Palmetto State did not stand alone for long. By February 1861, six other states—Texas, Florida, Alabama, Mississippi, Georgia, and Louisiana—had also seceded.

The concept of secession was an attempt to find constitutional legitimacy for separation from the United States. Grounded upon the notion that sovereign states voluntarily had joined together to establish a federal government of limited and specified powers, the logic of secession posited that any of the contracting parties had always retained the right to withdraw from said contract when violations of it had rendered it void—and the states would determine what constituted a violation. This argument drew upon the theory of nullification as advanced by James Madison and Thomas Jefferson in the Virginia and Kentucky Resolutions and elaborated upon by South Carolina's own John C. Calhoun. However, Jefferson, Madison, and (for a good part of his political career) Calhoun opposed secession: in their minds nullification was simply an extension of the notion of checks and balances applied to federalism—that is, the relationship between the central government and state governments—as well as a challenge to the assertion that the Supreme Court was the ultimate arbiter of constitutionality. Secession, however, extended the logic of nullification, for it followed that if a state and the central government continued to disagree over the constitutionality of a specific measure or act, the will of one would prevail, and devotees of state sovereignty believed that in such cases the state's judgment was superior to the nation's.

Needless to say, there was great debate over whether a right to secede did indeed exist. It was not to be found in the Constitution: at best it was extrapolated from contractual theories of government. It differed significantly from a right of revolution because secessionists denied the right of the central government to coerce seceding members to remain in the union. However, the failure of secessionists to win a majority of Americans to their point of view meant that any acquiescence to secession would be the result of policy, not constitutional principle. Nor did all white Southerners embrace the theory. "Secession is nothing but revolution," argued Colonel Robert E. Lee, United States Army, in January 1861. "The framers of our Constitution never exhausted so much labor, wisdom and forbearance in its formation, and surrounded it with so many guards and securities, if it was intended to be broken by every member of the Confederacy at will." For Lee, who sympathized with many of the grievances of secessionists, the Constitution served a larger purpose—the Union. In light of the present crisis, he remarked that "a Union that can only be maintained by swords and bayonets, and in which strife and civil war are to take the place of brotherly love and kindness, has no charm for me."

If the right of secession was the proposed means of separation, however, it did not explain the need for that separation. Why the Southern states seceded remains a point of heated contention, especially among those Americans who still take a passionate pride in the Confederate cause. Although some cite the protection of the principle of states rights, it is more accurate to say that Southern whites used the principle of states rights to protect *Southern* interests. Southern politicians had spoken forcibly in favor of federal power when it came to issues such as the protection of slavery in the territories or the recapture of fugitive slaves. They had not decried the strong-arm of federal authority when the Supreme Court handed down decisions protecting the rights of slaveholders, as in *Dred Scott* v. *Sandford*

(1857). Indeed, they had opposed Northern efforts to use states rights as a means to protect blacks accused of being fugitive slaves through the passage of personal liberty laws; several Georgia secessionists even highlighted alleged Northern violations of the Fugitive Slave Law to justify secession. States rights was a means to an end, not an end in itself. That the end usually involved slavery was worth noting.

Perhaps secessionists were closer to the truth when they justified secession on the grounds of protecting a particular way of life. But exactly what about the Southern way of life was under attack? What did Lincoln's election supposedly threaten? Although there was talk that contemplated import tariffs would have an adverse impact on the Southern economy, such legislation would be difficult to pass, and in any case tariff policy by itself was not worth the breakup of the Union. Much more telling were characterizations of Lincoln and his supporters as Black Republicans and abolitionists who would threaten slavery at every turn. Time and again spokesmen for secession pointed to slavery as the part of the Southern way of life that was now under attack. In so doing, they declared the peculiar institution as essential to their society—making its past, present, and future the central point of contention.

A majority of Deep South whites were convinced that slavery was no longer safe in the Union; to them, secession was an act of self-defense, not of defiance. Most agreed that Lincoln and the Republicans were antislavery if not abolitionist, even if they disagreed on whether his mere election constituted a sufficient threat to their way of life. Lincoln's election, charged Governor Joseph Brown of Georgia, meant "the total abolition of slavery, and the utter ruin of the South, in less than twenty-five years." The Charleston *Mercury* argued that emancipation would result in "the loss of liberty, property, home, country—everything that makes life worth having."

Large numbers of white nonslaveholders in the South also supported secession. Some did so because they hoped to become slaveholders in the future; others clung to a need to validate white supremacy, seeing the legal enslavement of blacks as a confirmation of their own racial superiority. Governor Brown emphasized this theme, telling his fellow Georgians that "the poor, honest laborers of Georgia, can never consent to see slavery abolished, and submit to all the taxation, vassalage, low wages and downright degradation, which must follow. They will never take the negro's place; God forbid." In so arguing, Brown asserted that all white Georgians, "poor and rich, have a common interest, a common destiny."

Southern whites were somewhat more divided over exactly how to proceed. The most fervent secessionists, aware that to wait for the slave states to act in concert might well slow the momentum of secession, advocated immediate, independent action by each dissatisfied state. A significant minority preferred cooperative, unified action; in the ranks of this group were found the so-called conditional unionists, who wanted to await overt antislavery action by the incoming Lincoln administration before deciding whether to secede. Only in Georgia and Louisiana did conditional unionists possess significant influence. But even in those states immediate secessionists carried the day, and by February they believed that they had achieved a peaceful separation. They would leave it up to the North to decide whether that peace would last.

Not all of the slave states chose secession in the winter of 1860–1861. A majority of white Southerners in the eight slave states that resisted the temptation to secede and then join the Confederacy prior to Lincoln's inauguration still believed that slavery was best protected *in* the Union. In *The Political Crisis of the 1850s* (1978), Michael Holt argued that residents of the upper South slave states also believed in the ability of the political system to craft a compromise to preserve the Union, citing as evidence the persistence of interparty competition in these states. But it does not necessarily follow that border-state voters believed that political parties on the national level would resolve the crisis. Rather, they were less likely than their counterparts in the lower South to exaggerate Northern antipathy toward slavery, for they interacted more frequently with free-state residents. Nor did slaves form as high a percentage of the border-state population. After all, it had only been with John Brown's abortive attempt at sparking a slave uprising at Harpers Ferry in October 1859 that party competition collapsed in the Deep South, as whites there united against the external threat of abolition and the internal threat of slave rebellion. Secessionist sentiment in the border states, while present, was still unable to carry the day in the absence of any provocative action by the Lincoln administration. People in these states realized that if secession led to war, the first battles would be fought on their soil. Thus a majority of border-state residents continued to seek a peaceful solution to the impasse.

Northern politicians reacted uncertainly at first to the crisis. In his final annual message (December 1860), the lame-duck Buchanan offered the novel theory that secession was unconstitutional but that the federal government had no power to coerce seceding states to remain in the Union. This proposal for inaction pleased nobody, although over the next several months Congress failed to pass any concrete proposals for reunion that smacked of coercion. Instead, an olive branch of sorts was offered in the form of a proposed constitutional amendment guaranteeing the perpetual pledge of the federal government not to legislate against slavery where it already existed. Some conservative Republicans even offered bills to organize the New Mexico territory (containing present-day Arizona and part of Nevada as well as New Mexico) without reference to slavery, while others revived proposals to extend the Missouri Compromise line defining the border between slavery and freedom at the latitude of 36° 30'. The latter proposal was at the core of Kentucky senator John J. Crittenden's compromise plan, which also prohibited the abolition of slavery in the District of Columbia, forbade federal interference with the interstate slave trade, and enhanced existing legislation for the recapture of fugitive slaves.

But most Republicans would have nothing to do with Crittenden's proposals, which took the form of unamendable and unrepealable constitutional amendments. Some Republicans found more attractive the New Mexico proposal, but before long it became evident that such an act could not pass Congress. From his home in Springfield, Illinois, Lincoln rejected any proposals that permitted slavery to expand. "On that point hold as with a chain of steel," the president-elect informed one spokesman. "The tug has to come and better now than later." To make concessions now would simply lead to more Southern demands; to retreat from the principles of the Republican creed would discredit the new party forever.

Other efforts at compromise met with similar fates. Republicans had little use for the proposals offered by a convention of elder statesmen led by former president John Tyler. These measures hoped to revive the Missouri Compromise's dividing line between slavery and freedom in the territories, guarantee the legality of slavery south of the line; make it more difficult for the United States to acquire additional territory (in an effort to avoid yet more slavery debates); declare that Congress could not interfere with slavery; call for the enforcement of the Fugitive Slave Law, with federal compensation to owners of escaped slaves; and reaffirm the cessation of the international slave trade. Whatever chance for success these proposals may have had in the past, they were now too little and too late.

Some in the North hoped for war. Among them was the black abolitionist Frederick Douglass. As David W. Blight has pointed out in *Frederick Douglass' Civil War: Keeping Faith in Jubilee* (1989), Douglass understood that the sectional upheaval and even war might well advance the cause of black freedom, certainly far better than would continued peace. "The contest must now be decided, and decided forever, which of the two, Freedom or Slavery, shall give law to this Republic," he announced. "Let the conflict come." And there were those who were perfectly willing to acquiesce in disunion—a sentiment not limited to conservatives who dreaded war. Several abolitionists announced that they preferred disunion to granting concessions to slaveholders. Wendell Phillips declared that the South's independence would mean "the jubilee of the slave." But these voices remained in the minority.

Republicans refused to consider letting the seceded states leave the Union. They rejected the notion that there was a right of secession, pointing out that there was no mention of it in the Constitution. Moreover, they deplored the possible consequences of establishing such a precedent. Secession rendered representative government impotent. "If any minority have the right to break up the Government at pleasure, because they have not had their way, there is an end of all government," asserted one Cincinnati newspaper. Lincoln's election was perfectly legitimate, Republicans pointed out; secessionists seemed bent upon ruling the Union or ruining it. Many Northern Democrats agreed, although they were far more willing to support compromise proposals. Many Northerners saw secession as an effort to break up the Union established through the efforts and sacrifices of the founding generation of the American republic, whose achievements they had long cherished. It was time, they believed, to stand firm on the issue of the preservation of the Union, even if they disagreed over the best way to attain that end.

Most Republicans, including Lincoln, anticipated eventual reunion through a peaceful resolution of the crisis that did not entail compromising party principles on slavery. They believed that secession was the work of a minority who had seized on the excitement of the moment to ram their program through. Let time pass, these Republicans believed, and cooler heads, belonging to Southern unionists, would prevail. By refusing to act hastily, Lincoln hoped to forestall secession in the eight slave states still in the Union. To lose a number of them would make the task of reunion all the more difficult, for the Confederacy would be immensely strengthened (and the Union correspondingly weakened) if several of these states joined those already seceded. At the moment, unionist sentiment held these states in the Union, but the grasp was a tenuous one that would loosen at the first sign of federally mandated force. Maintain the status quo, however, moderates reasoned, and secessionist fervor would die in the undecided areas and, eventually, even subside in the seceded states, opening up the best opportunity for peaceful reunion. This belief in the latent power of Southern unionism would remain a cornerstone of Lincoln's attitude toward the South for some time to come, and it shaped his approach to the challenges of waging war and defining a policy toward emancipation.

Inaction by the outgoing Buchanan administration and Congress bought time for proponents of peace. In the meantime, Southerners left cabinet posts (sometimes followed by charges of treasonous behavior) and their seats in Congress. But lines of communication remained open. One of the foremost advocates of a negotiated settlement leading to reunion was Secretary of State-designate William Henry Seward, the Republican senator from New York. Just two years before, Seward, at that time identified as a solid antislavery advocate, had spoken of an "irrepressible conflict"; his reputation as an extremist had contributed to his failure to secure the Republican presidential nomination in 1860, as many party leaders, overlooking Lincoln's statement that "a house divided against itself cannot stand," argued that the Illinoisan was far more moderate on slavery and related issues. Now Seward worked for time to allow Southern unionism to assert itself as a prerequisite to a peaceful settlement. At the least he hoped that by avoiding precipitate action, the North could forestall the spread of secession. If no more states joined the Confederacy, the new nation might not find itself able to survive, and before long there might be a chance for a rapprochement.

Meanwhile, the Confederates went about the business of setting up shop for themselves. On February 4, representatives from the seceded states met in Montgomery, Alabama, to frame a constitution and elect a provisional president. The first task took only four days; the resulting document resembled the United States Constitution in most particulars—although it contained several clauses specifically protecting slavery and others that espoused a state-centered federalism. This done, on February 9 the delegates named Jefferson Davis of Mississippi provisional president and Alexander H. Stephens of Georgia provisional vice president. Popular elections to be held in November would select an official president and vice president, each to serve a single six-year term, and delegations to the first formal Confederate Congress. In picking Davis and Stephens, the delegates purposely turned their backs on the "fire-eaters" (an appellation used to describe the most militant secessionists) and named well-known moderates to lead the new nation in the hope that they would attract broader support for the Confederacy in the upper and border South. A similar purpose was behind the convention's decision to ban the trans-Atlantic slave trade: the upper South already possessed a surplus slave population, and one of Virginians' chief sources of income was the selling of their slaves to other states. At the same time, however, by calling for 100,000 volunteer soldiers, the new Confederate government revealed an increasing willingness to accept the prospect of armed conflict.

Jefferson Davis seemed an ideal choice to head the new nation. Although he was no fire-eater, he was a staunch defender of Southern rights who had easily accepted secession. Davis, a West Point graduate, Mexican-American War hero, and former secretary of war, would have preferred to command the Confederate army, but he accepted his new responsibility willingly and with the hope that he could secure Southern independence peacefully if possible. "The man and the hour have met," proclaimed long-time fire-eater William Lowndes Yancey of Alabama in introducing Davis when the Mississippian arrived in Montgomery on February 16. Two days later Davis took the oath of office as the Confederacy's first chief executive. "Upon my weary heart was showered smiles, plaudits, and flowers," he told his wife, "but, beyond them, I saw troubles and thorns innumerable. We are without machinery, without means, and threatened by a powerful opposition; but I do not despond, and will not shrink from the task imposed upon me." Publicly, however, Davis sounded more confident: "Obstacles may retard, but they cannot long prevent, the progress of a movement sanctified by its justice and sustained by a virtuous people."

In making his cabinet appointments Davis had sought to balance sectional and political concerns. Robert Toombs of Georgia, a staunch secessionist, took over as secretary of state. The treasury went to South Carolina's Christopher G. Memminger. Alabama's Leroy P. Walker assumed control of the war department. Stephen Mallory of Florida received the navy department. Louisiana's Judah P. Benjamin was named attorney general. And John H. Reagan of Texas became postmaster general. Each Confederate state was represented in the new administration. Fire-eaters grumbled that they were underrepresented, but the moderation of the majority of the cabinet was designed to broaden support for the new nation. Much, however, would depend on the North's response to the establishment of the Confederacy.

In the last months of the Buchanan administration the outgoing president began to stiffen against secession. Out went several cabinet members accused of harboring secessionist sympathies, to be replaced by staunch unionists, including Edwin M. Stanton. Buchanan also decided not to evacuate federal forts in the South, most notably Fort Pickens outside Pensacola, Florida, and Fort Sumter, standing astride the entrance to the harbor of Charleston, South Carolina. On December 26, 1860, a federal detachment under the command of Major Robert Anderson had abandoned Fort Moultrie, on the shoreline just north of Charleston, and joined Sumter's garrison, much to the chagrin of South Carolinians, who immediately demanded that the Buchanan administration turn over Fort Sumter—to no avail. But efforts to reinforce and resupply the garrison failed when shore batteries opened fire on the *Star of the West*, a ship bearing relief supplies, on January 9, 1861. The next month Davis put General Pierre G. T. Beauregard, a dashing and able officer, in charge of the Charleston defenses, and assumed control of affairs there. Beauregard went to work improving the harbor's defenses and encircling Fort Sumter with cannon. Southern forces seized other U.S. arsenals and outposts in Confederate territory, so that by the end of February only Forts Pickens, Sumter, Jefferson, and Taylor, the latter two on the southern tip of Florida, remained in the hands of the United States.

It was in these circumstances that Abraham Lincoln left Springfield, Illinois, on February 11, 1861—the eve of his fifty-second birthday and the same day on which Davis left his plantation to head for Montgomery. As the president-elect travelled east by rail he reassured the crowds assembled at several stops that there was nothing to worry about, once terming the situation "an artificial crisis," but he added that he would work to hold the Union together, preferably by peaceful means. Many listeners approved of his declaration that at stake was the preservation of the notion of representative government. Others were not so well-disposed toward the incoming chief executive, and Lincoln had to sneak through Baltimore on a night train when news reached him of a possible assassination plot being hatched in that strongly pro-Southern city. It was not exactly the entrance he would have preferred to make, and it subjected him to ridicule.

On March 4, under the still uncompleted dome of the United States Capitol, Lincoln took the presidential oath of office. In his inaugural address he set forth his position. He held the Union perpetual and pledged to preserve it, but he would not initiate hostilities. "In your hands, my dissatisfied fellow countrymen, and not in mine, is the momentous issue of civil war," Lincoln warned secessionists. "The government will not assail you. You can have no conflict, without being yourselves the aggressors. You have no oath registered in Heaven to destroy the government, while I have the most solemn one to 'preserve, protect and defend' it." Still, he ended on a note of reconciliation, calling upon heritage and history as he reminded white Southerners of all they shared as Americans: "The mystic chords of memory, stretching from every battle-field, and patriot grave, to every living heart and hearthstone, all over this broad land, will yet swell the chorus of the Union, when again touched, as surely they will be, by the better angels of our nature."

In appointing his cabinet, Lincoln, like Davis, balanced various interests. Seward headed the list as secretary of state; Ohio's Salmon P. Chase, a leading antislavery advocate, became treasury secretary. For the War Department Lincoln reluctantly nominated Simon Cameron of Pennsylvania, to repay a political debt for his nomination, while Gideon Welles of Connecticut took over the navy department. Indiana's Caleb B. Smith cashed in on another political deal to secure Lincoln's nomination when he was named secretary of the interior. Maryland's Montgomery Blair became postmaster general, and Edward Bates of Missouri assumed the attorney generalship. In Lincoln's original cabinet, former Democrats were paired against former Whigs, the border states claimed two representatives, and the slate represented a spectrum of antislavery opinion. Seward, who had once been marked as a pro-abolition extremist, proved to be far more moderate than Lincoln on most matters, especially emancipation. During the next six weeks the secretary of state would do what he could to seek a peaceful solution to the crisis of secession, not always acting with Lincoln's knowledge or approval.

The First Shot

No sooner had Lincoln entered into his presidential duties than he faced his first crisis. On the eve of inauguration day Major Anderson had telegraphed Washington that the supplies in the Fort Sumter garrison would last only another six weeks. Over the next month Lincoln and his cabinet debated what to do. Would holding on to the fort cause war? Would giving it up represent a concession to the Confederacy? What impact would either action have on the wobbling loyalty of the border states? Representatives from these states as well as the Confederacy were in Washington anxiously awaiting the administration's next move. Most interesting was Seward's proposal to start a war with a European power in order to reunite all Americans against a common foe. Lincoln dismissed this farfetched notion and coolly responded to Seward's suggestion that he take over the management of policy by reminding the secretary who was president.

At first, a majority of the cabinet favored abandoning the fort. After some hesitation, Lincoln decided to maintain possession of it. Within two weeks several members of the cabinet came around to his point of view, supporting the president's decision to reprovision Sumter and retain both it and Fort Pickens. In taking this step, Lincoln was well aware that it might result in war. This did not mean that he had abandoned his hope of retaining the border states in the Union, nor did it mean that he wanted war. He would leave that decision to Davis. On April 6 he notified South Carolina's governor, Francis Pickens, that he was dispatching an expedition to Sumter to resupply the fort's garrison. This decision thwarted Seward's efforts to negotiate a peaceful solution based upon the Union's abandonment of the fort.

Now it was up to Davis. To allow Lincoln to resupply Sumter's garrison would cast doubt on the resolve of white Southerners for independence. Many observers would regard it as an unanswered slight upon Southern honor. Furthermore, if no action were taken, the initial enthusiasm for secession might wane, over time leading to the sober second thoughts that Seward predicted Southerners would have. To fire on Sumter might well inaugurate armed conflict, yet the speedy onset of hostilities might best serve the Confederate cause. If Lincoln chose not to respond to the bombardment of Fort Sumter—a highly unlikely possibility—Northern resolve would be shaken and Northern honor questioned. However, if Lincoln decided to meet force with force, escalating the conflict, several of the wavering border states, including the critical ones of Tennessee, North Carolina, and Virginia, would doubtless join the Confederacy, citing Lincoln's actions as the unconstitutional coercion for which they had been waiting. With these alternatives in mind, Davis did not hesitate. Back went word to Beauregard to open fire on Fort Sumter if Anderson did not capitulate.

On the evening of April 11, 1861, Beauregard called on Anderson to evacuate the fort. At first the fort's commander sought to buy time by announcing that before long the garrison would be "starved out" anyway, but when Beauregard, prodded by Davis, repeated his demand for an immediate surrender, Anderson refused. Dawn was still a few hours away on April 12 when a cannon ball blazed across the night sky and exploded over the fort. Immediately the batteries ringing the fort opened fire, pounding away at the brick walls; a shot snapped the flagpole. Anderson's cannons could offer only token resistance. The next day he agreed to surrender, and on April 14 his men marched out of the fort. The clash's only casualty occurred during a fifty-gun salute as the soldiers lowered the U.S. flag: an accidental explosion killed one of Anderson's men and injured several more. War had come to the United States.

CHAPTER TWO

War Begins

The news of Fort Sumter electrified Americans. In the North people rallied to the cause of the Union. Speeches and sermons declared that the rebellion must be crushed. Mass meetings passed resolutions brimming with patriotic fervor. For the moment most people forgot partisan politics. In Galena, Illinois, one of the town's leading Democrats took the podium to declare, "We will stand by the flag of our country, and appeal to the God of battles!" The enthusiasm brought all Northerners together. "At the darkest moment of the republic, when it looked as if the nation would be dismembered," reflected Ralph Waldo Emerson, the famed New England writer and speaker, "the attack on Fort Sumter crystallized the North into a unit, and the hope of mankind was saved."

Even as the flag of the United States came down from Fort Sumter, Lincoln met with his cabinet to prepare a proclamation calling for the formation of a 75,000-man volunteer militia to serve ninety days to quell the "insurrection." Out west in Galena, posters announced a meeting at the local courthouse to

meet the president's call. "Business ceased entirely; all was excitement; for a time there were no party distinctions; all were
Union men, determined to avenge the insult to the national flag,"
recalled a thirty-eight-year-old store clerk who had served in the
Mexican-American War. That night, enough volunteers stepped
forward to make a company, and the townswomen pledged to
sew a flag and uniforms. The Mexican-American War veteran
proved willing to drill the new recruits, but he declined the cap-
taincy of the regiment, believing that he was qualified to command a regiment. Eventually, Ulysses S. Grant would get his turn
to lead men in battle.

White Southerners also welcomed the news of war. "I find
our people everywhere are alive to their interests and their duty
in this crisis," observed Vice President Alexander H. Stephens.
"Such a degree of popular enthusiasm was never before seen in
this country." Here and there a unionist spoke up: a newspaper
editor from Knoxville, Tennessee, pledged to "fight the Secession leaders till Hell froze over, and then fight them on the ice."
But these protests were in the minority. The news of war served
to break the tension of the last four months. "The war spirit is
waking us all up," Mary Chesnut, wife of a former U.S. senator,
observed from Charleston.

In all of the bravado and boasting, few Americans on either
side were willing to contemplate what war might actually cost
them. Most anticipated a short and decisive conflict. What un-
folded over the next four years reminded many of those who
had been so eager to fight of the wisdom of the adage that one
should think carefully about what one really wants, for one might
just get it.

Mobilizing for Conflict

The combination of Fort Sumter's fall and Lincoln's call for troops
proved too much to bear for the cause of the Union in four of
the border states. As secessionists had anticipated, the advent of
hostilities, by rendering null the possibility of a peacefully negotiated settlement, led many wavering Southern whites to cast

their lot with the Confederacy. On April 17, Virginia seceded; Arkansas, Tennessee, and finally North Carolina followed. Missouri and Maryland teetered on the brink of secession, while Kentucky's legislature sought refuge in a declaration of neutrality. Of all the border states, only Delaware's loyalty to the Union remained secure. The Confederacy found itself greatly strengthened, for Virginia, Tennessee, and North Carolina were now its three-largest states in terms of white population, and the newly Confederate quartet doubled the new nation's manufacturing and food-production capability. The best prize of all was Virginia, with the armory at Harpers Ferry, the naval yard at Norfolk, the Tredegar Iron Works at Richmond, and a group of talented military leaders headed by Robert E. Lee joining the Confederate cause. (As Lee had just turned down command of the Union forces, it was apparent that both sides recognized his ability.) But significant white minorities in the border states, concentrated primarily in western Virginia and East Tennessee, opposed secession and resisted Confederate rule, and their regions became havens for Southern unionists.

With the departure of four upper South states, the balance sheet of the opposing forces came into clearer focus. Certainly the Union still held significant material advantages over its counterpart, with nine times the overall industrial capacity of the Confederacy. For every factory worker in the Confederacy there was a factory in the Union; there were more factories in New York alone than there were in the entire Confederacy. The North produced fifteen times the iron, thirty-eight times the coal, fourteen times the textiles, thirty times the footwear, and thirty-two times the firearms of the South. The Union was also far more urbanized: of the sixteen cities in the United States in 1860 with populations over 50,000 (nine of these with populations over 100,000), only New Orleans was located in the Confederacy. The story was nearly the same when it came to agriculture. The Union had nearly twice the improved farmland of the Confederacy, three times as many horses, nearly twice as much livestock, and far more foodstuffs. The Union also enjoyed significant advantages in its rail network, in terms both of total miles of track and the superior integration of its rail net—many railroads in the Confederacy were incompatible in terms of gauge (the width of the track), often making it difficult to move locomotives and rolling stock over long distances.

The Union had over three times the white population of the Confederacy—some 20 million to 6 million—although neither side could count on the full support of all its people. The Confederacy could also draw on the labor of some 3.5 million slaves. Nearly another half-million enslaved black people lived in the border states. Also, some 226,000 free blacks lived in the free soil North, and another 130,000 resided in the border states that remained in the Union, about the same number of free blacks that lived in the Confederacy. The slave population proved both a help and a hindrance to the Confederate cause. The presence of slaves allowed the Confederacy to mobilize a far higher percentage of the 1 million white males available for military service than could the Union, which could draw from some 3.5 million white males (and potentially several hundred thousand free black men) in recruiting its armed forces. However, as Union armies swept southward, the South's slaves could prove unreliable, even disloyal. Indeed, many took the first available opportunity to flee to Union lines. Finally, during the years 1861–1864, over a half-million immigrants entered Northern ports, increasing the Union population margin still more.

Nevertheless, numbers can be deceiving. And superior numbers did not guarantee the triumph of the Union. History is rife with cases in which the side that possessed more people and more resources managed to lose a war. Confederates could (and did) point to the American Revolution as merely the best-known case of the smaller side emerging victorious. Moreover, military and political considerations bolstered Confederate confidence. It would prove hard for the Union to reassert control over some three-quarters of a million square miles of territory. "They may overrun our frontier states and plunder our coast but, as for conquering us, the thing is an impossibility," observed one Confederate general. "There is no instance in history of a people as numerous as we are inhabiting a country so extensive as ours being subjected if true to themselves." The battlegrounds would be familiar and friendly terrain for many a Confederate soldier, and the notion of fighting to preserve one's home could prove a powerful stimulus for even those Confederates who had opposed secession or cared little about protecting slavery. In light of the advantages—both tangible and intangible—enjoyed by the defensive on the battlefield, the numerical inferiority of Confederate manpower need not have proved fatal. And the burden of the offensive rested with the Union.

Furthermore, it was not yet clear exactly how many states would join the Confederacy. The addition of Virginia, Tennessee, North Carolina, and Arkansas had immeasurably increased the Confederacy's chances for victory; should several other border states join the new American republic, it might prove too powerful for the Union to reclaim. For several weeks prospects seemed dark for the Union cause in Maryland. Its loss would strand Washington, D.C., well inside hostile territory. The strength of secessionist support in the eastern part of Maryland soon made itself felt. On April 19, as soldiers from the Sixth Massachusetts Infantry changed trains in Baltimore, a mob attacked them. After a clash in which four soldiers and a dozen citizens were killed, the regiment made its way to Washington, but secessionists burned railroad bridges and cut telegraph wires, effectively cutting the capital off from the rest of the North. Finally, several Union regiments, bypassing Baltimore by water, arrived, much to the relief of Lincoln and others.

Now Lincoln took steps to ensure that Maryland did not move any further toward secession. He suspended the writ of habeas corpus there, arrested dissenters, and dispatched Union soldiers to Baltimore and other strategic locations to secure lines of communication and transportation. These strong-arm tactics succeeded in deterring the state's secession, although some 20,000 Marylanders still enlisted in the Confederate army. Lincoln's drastic measures did not go unchallenged. One John Merryman, imprisoned in the first wave of arrests, appealed to Chief Justice Roger B. Taney (acting in his capacity as circuit judge for Maryland) for his release. Taney issued a writ of habeas corpus, declaring in *ex parte Merryman* that Lincoln's suspension of the writ was unconstitutional. Disagreeing, Lincoln directed federal officials not to give Merryman up, and Taney found himself unable to enforce his decision.

Force also decided the fate of secession in Missouri. Governor Claiborne Jackson tried to steer the state into the Confederacy by mobilizing secessionist sympathizers in the militia to try to seize the federal arsenal in St. Louis. But Captain Nathaniel Lyon, a passionate Republican, and Congressman Francis P. Blair, Jr., brother of Lincoln's postmaster general, promptly checked Jackson, transferring arms out of the arsenal even as they raised several regiments of German Americans to meet the advancing secessionist militia. On May 10 Lyon's men surrounded the secessionist encampment and forced its surrender. Marching the prisoners through St. Louis, however, provoked a riot, and in the ensuing exchange of gunfire two soldiers and thirty-one civilians were killed. Lyon's aggressive behavior led to mixed results: if St. Louis now rested firmly in Northern hands, elsewhere across the state hostilities commenced as Confederate and Union supporters raised their own regiments. Moderate efforts to construct a compromise ended in June when Lyon refused to contemplate alternatives short of a direct military confrontation. For the remainder of the war Missouri would be plagued by a bloody internal conflict.

As events in the border states came to a head, both Lincoln and Davis turned to the task of preparing for war. Before long it was apparent that Lincoln's original request for volunteer militiamen would not suffice. On May 3 he issued a call for additional volunteers to serve a term of three years and authorized the expansion of the regular army. Two months later, on July 4, Lincoln sought Congress's retroactive approval for his past actions while pushing for the raising of more men and money for the military. Davis already had secured (in March) the approval of the Confederate Congress to accept volunteers for twelve-month terms of enlistment.

Both presidents also confronted the problem of appointing generals to lead their new armies. Political considerations as well as military experience shaped the resulting selections on both sides. Lincoln, anxious to woo Radicals and Democrats alike, used several of his appointments as patronage. John C. Frémont gained a commission for his Republican credentials. Benjamin F. Butler secured a major generalship because of his popularity among Democrats. Nathaniel Banks won a pair of starred shoulder straps in recognition of his past influence among Republicans and Know Nothings. Several West Point graduates also returned to military service. George B. McClellan gave up a railroad presidency to take command of Ohio's soldiers; William T. Sherman, who had just resigned a position as superintendent of a Louisiana military academy and established himself in business at St. Louis, accepted a colonelcy after some hesitation. Ulysses S. Grant had to wait several months until the governor of Illinois put him in charge of an unruly regiment. It had not hurt Grant or Sherman that they, too, had political connections: Sherman's brother John was a Republican senator from Ohio, and he counted members of the Blair family as his friends, while Congressman Elihu Washburne took a great interest in the military prospects of his constituent Grant. Similar considerations guided Jefferson Davis's early appointments. To be sure, he recognized the military talent of Joseph Johnston, P. G. T. Beauregard, and Robert E. Lee, but he was also aware of the need to placate politicians and transcend old partisan rivalries. Virginia Democrats John B. Floyd and Henry A. Wise secured positions as generals, so did Democrat Gideon J. Pillow and Whig Felix Zollicoffer, as Davis worked to forge bipartisan support for the Confederacy in Tennessee. When Robert Toombs left the cabinet in July 1861, Davis, aware of the importance of maintaining the support of the Georgia secessionist, made him a brigadier general—although Toombs retained his seat in the Confederate Congress.

The military appointments of both chief executives was part of a broader effort to construct bipartisan coalitions to support the war effort. Lincoln went out of his way to seek the assistance of Democrats. Stephen A. Douglas, long Lincoln's foe in Illinois politics and one of his rivals in 1860, proclaimed his support of the administration from the beginning; his death soon afterward proved most unfortunate for Lincoln and the Democratic party, who both needed his leadership. As Lincoln sought common ground with Democrats, Davis worked to strengthen ties between the upper and lower South. In May the Confederate government decided to relocate its capital to Richmond, Virginia, a move that caused both sides to concentrate on the eastern theater as the theater of decision. With the two capitals barely one hundred miles apart, commanders on both sides found themselves saddled with the double burden of defending their own capital even as they tried to take their opponent's.

War Aims

At the beginning of hostilities it seemed rather easy to define what each side hoped to gain from the war. The Confederacy fought for its independence; the Union fought to reunite the country. Yet these goals were deceptive in their simplicity, for they begged the question of how each side would go about getting what it wanted.

The original seven states of the Confederacy did not simply seek to be left alone. Rather, from the beginning they looked forward to the prospect of adding more of their fellow slave states to the north. Davis had alluded to that hope in his inaugural, and news that Virginia's senators preferred Davis as president had played a role in the selection of the Mississippian. Others had cited the possible addition of more states in urging the Confederacy to take the initiative at Fort Sumter; days after the fort's surrender South Carolina Governor Francis W. Pickens wrote Davis that "if we can consolodate [sic] the slave holding race in one government it would give us the certainty of permanent peace & prosperity & secure the development of our peculiar form of civilization." Having welcomed North Carolina, Virginia, Tennessee, and Arkansas to the fold, many Confederates looked forward to the day when Maryland, Kentucky, and Missouri would join the new nation.

How best to achieve independence remained a challenging question. Should the armed forces of the Confederacy rest content with repelling invasions, or might they consider counterattacks, even invasions of the North? Would Confederates be satisfied with waging a passive defense? And did the Confederacy have to defend every square inch of land within its borders, or might it trade space for time while consolidating defensive positions? Finally, should the Confederacy rely primarily on its own ability to defend itself, or should it actively seek foreign assistance to secure its independence? Political and cultural as well as military concerns contributed to the answers that were offered. In some cases there was never total or lasting agreement.

Military policy proved especially problematic. The Confederacy simply did not have the manpower necessary to defend its entire territory. People who went to war to protect their homes might well find those homes left undefended against enemy invasion. Political necessity clashed with military reality: it made far more sense to gather forces in areas most likely to be targeted by Union offensives than to disperse men everywhere. A passive defense would minimize the handicap of having smaller armies, for the defender in Civil War combat could drive off a numerically superior force. But passivity was in short supply in a region where concepts of honor and courage demanded that one confront and challenge one's enemy—especially since Confederates had been quick to mock the willingness and ability of their counterparts to fight. Store clerks and menial laborers, Southern whites jeered, were no match for the gallant farmers and gentlemen planters of the South, trained as they were in riding and shooting. Besides, superior generalship might more than make up for inferior numbers, and counterattacks might well catch the enemy off balance: that they might also result in heavy casualties became significant only if the audacity, dashing, and derringdo of the smaller forces failed to clear the field.

The quest to invite foreign intervention likewise had its pros and cons, as well as a major flaw. Certainly the Confederacy would have a better chance to achieve victory on the battlefield if European powers joined it in its struggle for independence. On the surface it seemed as if such a policy would serve the interests of the British, whose textile manufacturers needed raw cotton. Several British and French government leaders foresaw advantages for their respective nations in a weakened (and divided) post-war United States. Yet one might invest so much faith in others as to ask less than was necessary of one's self. Reliance on foreign powers, in short, might lead to a slackening of the Confederacy's endeavors on its own behalf. Nor was it clear that the interests of European powers would favor intervention until Confederate independence seemed imminent—thus rendering it moot as a tool to gain that very independence.

If the Confederacy could maintain itself on the battlefield, it could win the war in one of several ways. It might crush Union armies, rendering the war for reunion an impossibility. It might achieve enough to persuade European powers to recognize its independence, which, while not guaranteeing a Confederate victory, would make it more likely. Or it might frustrate Union offensives to the point that the Northern public would grow tired of the war and sue for peace—and accept Confederate independence. Therefore, in order to win its objective, civilian support and morale was as essential to the Confederacy as military success—indeed, one would be rather difficult to sustain without the other.

For the Union to triumph, it had to meet several goals. European nations must be deterred from supporting, let alone formally recognizing, the Confederacy. Northern public opinion must continue to support the administration's prosecution of the conflict, or at least not become so demoralized that the South's separation became acceptable. Much more complicated was how to approach the problem of actually conquering the Confederacy. Throughout the conflict Union leaders drew distinctions between different classes of white Southerners. There remained die-hard unionists, such as Andrew Johnson of Tennessee and George H. Thomas of Virginia, but they were seriously outnumbered. Larger still were the number of Southern whites who would support (or at least acquiesce in) reunion but who opposed abolition. Finally, there were those white Southerners who were more or less committed to the Confederate cause. In the minds of many Union leaders, including Lincoln, support for the Confederacy could be undermined if Union policy disabused this large bloc of white

Southerners of the notion that the Republicans sought the immediate abolition of slavery. Lincoln and Seward (and others) held on a long time to the belief that old loyalties would revive over time if the Union followed a conservative course in waging the war. Abolition was not to be an aim of the conflict: the North was waging a war to preserve and restore the Union, not to create a new type of nation. Patience and a few triumphs on the battlefield might well lead to the collapse of the support of the Confederacy and an early end to the war. Thus the will as well as the ability of white Southerners to persist in their quest for independence were targets of Union policy.

These assumptions were reflected in General-in-Chief Winfield Scott's vision of Northern strategy. The Mexican-American War hero was feeling the impact of age—he was seventy-four—and his excessive weight and poor health rendered him unfit for the field. Nevertheless, he retained a keen appreciation of military strategy. He thought the best way to achieve victory would be through squeezing the Confederacy to death through a vigorous application of the naval blockade of the Confederates' ports and the seizure of the control of the Mississippi River. This accomplished, Scott believed that it would only be a matter of time before resurgent Unionists and frustrated Confederates would call for an end of Rebel resistance, resulting in a relatively bloodless triumph for the Union. Such a plan would take time to implement, but it promised to bring peace without inflicting too much damage.

This so-called Anaconda Plan of victory through strangulation of the enemy by the coils of military force demanded too much patience and assumed that Confederates would be passive victims, unable to use their own resources to hold out for more than a year without ample imports. But it did conform to early notions that the war for reunion should not foment revolution. In July 1861, Congress passed the Johnson-Crittenden Resolutions, offered by border-state leaders Senator Andrew Johnson of Tennessee and John Crittenden of Kentucky and declaring that the U.S. government's goal in the conflict was reunion, pure and simple. However much some northern Republicans might disagree with this limited policy, it provided as broad a base as possible for support of the Union by keeping abolition out of the government's war aims.

It was already apparent, however, that the future of slavery was so intertwined with the essence of the conflict that confronting the issue was unavoidable. The very act of waging war against slaveholders declared their property to be at risk. No

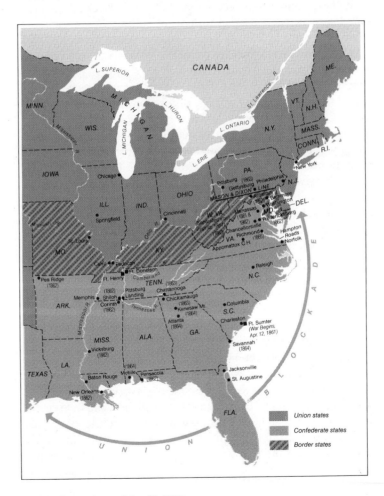

Major Campaigns of the Civil War

sooner had Benjamin F. Butler assumed command at Fort Monroe, Virginia, in May 1861, than he faced the question of what to do with black refugees who streamed into his lines seeking sanctuary. Slaveholders soon appeared, demanding the return of their property. Butler politely refused on the grounds that their work on the entrenchments had made the slaves subject to the laws concerning "contraband of war." After all, he reasoned, any property used in support of military operations was liable to seizure by enemy forces, and, as Southern whites had long insisted that slaves were property, certainly the laws of war applied in this case. While this line of reasoning may not have liberated the "contrabands" from slavery per se, it certainly liberated them from their masters. Before long other slaves, male and female, old and young, had made their way to Butler's lines, and the general had to apply his definition of contraband rather broadly to cover slave families as well as those blacks who had actually been made to toil as Confederate laborers. Butler's action, however, hardly set the Lincoln administration upon a course of emancipation, and other Union generals chose different approaches to slavery. As he advanced into western Virginia, George McClellan repeatedly reassured civilians of his intention to respect their property rights, including slaves—a position echoed by Union leaders elsewhere.

Therefore, as the war spilled over into the second half of 1861, supporters of the Union might say that they were fighting to preserve that union, and advocates of secession and the Confederacy might speak eloquently about their desire to preserve a way of life, but the very war that both sides chose to wage could not but change both the Union and the Southern way of life, in large part because that conflict, one way or another, sooner or later, would have to confront the issue of slavery. As Grant put it during the opening weeks of the war, "In all this I can but see the doom of slavery." The friction of war and the course of events, not a determination to adopt emancipation as a war aim, would erode what Alexander H. Stephens called the cornerstone of the Confederacy.

The First Battles

As both governments geared up for war, the armies encountered each other in a series of engagements whose significance far outweighed the number of men engaged. One of the most publicized of these clashes occurred near Fort Monroe, Virginia, at a crossroads called Big Bethel on June 10. The Federal attack was mismanaged, with several Union regiments firing into each other before retreating before a small Confederate force. Although in light of what was to come, the casualties—seventy-six Yankees and eight Rebels—were insignificant, Confederate newspapers declared that the clash proved that one butternut could whip ten Yankees (overlooking the fact that it had been friendly fire that had felled a good number of the Federals). Elsewhere, however, the news was not so good for the new republic. In late May, Union forces advanced into western Virginia, in part to secure the Baltimore and Ohio railroad, one of the few east-west links across the North. Under the overall command of McClellan, the Union advance drove away Confederate forces at Philippi on June 3, entered Romney ten days later, and on July 11 won a major victory at Rich Mountain, followed two days later by yet another triumph at Carrick's Ford. Much of western Virginia soon came under Union control, a source of great cheer to many of the region's citizens, some of whom were already beginning to contemplate the notion of declaring their region a separate state. Another Yankee column under the command of Robert Patterson crossed the Potomac on July 2 and entered the Shenandoah Valley of Virginia, a source of foodstuffs for the Confederacy as well as a possible corridor for a Rebel offensive into the North.

News of these military activities elsewhere made all the more visible the inactivity of Union forces based around Washington. Except for securing Alexandria and Arlington, Virginia, in May, little had happened, and Union recruits chafed for action. Their ninety-day enlistments would soon expire, and many soldiers feared returning home without a battle to show for their efforts.

Newspapers, led by Horace Greeley's New York *Tribune,* cried "Forward to Richmond!" When General Irwin McDowell, in charge of the forces assembled about Washington, warned Lincoln that his men and officers were not yet ready for combat, the president shrugged off the warning: "You are green, it is true, but they are green, also; you are all green alike."

McDowell's army was some 35,000 strong, while 15,000 more men under Patterson were stationed around Harpers Ferry in Virginia. Confronting McDowell was a Confederate force of some 20,000 under the command of the hero of Fort Sumter, P. G. T. Beauregard, gathered about Manassas Junction south of a creek named Bull Run, some twenty-five miles southwest of Washington; another Confederate force of 11,000, led by Joseph E. Johnston, waited opposite Patterson. While Patterson kept an eye on Johnston, McDowell planned to drive off Beauregard. The plan sounded good, but it was ill-fated from the start. McDowell marched on July 16, only to encounter countless delays as his inexperienced soldiers and subordinate commanders stumbled down the turnpike toward Centreville, Virginia. The news of this advance was quickly relayed to Confederate commanders by Rose O'Neal Greenhow and other Confederate spies, who had overheard details of the operation from loose-lipped civil and military authorities. Johnston, giving Patterson the slip, transferred his force by rail to Manassas Junction, arriving just as McDowell's army slowly made its way southward. As night fell on July 20, each side planned to attack on their right and parry on their left.

McDowell moved first. On the morning of July 21, the Yankees forded Bull Run and assailed the Rebel left. Beauregard and Johnston rushed over reinforcements to stave off a retreat, but the Union forces kept coming. Only McDowell's failure to coordinate attacks and press his initial success prevented him from driving the foe from the field. Eventually the Confederates rallied, due in large part to the steadfastness of a brigade of Virginians under the command of Thomas J. Jackson, a West Point graduate and a professor at the Virginia Military Institute. Jackson's belief in discipline and training were paying off this summer afternoon; his men, noting the odd habits of their commander, recalled that the VMI cadets referred to him as "Tom Fool," but that nickname would soon be replaced. A South Carolina brigadier, seeing the Virginians hold their ground, reportedly exclaimed, "There is Jackson standing like a stone wall! Rally behind the Virginians!" The Union advance became disorganized, then confused by the appearance of blue-clad Confederates on their flank. A withdrawal turned first into a retreat and then a rout, sweeping along in its wake Washington civilians who had brought picnic lunches along with them to view what they believed would be the only battle of the war. Some of the Yankees did not stop fleeing until they had returned to their camps outside the capital. The Confederates were as scattered by their victory as their opponents were by their defeat, rendering a pursuit impracticable. Union casualties totalled nearly 3,000, including approximately 1,200 prisoners; the Confederates lost less than 2,000 and gained a hero in "Stonewall" Jackson.

The North was shocked by the news of the debacle at Bull Run. A few people grew faint of heart; the once-belligerent and always mercurial Greeley now begged Lincoln to sue for peace. But if the Yankee army had stampeded, the Northern public stood fast. Recruiting thrived, and Congress passed measures to carry on the conflict, including an income tax to fund the war effort. More significant was the passage of legislation that challenged the intent of the Johnson-Crittenden Resolutions. Employing the same reasoning first offered by Butler, the First Confiscation Act declared that property—including slaves—employed in support of the Confederate war effort was subject to seizure by U.S. authorities. If this was not a measure of emancipation, it certainly was an escalation of the conflict, and it forecast sterner measures.

There were other changes. Lincoln decided to replace McDowell with George B. McClellan. Fresh from his victories in western Virginia, McClellan, with his talent for organization and inspiration, was exactly what the newly christened Army of the Potomac needed as it recovered from the doldrums of its defeat at Bull Run. The president also now recognized that it took time to transform recruits into soldiers, and in McClellan he had a general who would take all the time he could get to ready his men for action. Other legacies proved more durable. If Bull Run had alerted the Union to the need to take more vigorous steps to conduct this war, it also left Northerners uneasy about the alleged superiority of their foes. On the other side, imbued with confidence in the aftermath of victory, the Confederacy did not quite comprehend that Bull Run was simply the opening act.

But news from Missouri also brought smiles to Dixie. Back in June, Lyon had advanced into central Missouri, driving away Confederate militia at Boonville, and then continued marching toward the southwest corner of the state. After Bull Run, Lincoln appointed John C. Frémont to command Union forces in the area. Frémont, who initially had come to public attention as a result of his exploration of the Rockies, had earned a military reputation in California during the Mexican-American War and political prominence as the first presidential candidate of the Republican party. Once arriving in St. Louis at the end of July, he found it impossible to help Lyon in his offensive while shielding Illinois from Confederate forces in southeast Missouri. Thus shorn of expected reinforcements, Lyon, struggling to hold his 6,000-man force together in the face of dwindling supplies, short-term enlistments, and an opposing force nearly twice his strength, decided to launch a bold blow at the Confederate camp at Wilson's Creek. Although the surprise attack at dawn on August 10 scored initial successes, Lyon's chances for victory faded after Union forces mistook a blue-clad regiment from Louisiana for one of their own, allowing it to open fire with devastating results. Lyon was killed; his army retreated from the field and made its way back toward the center of the state, leaving western Missouri vulnerable to a Confederate counterstroke.

The last four months of 1861, however, saw Union forces establish several footholds in Confederate territory. In his first campaign, Robert E. Lee, placed in command of a Confederate force in western Virginia, failed to drive Union forces out of his area, although he at least retained control of the Shenandoah Valley. With the consolidation of Union control over this region, the way was clear to establish West Virginia as a separate state, an opportunity eagerly seized by local unionists. Elsewhere in the East there was relatively little action. McClellan methodically drilled and disciplined his men, while doing his best to fend off suggestions to advance. Slowly but surely his relationship with Lincoln began to erode, in large part because McClellan treated the president with contempt. He styled Lincoln "the original gorilla" and snubbed the commander-in-chief several times. But the president was willing to tolerate much if McClellan would fight and win. In fact, in November he elevated McClellan to the position of general-in-chief, displacing Scott.

Republicans and some war Democrats suspected that McClellan's apparent lethargy was in reality an unwillingness to fight an aggressive war. These suspicions seemed confirmed when a Union reconnaissance patrol of the Confederate position at Ball's Bluff, Virginia, on the south bank of the Potomac, turned into a military fiasco. A Rebel ambush inflicted nearly a thousand casualties; among the dead was Colonel Edward Baker, senator from Oregon and a close friend of Lincoln's. Outraged, congressional Republicans in December established the Joint Committee on the Conduct of the War. The committee's first target was General Charles P. Stone, commander of the ill-fated Ball's Bluff expedition. Like McClellan, Stone opposed emancipation; he had returned fugitive slaves to their owners. Rumors circulated that he even had conducted clandestine conversations with Confederate officers. Stone soon found himself in jail; McClellan deplored the result of the committee's investigation as another example of political interference.

In the West both sides sparred for position. In the aftermath of Wilson's Creek, Confederate forces advanced northward through western Missouri, reaching the Missouri River at Lexington, where they captured a Yankee garrison. Guerrilla activities redoubled as well. Frémont seemed helpless and befuddled. On August 30, he declared Missouri to be under martial law, promised to execute captured guerrillas, and confiscated the property of all Confederate sympathizers in the state—including slaves. The order went too far. Although abolitionists and other antislavery advocates celebrated Frémont's proclamation, it promised to escalate the bitter exchanges between the region's guerrillas and unionist citizens. In the border states it intensified the sentiments of secessionist slaveholders while weakening the allegiance of many unionist slaveholders—this at a time when the fate of Kentucky had yet to be determined. Lincoln had no choice but to intervene. When Frémont refused his request to modify his proclamation by putting it in line with the First Confiscation Act, Lincoln ordered the general to rescind it. "To lose Kentucky is nearly the same as to lose the whole game," the president observed. "Kentucky gone, we cannot hold Missouri, nor, as I think, Maryland. These all against us, and the job on our hands is too large for us."

If Frémont's blunder had almost cost the Union Kentucky, within a week a Confederate misstep reversed the course of events. Kentucky's neutrality proved too precarious to preserve, although neither Union nor Confederate forces wanted to precipitate a decision, for whoever challenged the state's neutrality risked losing its allegiance. During the spring and summer, both sides recruited soldiers from the Bluegrass State, while Confederates siphoned off horses and food. As September began, Confederate forces crossed the Kentucky border to secure Columbus, a town overlooking the Mississippi River. In response, newly promoted Brigadier General Ulysses S. Grant ferried several regiments from Cairo, at the southern tip of Illinois, along and across the Ohio River to Paducah, Kentucky, located at the mouth of the Tennessee River and just a few miles downriver from where the Cumberland River empties into the Ohio. The rapid move preempted a Confederate advance on the Kentucky town. Grant then issued a proclamation to Paducah's citizens that stood in stark contrast to that issued a week earlier by Frémont, for Grant promised to leave slavery alone. Whatever pretenses of neutrality remained in Kentucky quickly dissipated, and a majority of the state's citizens proclaimed their allegiance to the Union.

Grant was an unlikely hero. An Ohio native, he graduated in the middle of his class at West Point and demonstrated bravery under fire and initiative during the Mexican-American War.

Marrying Julia Dent, daughter of a Missouri slaveholder, in 1848, he became disenchanted with army life when a transfer to the West Coast separated him from his family. He resigned his captain's commission in 1854 amid rumors of intoxication, giving rise to the myth of a besotted man whose biggest battle was with the bottle, and stumbled through a succession of jobs in civilian life. Finally placed in charge of a regiment in June 1861, Grant soon became a brigadier general with the assistance of Congressman Washburne. Within weeks he was ordered to attack an enemy camp in Florida, Missouri. Uneasy on the eve of what he anticipated to be his first battle as a commander, propelled forward primarily by his fear of cowardice, he discovered that the enemy forces, commanded by a Colonel Harris, had fled. "It occurred to me at once that Harris had been as much afraid of me as I had been of him," he later recalled. "This was a view of the question I had never taken before; but it was one I never forgot afterwards. From that event to the close of the war, I never experienced trepidation upon confronting an enemy, though I always felt more or less anxiety. I never forgot that he had as much reason to fear my forces as I had his."

Two months after taking Paducah, Grant again showed initiative. This time it led to a battle along the Mississippi. With a force of some 3,000 men aboard several steamboats, he moved down the Mississippi to Belmont, Missouri, opposite Columbus, Kentucky, and attacked a Confederate encampment there on November 7. At first the Union attack swept the enemy from the field, but the Rebels, reinforced from Columbus, launched a counterattack that nearly pushed Grant's men into the river. Grant himself narrowly escaped capture, then death, as his soldiers scampered aboard their transports and made their way back upriver. But he had survived his first experience of command in combat, and the Confederate high command, in its concern about protecting Columbus against a renewed effort, paid less attention to the possibility of another Yankee thrust into western Tennessee along the Tennessee and Cumberland rivers.

Also on November 7, Union forces landed at Port Royal, South Carolina, some fifty miles up the coast from Charleston, and fanned out across Hilton Head and St. Helena islands. The Confederates conceded the landing, although possession of Port Royal proved the first of several steps in helping the Union establish bases from which to mount a more effective blockade of Confederate ports. Meanwhile in the Deep South, after several attempts Yankees occupied Ship Island, offshore Mississippi in the Gulf of Mexico, thus establishing a staging point for possible future operations against New Orleans and Mobile, Alabama.

The Port Royal operation carried with it other consequences. If Confederate civilians fled before the appearance of Yankee soldiers, their black slaves stayed behind. Although most of these people did not fall under the provisions of the First Confiscation Act as "contrabands," they were obviously no longer under the control of their masters. Instead, they were put to work harvesting the area's plantation corps, while philanthropists and educators hustled south, eager to see what they might do to assist the former bondspeople in the transition from slavery to freedom.

Union commanders elsewhere confronted the problem of an influx of ex-slaves on their front lines. Within days of the fall of Port Royal, McClellan impressed upon his western subordinates that "we are fighting solely for the integrity of the Union, to uphold the power of our National Government, and to restore to the nation the blessings of peace and good order." One of those subordinates, Henry W. Halleck, who replaced Frémont in November, issued orders closing Union lines to black refugees.

The problems presented by slavery were obvious to Grant. In the aftermath of the clash at Belmont, he reaffirmed that the primary goal of the conflict was reunion. "My inclination is to whip the rebellion into submission, preserving all constitutional rights," he declared. "If it cannot be whipped in any other way than through a war against slavery, let it come to that legitimately. If it is necessary that slavery should fall that the Republic may continue its existence, let slavery go." Still, to Grant, that moment had not yet come. He instructed subordinates to return the escaped slaves of unionist masters, although he refused to do the same for secessionist slaveowners. Nor was he willing to allow secessionist civilians to misbehave. When news came that his pickets had been shot by civilians, he ordered the ouster of all civilians from the vicinity; anyone who violated this directive was "liable to be shot." Nevertheless, he would not provoke civilian resistance, warning his men that to act abrasively toward the populace "makes open and armed enemies of many who, from opposite treatment would become friends or at worse non-combattants."

Although Bull Run and Wilson's Creek were the two most notable battles of 1861, these Yankee defeats overshadowed far more significant accomplishments. Military and political action combined to keep Missouri, Kentucky, and Maryland in the Union; the capture of Port Royal proved immensely beneficial to the blockade, and in the West, Union forces were poised to advance along the Mississippi, Tennessee, and Cumberland rivers. In the East, McClellan had done wonders with his army in training camp; whether he could do the same in the field remained an open question.

The European Response

Confederates still harbored hopes that America's civil war would soon become an international conflict. The example of the American Revolution, considering the assistance that had been rendered the revolutionaries by France, Spain, and the Netherlands, offered grounds for such hope. Lincoln's decision to impose a naval blockade of the Confederacy further fueled these hopes, for in response on May 13, 1861, Great Britain proclaimed its neutrality in the conflict—thus recognizing the Confederacy as a belligerent, although not as an independent nation. This status enabled Confederate representatives to negotiate international loans and make purchases abroad, and it also endowed Confederate naval forces with the maritime rights of a belligerent.

Britain's decision to recognize a state of belligerency for the Confederacy angered many Northerners, who argued that this was only one step away from recognizing Confederate independence. In reality, however, Lincoln's decision to blockade the Southern ports had left British officials with little choice. But before long, Confederate leaders sought still more. Harkening back to prewar declarations about cotton's clout, they decided to embark on a voluntary program of economic coercion with "King Cotton" as the ultimate weapon. Across the South, newspaper editorials called upon planters to refuse to put up their cotton for export, reasoning that the resulting shortage of raw cotton for British textile mills would force Great Britain's hand. The King Cotton strategy did not reap immediate dividends, largely because in the late 1850s Southern cotton crops had been so large that surplus raw cotton currently swelled English storehouses. It would take some time to deplete those stores. Moreover, it overlooked the fact that the English actively traded with the North as well as the South, so that initiating a war with the North would damage other British industries. Finally, the rapid diversification of the British industrial economy already meant that the textile industry no longer played as large a role as it once had in Great Britain's overall prosperity.

Instead, European powers took advantage of the Civil War to press home their interests in the Western Hemisphere. Chief among those concerns was the failure of the Mexican Republic to pay off its European creditors. France, England, and Spain finally decided that military intervention might force due payment. Eventually, England and Spain withdrew their portion of the military contingent in Mexico, but France's Napoleon III, searching for ways to achieve a more permanent presence there, in 1863 hit upon the idea of establishing a puppet regime in Mexico City headed by the Austrian archduke Maximilian. In this he hoped to promote French interests in Europe, by forging an alliance with the Hapsburgs, while expanding France's presence in North America. However, many Mexicans did not welcome such interference. Under the leadership of Benito Juárez they warred against the invader. While Lincoln, Seward, and other Northern officials were sympathetic to Juárez, they realized that they could do little about Maximilian for the moment. Confederate leaders, hoping to attract French support, were willing to risk the establishment of a European-supported regime to the south in exchange for assistance in their own war for independence—although some diplomats expressed concern over rumors that Napoleon III's interest extended north towards Texas and New Mexico as well.

The irritant of European intervention in Mexico, was soon overshadowed by a far more dangerous crisis. On November 8, 1861—one day after Belmont and Port Royal—Captain Charles Wilkes of the United States Navy, commanding the *U.S.S. San Jacinto*, stopped a British mail packet, the *Trent*, in the Caribbean, intercepting its voyage from Cuba to St. Thomas. Union sailors seized two passengers, James Mason of Virginia and John Slidell of Louisiana, and took them aboard Wilkes's vessel, which then made its way to Boston. The two men were Confederate diplomats en route to Europe—Mason to London and Slidell to Paris—to seek European recognition of their new nation's independence.

Although Northerners hailed Wilkes as a hero, his action enraged British leaders, who spoke of war. The Royal Navy's North Atlantic Squadron was bolstered, while the British army made plans to send forces to Canada. However, at this time a war between Britain and the United States would have been in neither nation's interest, and before long both sides acted to dampen the crisis. The British wanted an immediate apology and the release of the two commissioners; Prince Albert added a statement to the formal demand that cleverly offered the Lincoln administration an out by suggesting that Wilkes had acted on his own, not under orders. Lincoln and Seward, fully aware that it was not a good time to commence a second war, acquiesced. Seward disavowed Wilkes's action, claiming that the captain had failed to observe international maritime law by not hauling the *Trent* into prize court for adjudication. Lincoln then authorized the release of Mason and Slidell, who did then make their way overseas. These measures proved sufficient to quell a possible trans-Atlantic war—at least for the moment.

The *Trent* affair had brought the United States and Great Britain to the brink of war at a time when the Confederacy could have benefitted significantly from such a contest. (It remains unclear exactly how close war had come.) Whether Great Britain would continue in its neutrality in America's civil war depended in large part on what happened in the battlefield in 1862.

CHAPTER THREE

The Limited War

As 1862 opened, both the Union and the Confederacy prepared for what portended to be the pivotal year of the conflict. Union armies were poised to move into the Confederacy, where the equally confident butternuts eagerly waited to do battle. Most observers looked toward Virginia for the decisive clash. For months General-in-Chief George B. McClellan had been drilling his men while he awaited the perfect opportunity to advance. Nor was his attention confined to his own Army of the Potomac, for as commanding general McClellan had to supervise the operation of all the blue-clad armies. When he had taken over the top spot in November 1861, he had found "everything at sixes & sevens—no system, no order—perfect chaos." He pledged that before long he would "soon have it working smoothly." Meanwhile he put up with the criticisms of Lincoln, other Northern politicians, and editors, all of whom were impatient for "Little Mac" to make something happen.

Months passed without McClellan moving. It seemed as if the Army of the Potomac, as well-trained and as well-supplied as it was, would never march off the parade ground and into battle. "Things seem to move as slow as ever," noted one Massachusetts officer, "and we seem to get no near[er] to the end, and it seems to be a war for the preservation of slavery more than anything else." Republican congressmen grumbled that it was time to attack; so did the new secretary of war, Edwin M. Stanton, whom Lincoln appointed to replace Cameron after it became evident that his first choice was unable to administer the war effort efficiently. Stanton, never one to mince words, declared that "the champagne and the oysters on the Potomac must be stopped." At last Abraham Lincoln ran out of patience. On January 27 he issued General War Order No. 1, instructing all Union armies to move forward by Washington's birthday (February 22); four days later a second order directed McClellan to advance against Manassas Junction. "All quiet along the Potomac," once a phrase connoting relief, now was uttered with derision by Northerners.

Forts Henry and Donelson

While all in Washington were still waiting for McClellan to move, the first Yankee thrusts deep into Confederate territory took place in the western theater. In January, Union troops under the command of George H. Thomas routed a Confederate force at Mill Springs, Kentucky, solidifying Federal control of that crucial state. Lincoln hoped that the victory would inaugurate an offensive into East Tennessee, a haven of Southern unionists, but it soon became apparent that such an operation would have to wait due to logistical problems. Instead, the first major Union success occurred in West Tennessee. For some time several military planners had eyed the Tennessee and Cumberland rivers, along with the Mississippi, as providing natural areas of invasion. To exploit this opportunity Union planners had worked hard on constructing a riverline navy, a mix of steamer transports, ironclads, and rams to support army operations in the region. It proved easier to move and to supply soldiers by water than over land, and gunboats offered fire support during many land battles.

The Confederates, realizing this, had built a brace of makeshift forts, christened Henry and Donelson, respectively, to protect the area in which the two rivers neared the Kentucky border, a point at which the two rivers ran less than a dozen miles apart. In February 1862, Ulysses S. Grant and Flag Officer Andrew Hull Foote secured the approval of Grant's superior, Henry W. Halleck, to take the forts. Fort Henry fell first, on February 6, its walls crumbling under the combined impact of cannon fire from Foote's gunboat flotilla and flooding as a result of heavy rains, allowing one of the Union vessels to demand the fort's surrender even before Grant's soldiers arrived.

Grant then turned east towards Donelson, a far firmer structure. There Confederate commander Albert Sidney Johnston had posted some 17,000 men under the command of John B. Floyd and Gideon Pillow to stop Grant, whose original force of 15,000 was being augmented daily by reinforcements until it exceeded 25,000. The Yankees prepared to lay siege to Donelson, but the fort's cannon beat back an attack by Foote's gunboats. The Confederates, believing that they could not withstand a siege, planned a blow against Grant's right flank, hoping to pry it back so as to open an avenue for escape. On February 15, some 10,000 Rebels launched their assault. Initial success disorganized the Confederates as much as it did Grant's men, and Grant ordered counterattacks all along the line. By nightfall the Confederates had been driven back to their original positions; elsewhere Union advances had breached Donelson's fortifications. Floyd and Pillow deemed their position hopeless; afraid that they would be singled out for harsh treatment should they be taken prisoner—Pillow had once been a major general in the Mexican-American War, while Floyd, as James Buchanan's secretary of war, had supposedly dispatched arms and munitions to federal armories in the South, where they soon fell into Confederate hands—they decided to flee, leaving Simon B. Buckner with the burden of surrendering those who remained. Perhaps Buckner thought that his prewar friendship with Grant would allow him to work out some sort of lenient arrangement for the capitulation of the garrison, but the Union general's response to his entreaty cut short

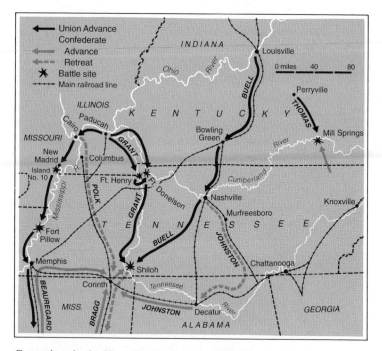

Campaigns in the West, February to April 1862

any such notions. "No terms except unconditional and immedi-
ate surrender will be accepted," Grant bluntly told Buckner. The
Confederate commander reluctantly submitted, and some 15,000
Rebels soon headed north to prison.

At last Northerners had cause to celebrate. "Unconditional
surrender" became both a slogan and a nickname for the Union
commander's malleable initials. The surrender was the largest
ever on the North American continent. Johnston proceeded to
evacuate Nashville; soon Federal forces were threatening
Memphis and poised to invade Mississippi. Lincoln promoted Grant to major general, while Northerners, reading reports that Grant had rallied his troops with a cigar in his hand,
showered the pipe-smoking general with boxes of Havana's finest; Grant, not wanting to waste the gifts, commenced a cigar-

smoking habit that would ultimately lead to his contracting throat cancer over two decades later. But a more immediate threat to the career of the North's newest hero soon surfaced. Communications between Grant and Halleck after Donelson were broken by a disloyal telegraph operator; Halleck, somewhat jealous of Grant's new fame and always a stickler for form, assumed that Grant was deliberately ignoring him and acting without authority. Reporting his suspicions to McClellan, he added that rumors had reached him that Grant "had resumed his former bad habits"—a reference to Grant's fondness for alcohol (although there was no evidence to substantiate these stories). Little Mac authorized Halleck to shelve his subordinate. Grant protested and requested to be relieved of duty rather than accept such a demotion; Halleck backed down after the Lincoln administration instructed him to prove his charges against the victor of Fort Donelson.

Shiloh

Grant joined his army, now encamped on the west bank of the Tennessee River at Pittsburg Landing, twenty miles northeast of Corinth, Mississippi, an important rail junction and the target of the next offensive. Halleck ordered Grant to await the arrival of another column under the command of Major General Don Carlos Buell before advancing; Buell's leisurely advance gave Grant plenty of time to drill his new recruits, including a green division encamped around Shiloh Church under the command of William T. Sherman. For Sherman, the assignment represented a second chance. Placed in charge of Union forces in central and eastern Kentucky in October 1861, he had, in a tremendous bout of overestimation, insisted that his forces were insufficient for the task before him in such passionate tones that observers suspected him of cracking under pressure. A few even judged him insane. Eventually Lincoln had set Sherman aside; only now did the general seem ready to resume field duty.

So confident was Grant of taking the offensive that he failed to lay out his camps in a fortified defensive position; Sherman, determined to disabuse his previous critics, dismissed reports of

Confederate forces just beyond his lines as products of an excessively vivid imagination. Grant informed Halleck on April 5 that he had "scarcely the faintest idea of an attack (general one) being made upon us, but will be prepared should such a thing take place." Sherman was more blunt. Responding to reports of enemy activity, he told one jumpy colonel, "Take your damn regiment back to Ohio. There is no enemy nearer than Corinth."

But there were Rebels in those woods, and they were ready to take advantage of Grant's confidence and Sherman's bravado. By foot and by rail Albert Sidney Johnston had concentrated some 40,000 Confederates at Corinth, determined to strike a blow at Grant before Buell arrived to reinforce him. As April began the Rebels moved northward towards Pittsburg Landing, but the advance proved so ponderous and noisy that P. G. T. Beauregard and other subordinates advised Johnston to abandon the offensive. The Confederate commander demurred: "I would fight them if they were a million."

It was early morning on Palm Sunday, April 6, when Union patrols detected the advancing enemy. The Federals in camp dressed hastily, and stumbled into line just as the Rebel onslaught lit into them. Many rookie recruits broke at their first sight of the enemy; more stood firm, however, and before long both sides were engaged in a slugfest. Grant rallied his troops, sent for reinforcements, and organized a defense that gave ground grudgingly. Repeated Confederate assaults pushed the bluecoats back towards the steamboat landing. Grant's preparations for a final line of defense were immensely aided when one Federal division, posted in a sunken road, withstood a series of assaults, the air about them so thick with bullets that soldiers later christened the area the Hornet's Nest. Among its victims was Johnston, who was hit in the leg. By the time the Confederates overwhelmed the defenders, Johnston had bled to death, Grant's lines were set, and lead elements of Buell's force had arrived. As night and rain fell the Union line held. Sherman, who had distinguished himself during the day in rallying his troops despite suffering three wounds, found Grant, dripping wet, smoking a cigar under a tree, preferring the rain to the dreadful sounds of the wounded and dying in a nearby cabin turned field hospital. It had been a rough day, Sherman suggested; Grant, assenting, replied, "Whip 'em tomorrow, though."

During the night Grant was reinforced by the bulk of Buell's men and another of his own divisions. Stragglers, having regained some control over their fear, rejoined the ranks. At dawn on April 7, the Yankees counterattacked, and by day's end they had driven the Rebels, now commanded by Beauregard, back whence they came. But Grant's men were too exhausted to pursue the fleeing enemy, and Buell seemed unwilling to do so. Both attitudes were understandable. In two days of combat the bluecoats had lost some 13,000 men killed, wounded, and missing, the majority from Grant's command; Confederate losses exceeded 10,000. More Americans fell at Shiloh than had fallen in all previous American wars combined. Grant later recalled that it had been nearly impossible to avoid stepping on dead bodies as one crossed the field. Although he had emerged the victorious general, the fact that his men had been unprepared to meet the initial assault and had suffered immense casualties led to charges of military incompetence, more unwarranted whispers about the general's drinking, and demands for his removal. Overlooked was the fact that he had turned back the Confederacy's last major bid to regain control of West Tennessee and break the momentum of the Union offensive.

Grant survived Shiloh, but it was a close call. Halleck came down to Pittsburg Landing and took personal command of the combined armies of Grant, Buell, and Major General John Pope, the latter fresh from overwhelming a Confederate garrison on the Mississippi labelled Island No. 10, located near the Kentucky-Tennessee border. This large force then crept down toward Corinth, where Beauregard awaited their arrival. Grant was named second-in-command of the combined Union force, but he felt that he was being bypassed; at one point he prepared to take a leave which might have taken him completely out of the war. Eventually, Grant decided to stick around. He might get another chance.

Elsewhere in the Mississippi River valley and adjoining areas Union forces were also meeting with success. In Arkansas, bluecoats under General Samuel R. Curtis beat back a Confederate assault at Pea Ridge, securing Missouri and a foothold in Arkansas. Pope's victory at Island No. 10 had secured Union control of the Mississippi River from the north all the way down to Fort Pillow, north of Memphis. Even more spectacular was the surrender of New Orleans to a flotilla under the command of Flag Officer David Glasgow Farragut, a native Tennessean whose naval service extended back to the War of 1812. In April 1862, Farragut's force, carrying 15,000 soldiers led by Benjamin F. Butler, approached the forts protecting the mouth of the river. When a week-long naval bombardment failed to dislodge the defenders, Farragut decided to run his flotilla past the forts before dawn on April 24, the gutsy officer slipping by with only one ship lost and three disabled. Five days later Farragut's sailors and marines stepped ashore at New Orleans; their landing was unopposed, for the city's militia had fled. The forts near the river's mouth surrendered to Butler, who then moved upriver to occupy New Orleans. Thus the Confederacy lost its largest city and leading port.

Although the pace of Union victories slowed in May, by month's end things picked up again. Halleck finally readied an assault against Beauregard at Corinth, but the Confederate commander, anticipating such a move, evacuated the city on the night of May 29. Halleck's half-hearted effort at pursuit proved fruitless. As Grant later derisively remarked, the campaign "was a siege from the start to the close." On June 6, a Union naval force spearheaded by several ironclad rams collided with a similar Confederate force near Memphis. To the shock of Memphis's citizens, who had lined the river banks to cheer their boys on, the Yankee vessels bashed the Rebel fleet and took the city.

There the string of Union successes ended. Halleck dispersed his combined force, instructing Buell to march east toward Chattanooga while the remaining regiments either reinforced other armies or settled down to occupation duty in West Tennessee. Farragut's fleet moved upriver, capturing Baton Rouge and Natchez, but it proved unable to take Vicksburg on its own, leaving the Confederates in control of that key position. Once again, all eyes turned to Virginia.

Rebels Resurgent in Virginia

As Grant and Foote took Henry and Donelson, combined army-navy forces also scored several successes along the Atlantic sea-coast. Building on the triumphs of 1861 along the Carolina coast at Cape Hatteras and Port Royal, another expedition, 7,500 strong and under the command of Ambrose E. Burnside, landed at North Carolina's Roanoke Island and captured its 2,700 de-fenders. Within weeks Union forces occupied several more ports. Two months later Federal siege artillery pounded Fort Pulaski, Georgia, and forced the Confederates to abandon it. As a result, the port of Savannah was virtually closed. Along the Atlantic, only Charleston and Wilmington remained open as major ports for Confederate shipping, and the Union's naval blockade now focused on intercepting traffic to and from these ports as well as tracking down smaller and more elusive vessels that sought ref-uge in inlets and other natural hideouts.

These Union victories, along with Grant's triumphs in the West, made McClellan's inertia all the more apparent and frus-trating. Lincoln pressed him to advance south against the Con-federate position at Manassas Junction, but the general preferred a different approach. He planned to transport most of his force by water to Urbanna, Virginia, on the south bank of the Rappahannock River less than fifty miles north of Richmond. Confederate commander Joseph E. Johnston, he argued, then would be forced to abandon his position and attack before the Union army seized the Confederate capital. Lincoln reluctantly assented to the plan, but only after establishing a deadline for moving and securing a guarantee that the general would leave behind sufficient force to defend Washington.

Before McClellan moved, however, Johnston retreated south from Manassas across the Rappahannock. Little Mac's chagrin turned to humiliation when newspapermen revealed that the rows of cannon Johnston reportedly would use to blow away assault-ing infantry were in reality simply logs painted black—"Quaker guns," as the soldiers dubbed them. That McClellan had known of these phony emplacements for weeks did not diminish the criticism he heard. Undeterred, he simply recast his plan, this time choosing to land his force at Virginia's Fort Monroe and advance along the peninsula between the York and James rivers to Richmond. He again assured Lincoln that he would leave behind a force sufficient to protect the capital.

Then alarming news reached Washington. Upon seizing the naval yard at Norfolk back in 1861, Confederate authorities had been able to salvage the hull of the frigate *U.S.S. Merrimack*. In haste they ordered the construction of an ironclad ram, christened the *C.S.S. Virginia*, on top of the *Merrimack*'s wooden hull. At first Gideon Welles, Lincoln's navy secretary, had been focusing on the building of more sailing vessels for the blockade fleet, but after Northern newspapers got wind of the Confederate ironclad's construction, their alarmist reports moved Congress to pressure Welles to respond in kind. Yankee shipbuilders quickly got to work. Early designs were far more suitable as gunboats for use in the riverline navy in the West. Only when John Ericsson, famous for his various innovations in ship design—most notably the screw propeller—submitted his blueprint did Union authorities find a rival worthy of the *Virginia*. Ericsson's design featured a hull overlaid by an iron-plated deck, which was barely visible above the waterline, topped by a revolving turret mounting two cannon. Some said that the new vessel would look like a cheesebox on a raft, but it promised to be quick and maneuverable. With some misgivings and reservations Welles and his advisers gave Ericsson a contract. By the end of January, the *Monitor*, as Ericsson called his warship, was launched. Several weeks of outfitting remained. Would it be finished in time to check the *Virginia*?

The answer would come none too soon. On March 8, 1862, the *Virginia* steamed into Hampton Roads, where several wooden Union warships were protecting Fort Monroe and blockading the entrance to the James River. The *Virginia* first headed for the *U.S.S. Cumberland*; after peppering her with several broadsides, the *Virginia*'s ram tore into the *Cumberland*'s hull, sinking the Federal frigate. The crews of the other assembled ships looked on helplessly, their cannon balls bouncing off *Virginia*'s plates, although the ironclad did suffer some damage. Then the *Virginia* turned to its second victim, the *U.S.S. Congress*, claiming victory when the ship's powder magazine exploded. Only darkness prevented the *Virginia* from making equally short work of a third ship, the *U.S.S. Minnesota*, which had run aground while trying to assist its fellow ships. Tomorrow, the Confederates figured they would finish the job, their easy victory closing off the Union's most important base for its naval blockade.

When the sun rose and *Virginia* prepared to renew battle on March 9, however, it met the *Monitor*, which had arrived during the night. For several hours the two ironclads pounded away at each other, with the more maneuverable *Monitor* making circles around the *Virginia*. Finally the Confederates took advantage of an opportune shot that hit the *Monitor's* turret, wounding its commander, to make good their return to harbor at Norfolk. Though both sides claimed victory, it was the *Monitor* that had achieved its goal of protecting the key blockade station at Fort Monroe. The news brought Lincoln and his cabinet great relief, for rumors that the *Virginia* had finished in Hampton Roads and was headed for Washington had led to panic in the Union capital.

In the aftermath of this excitement McClellan pressed once more to launch his amphibious plan of attack. With the *Virginia* back in Norfolk and under the watchful eye of the *Monitor*, the way seemed open for the transfer of the Army of the Potomac to the James River. Lincoln agreed, but only after stripping McClellan of his responsibilities as general-in-chief to allow him to concentrate on his own campaign. On March 17, Union soldiers boarded transports at Alexandria, Virginia, and set sail for Fort Monroe. Nearly three weeks later the troop transfer was complete. There was only one hitch. Lincoln discovered that McClellan had been less than candid when he had promised to leave behind sufficient force to defend Washington, for the general's troop-strength figures included several miscalculations and embraced forces in the Shenandoah Valley, which were too far away to be of immediate assistance should Washington find itself under attack. Lincoln and Stanton, already worried about the security of the capital in light of the *Virginia* panic, had grown even more concerned when reports of a battle between a Confederate force under Stonewall Jackson and a Union contingent at Kernstown, Virginia, on March 23, alerted them to the possibility of danger from the Shenandoah. To secure the safety of the capital, they decided to withhold from McClellan's offensive an infantry corps under the command of Irwin McDowell, despite McClellan's protest that the decision was "the most infamous thing that history has recorded."

Grumbling, McClellan turned his attention to the problem in front of him. If he was to advance up the peninsula between the James and York rivers to Richmond, he must first overcome a Confederate garrison at Yorktown, site of the climactic battle of the Revolutionary War. The Confederate commander at Yorktown, John B. Magruder, found his prewar experience as an amateur thespian quite useful as he put on a little production to play on McClellan's fears. Marching regiments to and fro, with flags flying and bugles blaring, he convinced the Union commander that his force was far more formidable than the 10,000 he actually commanded. McClellan prepared to besiege the Confederates, while still complaining about the continued absence of McDowell's corps. Watching from Washington, Lincoln, pointing out that delay would only allow the Confederates to bolster their position, urged his general to attack immediately. He would defend McClellan from his critics: "But you must act." The general, smarting under the admonishment, told his wife, "I was much tempted to reply that he had better come and do it himself."

The Army of the Potomac sat in its entrenchments for nearly a month, McClellan held in check by his fear of being outnumbered and his concern that the *Virginia* might suddenly appear to wreak havoc behind his lines. He therefore emplaced siege artillery with the expectation that he would simply blast away at the Confederate lines. Anticipating this, Johnston planned a withdrawal; on May 3 the Confederates slipped away. McClellan ordered a partial pursuit, and three Union divisions collided with the Rebel rearguard at Williamsburg on May 5. Johnston continued to retreat. Within ten days he had reached the outskirts of Richmond. McClellan followed deliberately, while Lincoln, arriving at Fort Monroe on May 6, took matters into his own hands and directed several gunboats and regiments to take Norfolk. Abandoning the city, the Confederates ran the *Virginia* aground and set it on fire.

The prospects for the capture of Richmond seemed bright. McClellan called once more for McDowell to reinforce him, confident that only then would he be strong enough to overwhelm the Confederates. To avoid such a disaster, Robert E. Lee, now Jefferson Davis's military adviser, instructed Jackson to maneuver his forces in the Shenandoah Valley to threaten Washington and thus draw away potential reinforcements for McClellan. Stonewall played his part to the hilt. A series of marches and countermarches confused his Yankee opponents, and when Jackson hit, he hit hard, defeating Union forces under John C. Frémont and Nathaniel Banks in a brace of battles in the valley in May. Holding McDowell in reserve, Lincoln directed one of his divisions under James Shields to pursue Jackson in an effort to trap the wily rebel. Jackson returned south through the valley, drawing the Yankees in pursuit, fended off an attack by Frémont at Cross Keys on June 8, then drove back Shields at Port Republic the following day before withdrawing to the Blue Ridge Mountains. The Confederate commander had exploited his mobility, the terrain, and the lack of coordination among his confused opponents to claim success despite having faced double his numbers. Meanwhile, McDowell remained in central Virginia, and McClellan, who was once more calling for reinforcements, seized upon the absence of McDowell's men to explain his inability to take Richmond.

While Jackson dodged his pursuers, Johnston decided that it was time to snap back at McClellan. Noting that the two wings of the Army of the Potomac presently were divided by the swollen Chickahominy River, the Confederate general decided to hit McClellan's position south of the river at Fair Oaks (also known as Seven Pines) on May 31. But his overly ambitious plan of attack, requiring precision in coordination, soon gave way to a series of piecemeal assaults, which the Army of the Potomac beat back over two days. McClellan, however, disturbed by the "sickening sight of the battlefield, with its mangled corpses & poor suffering wounded," lost his stomach for another engagement: "Victory has no charms for me when purchased at such a cost." He would never again venture too close to the field of battle, despite a celebratory order of his which, in anticipation of future clashes, declared, "Soldiers! I will be with you in this battle, and share its dangers with you." Meanwhile Johnston, who had far fewer qualms about being under fire, paid for it when he was wounded on the evening of the first day, leaving him unfit for duty. After the battle Jefferson Davis asked Robert E. Lee to assume field command of the Army of Northern Virginia.

Lee's record thus far in the war was less than expected for someone possessing such promise. A model cadet at West Point, he had distinguished himself during the Mexican-American War and earned a reputation as one of the army's finest officers. Nevertheless, he had failed to shake the Union's hold on western Virginia in the fall of 1861 and his work preparing defenses along the Atlantic coast received little attention. For the past several months he had manned a desk at Richmond as Davis's adviser. McClellan welcomed the change in commanders, judging Lee "too cautious & weak under grave responsibility" and "likely to be timid & irresolute in action." Nor were the Confederate soldiers enamored of their new commander, referring to him derisively as the "King of Spades" when he ordered them to entrench fortifications. But a discerning observer claimed that Lee's aristocratic reserve concealed the soul of a gambler: "His name might be Audacity. He will take more chances, and take them quicker than any general in this country."

Before long it became apparent that Lee's orders to throw up earthworks were a prelude not to a stubborn defense but to a daring counterattack. Deceiving his opponent into believing that a reinforced Stonewall Jackson would renew his exploits in the Shenandoah Valley, Lee decided instead to bring Jackson's men to Richmond to hit McClellan's right, which still dangled above the Chickahominy in anticipation of McDowell's arrival. If it gave way, Lee could then strike at McClellan's supply depot. For the first time the Confederate commander revealed his favorite mode for bringing on an offensive battle. He would use one part of his army to pin his opponent in place, move a second force to the enemy flank, and finally strike a devastating blow.

Lee first dispatched cavalry commander James Ewell Brown "Jeb" Stuart on a raid around McClellan's entire army to disrupt supply lines, gather intelligence, and generally stun and fluster McClellan. Stuart took off on June 12, and over the next three days he led his 1,200 cavalrymen on a tour around the Army of the Potomac, losing only one man in the process. Lee, having thus received the information he desired, put his plan of attack in motion. Jackson's 18,000 men came by rail and foot to a position north of McClellan's right, some 30,000 men under Fitz-John Porter, McClellan's favorite subordinate. At the same time, Lee, leaving just enough men to hold his newly constructed Richmond defenses, shifted the majority of his army, some 45,000 men, opposite Porter's lines. McClellan cooperated with Lee's plan by staying in place while wiring Washington for more reinforcements, claiming that Lee's force was double his at 200,000. However, Stuart's raid had alerted him to the vulnerability of his supply line, and he began to contemplate shifting his base of operations.

But it was McClellan who, looking to commence his final campaign against Richmond, precipitated battle on June 25. The next day Lee answered, attacking Porter, but Jackson's men failed to appear on Porter's flank as planned. That night Porter withdrew to Gaines's Mill, where he formed a defensive perimeter, and on June 27 Lee attacked again. Jackson, although tardy once more, finally arrived in the afternoon and assisted in an assault that finally broke the Union line just before dusk. Under cover of darkness Porter's men made their way across the Chicka-

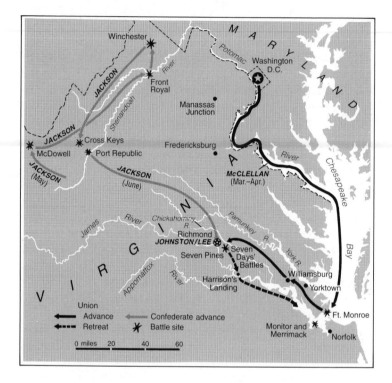

The Peninsula Campaign, 1862

hominy to rejoin their comrades, who had been waiting while McClellan, duped once more by Magruder's noisy theatrics, steeled himself for an attack.

As Porter retreated, McClellan, now truly worried about the threat to his supply line, decided to move the source of his supplies back to Harrison's Landing on the James River. He would then pull his men back to defend this new supply base. The retreat might well be risky, he believed, but it was not his fault, for, as he telegraphed Stanton, "I have seen too many dead and wounded comrades to feel otherwise than that this Government has not sustained this army. . . . If I save this army now, I tell you plainly that I owe no thanks to you or to any other persons in Washington. You have done your best to sacrifice this army." The last two lines never reached Stanton, for they had been deleted by an officer who realized their probable impact on the irascible secretary; moreover, as McClellan had directed operations from behind his lines—so much for sharing the dangers of battle—he personally had seen precious little of the carnage.

Lee pursued the retreating Yankees but failed to inflict significant damage. By July 1, McClellan had established a solid defensive position at Malvern Hill, some six miles north of Harrison's Landing. From atop the hill, Union artillery possessed a clear field of fire, but, nevertheless, Lee decided to launch yet another assault. As they charged up the hill, the attackers were mowed down by cannon fire. As one of Lee's generals later recalled, "it was not war—it was murder." On the following day McClellan, despite the urging of subordinates to mount a counterattack, moved his men to Harrison's Landing. The Seven Days—as people called the series of battles between Lee and McClellan—were over.

Although the Confederate army had suffered 20,000 casualties to the 16,500 lost by the Army of the Potomac (including 6,000 captured) and had broken the Union lines only at Gaines's Mill, Lee had succeeded in driving McClellan away from Richmond. The Confederate commander was unhappy that he had not achieved more, for he had entertained hopes of destroying his opponent in a climatic battle. He blamed his failure to do so in part "because I cannot have my orders carried out"—a reference to the failure of his subordinates, notably Jackson, to fulfill their obligations. Lee had expected too much too soon from people who had not fought together before and who lacked the tight coordination required for successful offensive operations. It would not be until a year later that the high command of the Army of Northern Virginia would again perform so poorly. In the interim, it would perfect the approach to battle of pin-flank-attack to drive the Yankees from several more fields. As for McClellan, while his army had fought well, he had passed up a major opportunity to strike a decisive blow and had seemed more anxious to attack the administration on paper than the Confederates in battle. There would be no quick victory. Lincoln began to cast about for alternatives.

Confederate Escalation

On February 22, 1862, Jefferson Davis shed the prefix of provisional from his position as president of the Confederacy. The first formally elected Confederate Congress assembled in Richmond to hear him outline the goals of his administration. Although the news of Donelson's surrender dampened some spirits, Davis seemed as resolute as ever. It was time to mobilize for a longer struggle. The first step was conscription. On April 16, in response to Davis's request, the Confederate Congress passed legislation making all able-bodied white male citizens between the ages of eighteen and thirty-five liable for three years of service—the first draft in American history. The terms of enlistment for those soldiers who had signed up for twelve months was extended for another two years—just as many of those men were counting the weeks before they returned home. Draftees could hire substitutes drawn from those men not subject to conscription; several exempt categories were soon added, including public employees, teachers, laborers in industries critical to the war effort, apothecaries, hospital workers, and clergymen. Not surprisingly, the number of Southern whites employed in these areas surged upward within months of the conscription announcement. But the institution of the draft actually encouraged enlistments—volunteers could form their own regiments, while conscripts filled the ranks of existing units—and Confederate ranks swelled by upwards of 200,000 men.

But worse in the eyes of those who thought the government too bold in mandating conscription was its imposition of martial law and the suspension of the writ of habeas corpus by the Davis administration. The Confederate Congress had authorized Davis to take such measures in areas under direct threat of enemy attack in the aftermath of the surrender of Fort Donelson. The Confederate president, who had just pointed with pride to his observance of civil liberties in marked contrast to the Lincoln administration, did not hesitate to wield his new power, most notably in Richmond.

Angry Confederates protested such measures. How could a government founded upon the notion of state sovereignty violate that very principle by adopting measures that smacked of strong central government? Was there any real difference between dictatorship from Richmond and dictatorship from Washington? Georgia governor Joseph E. Brown declared that conscription was "at war with all the principles for which Georgia entered the revolution." He was convinced that Southern whites "have more to fear from military despotism than from subjugation from the enemy." Others took a more realistic stance. Louis T. Wigfall, senator from Texas, warned his colleagues that it was time to "cease this child's play. . . . No man has any individual rights, which come into conflict with the welfare of the country." Other Confederates were willing to make these compromises if they led to victory.

Nevertheless, these and subsequent acts began to expose the tensions inherent in the Confederate experiment. For years slaveholders had challenged the right of government to infringe upon their rights of property in slaves. Now the Confederate government impressed slaves into service for the war effort. Slaveholders had always emphasized the importance of white solidarity, reminding nonslaveholding whites that the major dividing line in Southern society was race, not class. Subsequent conscription legislation, however, exempted those slaveholders or overseers who owned twenty or more slaves from the draft, lending credence to the sentiment that it was a slaveholder's war but a poor man's fight. Many white southerners had preached the virtues of limiting the exercise of centralized power and states rights, only to see the Confederate government wield powers and claim authority for actions that presaged the evolution of the very sort of political institution they had seceded to escape. Some white Southerners had joined the cause to protect their homes from the Yankee invader; Confederate military planners had to keep this sentiment in mind when they weighed giving up territory to improve their overall defensive position. Yet these tensions would not pull apart the Confederacy so long as its armies enjoyed success on the battlefield. Confederate military leaders looked to launch counteroffensives to rouse morale at home as well as to dampen the resolve of the Yankees—and, perhaps, gain enough momentum to entice foreign intervention. Defeats would only foster dissent and protest.

If anything, the Confederate commitment to continue the conflict intensified in 1862, at least according to those Union generals in the field who found the Rebels as determined as ever. In the aftermath of Shiloh, Grant believed that one more victory in the West might well tip over the Confederacy. But the capture of Corinth proved anticlimactic. As Grant and Sherman administered occupied West Tennessee, they discovered that sympathy for secession remained strong among the area's residents despite the officers' best efforts to promote a sense of reconciliation. Civilians proved recalcitrant, and guerrillas prowled the countryside, attacking Yankee detachments. The latent unionism that Lincoln and others assumed was there was nowhere to be found. "We curry favor of these secessionists," one Yankee noted, "and real Union men do not fare as well as they; we are obsequious to them, we feed them, we guard their property, we humble ourselves to gain their favor, and in return we receive insult and injury." Soldiers "very naturally ask is this the way to crush the rebellion. . . . The iron gauntlet must be used more than the silken glove to crush this serpent."

Therefore it was the behavior of Southern civilians, not the intensity of the Confederate attack at Shiloh, that proved decisive in changing the minds of Grant and Sherman about the duration and scale of the conflict. Such behavior, especially when it came to guerrilla operations, blurred the distinction between combatant and noncombatant and marked a distinct escalation of the conflict. Grant and Sherman responded in kind, shutting down secessionist newspapers, ousting Confederate sympathizers from their lines, promising to execute any captured guerrillas, and levying assessments on secessionist families to compensate for losses suffered by the Union army.

John Pope provided observers with a hint of what was to come when Lincoln ordered him east to take charge of the newly formed Army of Virginia, cobbled from the forces that had opposed Jackson in the spring. The new commander exhibited an enthusiasm for escalating the conflict notably absent in McClellan and a bravado that irritated many of his own soldiers as well as his opponents. Arriving in Washington just as Lee opened his offensive against McClellan, in mid-July, Pope issued a series of orders authorizing his men to live off the land, punish civilians in retaliation for guerrilla activities, and deport to the Confederacy any civilian who failed to take a loyalty oath to the Union. Confederate leaders denounced these measures, much as they did similar orders issued by Grant and Sherman. "I want Pope suppressed," Lee told Jackson. "The course indicated in his orders . . . cannot be permitted and will lead to retaliation on our part."

In the summer of 1862 William T. Sherman declared that the Union strategy of conciliation of civilians in occupied areas had proven a failure. He predicted that "the war will soon assume a turn to extermination, not of soldiers alone, that is the least part of it, but the people." As usual, Sherman's words were far stronger than his actions, and Union commanders did not resort to measures common to twentieth-century conceptions of total war. But there was no doubt that the conflict was escalating beyond its original boundaries, and this escalation was due in large part to the persistence of Confederate resistance, the mobilization of Confederate resources, and the increased central authority of the Davis government. These measures, and the Union responses to them, intensified the conflict and broadened its scope beyond the battlefield. The hopes of Yankees and Rebels alike that they were fighting to preserve something were eroding precisely because of the war they were fighting.

CHAPTER FOUR

War Becomes Revolution

In the summer of 1862 the scope and intensity of the American Civil War began changing in response to events. Saving the Union was one thing: restoring it was proving impossible. As Lincoln himself was fond of saying, "Broken eggs cannot be mended." Hopes for early victory were vanishing, both sides were already acting in ways unforeseen at the outset of the conflict. Back in New York City, George Templeton Strong, depressed by the news from Richmond, found it "hard to maintain my lively faith in the triumph of the nation and the law. . . . On the other hand, the government seems waking up to the duty of dealing more vigorously with rebellion by acts of emancipation and confiscation."

There were others who welcomed the escalation of the conflict, for it meant that at last the Lincoln administration would embrace emancipation. "The American people and the Government at Washington may refuse to recognize it for a time," Frederick Douglass had warned in 1861, "but the 'inexorable logic of events' will force it upon them in the end; that the war now being waged in this land is a war for and against slavery."

Now in the summer of 1862 he pressed his argument with renewed fervor. "They have fought the rebels with the olive branch," he declared. "The people must teach them to fight with the sword. They have sought to conciliate obedience. The people must teach them to compel obedience." The lesson of the conflict was clear to him. "The South says that the Union must die that slavery may live. The North must be brought to say, slavery shall die that the Union may live."

Toward Emancipation

At first, Abraham Lincoln did what he could to limit the boundaries of the conflict. The Union, he pledged, was not committed to a war of abolition; generals were not to disturb citizens in enemy territory unless absolutely necessary, and the government would take no untoward measures against slavery or Confederates. The reasons for such an approach were obvious. To commit the North to abolition as a war aim would erode Unionist support in the border states, placing their future loyalty to the Union in jeopardy, while only stiffening Confederate resistance. If the Union army treated Southern civilians roughly, it would confirm Confederate claims that the bluecoats were barbarians and vandals seeking to destroy the South at their first opportunity, which, again, would intensify and widen resistance. By waging a limited war, Lincoln hoped that it would be easier to secure peace.

Yet there were problems with this limited approach. In seeking to make reunion easier, Lincoln was making it harder for Union arms to triumph on the battlefield. Slave labor provided the Confederacy with a valuable military resource. It allowed a higher percentage of whites to be mobilized for military service without hurting Southern production levels. Of course, slaves worked plantation fields, but they could also be found working salt, iron, and lead mines, and slave labor filled many positions at the Tredegar Iron Works and other Confederate manufacturing establishments. Slaves also accompanied Confederate armies as cooks, wagoners, and laborers; in the Union army, soldiers had to be detailed to those duties, reducing the number of men available for combat. In short, by not touching slavery, Union authorities refused to strike directly at one of the foundations of Confederate military power.

Ignoring slavery also proved impractical in practice, for the mere presence of an invading army could not but affect the peculiar institution. Black refugees flooded into Union lines; hot on their heels were slaveowners demanding the return of their human property. Some of these slaveholders protested that they were loyal Unionists, although in many cases their loyalty to the North may have been conveniently revitalized primarily by the necessities of the situation; others unabashedly professed their allegiance to the Confederacy, utterly unconscious of the irony of demanding that a government whom they were battling and had denounced should honor their constitutional rights. In either case, whatever Union officers and soldiers chose to do with the refugees represented a political statement about the scope of Union war aims. To return fugitives would confirm the administration's pledge not to disturb slavery; to refuse to do so, even on the grounds that the property of rebels was subject to confiscation as contraband of war, made slavery a target of military operations. Complicating matters still further was the reluctance of the administration to promulgate a uniform policy regarding the issue.

In the absence of an explicit directive from Washington, commanders on the scene had to devise their own answers to the questions raised by fugitive slaves and their indignant masters. Congress had approved the Butler formula based on the notion of "contraband of war" in passing the First Confiscation Act in August 1861. Frémont's Missouri proclamation had promised to escalate the conflict still more until Lincoln countermanded it. Events at Port Royal in the fall of 1861 had compelled new policies, as had the penetration of Union armies along the Mississippi and Tennessee rivers in 1862. But it was the action of General David Hunter in South Carolina that provoked the most comment during the spring of 1862. Thousands of black refugees had flocked to Union enclaves along the South Carolina coast in the aftermath of the capture of Port Royal. Hunter, who took command in March, acted upon his abolitionist beliefs and actually organized several black regiments. On May 9, he issued a proclamation abolishing slavery in South Carolina, Florida, and Georgia. Ten days later Lincoln revoked it. The president made it clear that only *he* would decide when such a step was necessary—although he no longer denied the possibility. Indeed, he warned that it might soon become probable: "You can not if you would, be blind to the signs of the times."

One had only to look around to see what Lincoln meant. If slavery was vulnerable on the battlefield, it was also becoming more so in the halls of Congress. When it reconvened in December 1861, a majority of Republicans wanted to take more decided steps against slavery. By a party vote, the House refused to renew the Johnson-Crittenden Resolutions; furthermore, several congressmen announced that they intended to introduce measures striking directly at slavery. Lincoln, still concerned about the impact of such legislation upon the border states, sought to limit its impact. Yet he also hinted that he was for emancipation on certain terms. His approach featured the twin principles of a gradual, compensated emancipation and the colonization of newly freed blacks. "In considering the policy to be adopted for suppressing the insurrection," he explained, "I have been anxious and careful that the inevitable conflict for this purpose shall not degenerate into a violent and remorseless revolutionary struggle." This was underlined when he recalled Secretary of War Simon Cameron's report to Congress in order to strike a recommendation it contained to enlist black soldiers in the Union army.

Many congressional Republicans chafed at the president's cautious conservatism. While the most earnest Republicans (commonly denoted as Radicals) were not a majority in Congress, they influenced party deliberations and dominated the institutional structure of the legislature. They pushed for a more aggressive prosecution of the war and wanted to widen its scope to include emancipation, which they considered a moral imperative. These men did not fear the revolutionary consequences that a widened conflict would bear: indeed, many Radicals, led by Representative Thaddeus Stevens and Senator Charles Sumner, embraced them. More moderate Republicans favored emancipation but sought more pragmatic grounds on which to base it. They found such rationales in military necessity. How one achieved emancipation was as important in their eyes as that it be achieved.

As 1862 opened, Republicans in Congress began to move against slavery. On March 13, Congress instructed military commanders not to return black refugees to whites claiming to be their masters; the next month it provided for the abolition of slavery in the District of Columbia, with compensation to former slaveowners, and adopted Lincoln's proposal to provide federal compensation for voluntary emancipation. In June, Congress barred slavery from the territories, while the Senate ratified a treaty with Great Britain to crack down on smugglers defying the ban on the Atlantic slave trade. But Congress's strongest antislavery measure of the season was the Second Confiscation Act, passed on July 17, 1862. It provided for the seizure and eventual confiscation of secessionists' property and declared free the slaves of secessionists should such slaves come under Union control. Lincoln viewed the new legislation warily. He believed that it was unconstitutional to confiscate property beyond the life of the individual who committed treason—an interpretation which would seriously curtail the impact of the new measure. However, he had no objection to its emancipation clause.

The shift toward limited emancipation alienated a good number of Northern Democrats. Many of them held fast to the goal of reunion but attacked the administration's conduct of the war, especially as they saw it gravitate toward emancipation. The most hostile of these Democrats were labelled "Copperheads" by their Republican opponents, although it would be more correct to characterize them as peace Democrats. Led by Ohio congressmen Clement L. Vallandigham and Samuel S. Cox, these Democrats generally sought reunion through peaceful negotiation; at times it seemed that they were willing to accept Confederate independence rather than see slavery's demise. They rallied their forces around the cry, "The Constitution as it is and the Union as it was." Other Democrats were more supportive of the war effort but remained critical of administration measures, most notably the drift toward abolition.

This Democratic opposition had a mixed influence on Congress's Republican majority. When divisions among Republicans became noticeable, Democrats could join with either faction to defeat the initiatives of the other. Thus, Republicans had to hammer out legislation agreeable to both sections of their party if they were to assure its passage. Whether this fact of political life actually muted Republican factionalism or simply compelled intraparty cooperation is a different matter, for party unity was rarely due to party harmony. Republicans may have been united on basic goals, but they often divided on the best way to obtain them. One way for Radicals to express their dissatisfaction with administration policy was to call for investigations by the Joint Committee on the Conduct of the War. At times the committee's actions against Union generals may have assisted Lincoln in waging war as he wanted do to so, but on the whole one is forced to agree with Allan G. Bogue's assessment in *The Congressman's Civil War* (1989) that the committee's "activities undoubtedly influenced him but seldom with the end result that congressional radicals would have found most satisfactory." Much the same can be said for how Lincoln responded to congressional Republicans' demands that he move more quickly toward a policy of emancipation, for the president still had plenty of critics who thought that any movement against slavery was unwise.

One of those who warned Lincoln of the dire consequences of escalating the war through emancipation was George B. McClellan. When Lincoln visited Little Mac at Harrison's Landing in July, the general handed him a letter outlining his own views on the situation. "Neither confiscation of property, political executions of persons, territorial organization of states or forcible abolition of slavery should be contemplated for a moment," he warned, adding, "A declaration of radical views, especially upon slavery, will rapidly disintegrate our armies." In offering such advice, McClellan was simply reiterating long-held beliefs. Events, however, were pushing the president in a different direction.

Lincoln searched for middle ground. At a White House meeting he pressed representatives from the border states once more to accept some form of compensated emancipation. Should the border states accept such a proposal, the president averred, the Confederacy might well crumble, having lost whatever hopes it entertained of absorbing new members. Moreover, should the border states fail to act now, slavery might well be "extinguished by mere friction and abrasion—by the mere incidents of the war. It will be gone, and you will have nothing valuable to show for it." Reiterating his advocacy of a follow-up policy of colonization, Lincoln concluded that he was nonetheless under increasing pressure to do something about slavery. Unmoved, a majority of the delegation responded several days later that compensated emancipation would be both costly and counterproductive to encouraging the growth of Unionist sentiment in the border states.

Thus rebuffed, Lincoln realized that he would have to move ahead on emancipation along a different road. When one Democrat forwarded the observations of Louisiana's military governor that administration measures tending toward abolition were eroding unionist sentiment, the president, tired of courting a near-dormant Southern unionism, responded that more extreme measures might well follow if Louisiana did not return to the Union, and soon: "If they will not do this, should they not receive harder blows rather than lighter ones? . . . It may as well be understood, once for all, that I shall not surrender this game leaving any available card unplayed."

Lincoln's course toward emancipation was thus shaped by several considerations. Despite a series of military victories in the West, the failure of McClellan's Richmond offensive promised to prolong the conflict. It was now evident that while limiting the war had kept several border states in the Union, it had done nothing to erode the Confederate will for independence. Furthermore, what unionism remained in the South appeared hesitant to assert itself, as the situation in Louisiana demonstrated all too clearly. The border states remained a critical variable in his calculations, but by now Union forces had a fairly firm grasp on them. In short, present policy—especially in regard to slavery—had already achieved all that it could; to persist in it without gaining compensating advantages would clearly complicate the chances for military victory. "This government cannot much longer play a game in which it stakes all, and its enemies stake nothing," Lincoln observed. "Those enemies must understand that they cannot experiment for ten years trying to destroy the government, and if they fail still come back to the Union unhurt."

On July 22, 1862, Lincoln shared with his cabinet a short draft of a proclamation of emancipation. The first paragraph put into effect the sixth section of the Second Confiscation Act, which said that the president could authorize the seizure of secessionists' property after a warning period of sixty days. After promising to push once more for the acceptance of compensated emancipation, the second paragraph disclosed his intention to emancipate all slaves in states under Confederate control as of January 1, 1863, justifying such an act as a war measure to secure reunion. The ensuing discussion revealed high-level divisions about the consequences of going ahead with such a declaration—about which Lincoln had already thought much—and about the wisdom of issuing it at that point in time. Lincoln conceded Seward's point that perhaps it would be better to issue the proclamation in the wake of a Union victory, and so he shelved for the moment the second paragraph. The first paragraph was issued as a military order three days later. At the same time Lincoln instructed the military to seize whatever property it needed to fight the war—including blacks, who might work for the Union army and navy—and to destroy whatever might assist the enemy.

Lincoln was not oblivious to the potential political impact of his decision. Radicals and abolitionists, of course, would welcome any step toward emancipation, even as they might press for a firmer denunciation of slavery. Other Republicans accepted the military necessity of striking at slavery but worried about its political consequences. At greatest risk was the support of the Northern War Democrats. While a majority of the Democratic party supported the war effort, they still wanted the North to fight a war of reunion and reconciliation—not a war of emancipation. They feared that emancipation might well raise the stakes of the conflict, with many Confederates pointing to such a policy as evidence that they had been correct about the North's designs on slavery since day one. Lincoln was well aware of his detractors, but conciliation had proven barren in results. "What would you do in my position?" the president asked a Louisiana unionist. "Would you drop the war where it is? Or, would you prosecute it in the future, with elder-stalk squirts, charged with rose water? Would you deal lighter blows rather than heavier ones? Would you give up the contest, leaving any available means unapplied?"

Over the next several months, Lincoln shared his thinking on emancipation with others in a series of letters, public as well as private, and in response to delegations who visited the White House to present their positions on the issue. To a group of black ministers he made clear once more his preference for colonization—in part because he knew that colonization would make emancipation more acceptable to white racists. Racial prejudice was a fact, the president asserted; it was something he could not change. To a delegation of antislavery ministers from Chicago, he asked what effect a proclamation of emancipation might have, for he could not enforce it in the Confederacy. "Understand, I raise no objections against it on legal or constitutional grounds," he carefully added, "for, as commander-in-chief of the army and navy, in time of war, I suppose I have a right to take any measure which may best subdue the enemy"—thus establishing the very basis of such a proclamation. It was best for all to understand, Lincoln explained, that "I view the matter as a practical war measure, to be decided upon according to the advantages or disadvantages it may offer to the suppression of the rebellion."

Lincoln made his position most clear in responding to newspaper editor Horace Greeley's plea for emancipation on the editorial pages of the New York *Tribune*. Bearing the headline "The Prayer of Twenty Millions," Greeley's public letter charged that the president was "unduly influenced by the counsels. . . of certain fossil politicians from the Border Slave States" and thus had impaired the success of the war effort by a "mistaken deference to Rebel Slavery." It was clear to the editor that "all attempts to put down the Rebellion and at the same time uphold its inciting cause are preposterous and futile." Declining to discuss the more provocative and personal aspects of Greeley's column, Lincoln moved to the heart of the matter to define his policy.

I would save the Union. I would save it in the shortest way under the Constitution. The sooner the national authority can be restored; the nearer the Union will be "the Union as it was." If there be those who would not save the Union, unless they could at the same time *save* slavery, I do not agree with them. If there be those who would not save the Union unless they could at the same time *destroy* slavery, I do not agree with them. My paramount object in this struggle *is* to save the Union, and is *not* either to save or to destroy slavery. If I could save the Union without freeing *any* slave I would do it, and if I could save it by freeing *all* the slaves I would do it; and if I could save it by freeing some and leaving others alone I would also do that. What I do about slavery, and the colored race, I do because I believe it helps to save the Union; and what I forbear, I forbear because I do *not* believe it would help to save the Union. I shall do *less* whenever I shall believe what I am doing hurts the cause, and I shall do *more* whenever I shall believe doing more will help the cause. . . . I have here stated my purpose according to my view of *official* duty; and I intend no modification of my oft-expressed *personal* wish that all men every where could be free.

As Lincoln well knew, whether the Union would be saved in the end depended on events on the battlefield. "You are quite right, as to the importance to us, for its bearing upon Europe, that we should achieve military successes," he told a European correspondent, "and the same is true for us at home as well as abroad." Along with many other Americans and more than a few Europeans, he now turned his attention to the armies in the field.

Confederate Counteroffensives: Lee Moves North

Confederate successes in the summer of 1862 revived European interest in mediation and intervention. Napoleon III pushed for a joint Anglo-French recognition of the Confederacy, and Parliament debated the wisdom of the proposition. Lee's triumph outside Richmond had gained so much attention abroad that Union advances elsewhere were forgotten for the moment. At a time when British textile mills were at last exhausting their pre-war surplus of raw cotton, resulting in unemployment and working-class unrest, it seemed as if the Confederacy was on its way to gaining foreign assistance. John Slidell recognized this when he sought recognition and assistance in breaking the Union blockade from France in exchange for several hundred thousand bales of cotton and the promise of an alliance in Mexico.

It seemed a moment of decision for the Union as well. As Lincoln moved against slavery, he also reconsidered the military situation. In the wake of McClellan's "change of base" during the Seven Days, he decided to appoint Henry W. Halleck general-in-chief. It was a reasonable choice; forces under Halleck's command had won several significant victories, and it looked as if he was the most successful Union general to date. Leaving Grant in command of West Tennessee—but only after offering the command to someone else—Halleck travelled east in July to direct affairs from Washington. The coming months would show that he was unequal to the task before him.

Having checked McClellan's advance on Richmond, Lee turned north to face John Pope and his Army of Virginia. He directed Jackson to move northward through central Virginia to check any Yankee advance. When Lincoln and Halleck, responding to the Confederate thrust, decided that McClellan should abandon his foothold on the James River and reinforce Pope, Lee moved to join Jackson with the intention of crushing Pope before McClellan arrived—a process made far easier by McClellan's lackadaisical compliance with orders. After tangling with Pope's army at Cedar Mountain on August 9, Jackson marched toward Manassas Junction, destroying the Union supply depot there before Pope could respond. He then moved off to the west, waited until Pope arrived, then pinned the Federals down on the old Bull Run battlefield at the end of August. The ensuing battle, known to Confederates as "Second Manassas," ended much as had the previous clash. Repeatedly Pope ordered assaults against Jackson, to no avail, even though at one point the Rebel defenders, out of ammunition, could only throw rocks at the attackers. Then Lee and his other corps commander, James Longstreet, arrived. Longstreet was a solid commander, but he was prone to second-guess Lee and other commanders, a habit that was to have dire consequences. In this case, however, his advice to Lee—to wait until the moment was right to attack—paid off. Confederate cannon blasted bluecoat columns; then Longstreet's corps, 29,000 strong, flanked Pope, overrunning a small brigade of New York Zouaves (so-called because of their distinctive uniforms, complete with baggy red pants) shielding the Union left. Pope recovered just in time to fend off the attacking Rebels before pulling his forces back toward Washington. Attempts by Lee to pursue Pope were stopped short by the Union rearguard at Chantilly in a spirited battle on September 1.

As Pope's disheartened men made their way back to Washington, the Lincoln administration, afraid for the safety of the capital, reacted quickly. Halleck simply broke down, confessing that he was nearly useless when it came to exercising real responsibility. Although Lincoln suspected McClellan of having acted in bad faith by not arriving punctually to reinforce Pope, he also recognized that Little Mac's talents at reorganizing and rallying troops were unsurpassed. Without a moment to lose, the president, acting against the advice of his cabinet, placed McClellan in charge of the mass of Union soldiers around Washington. Soldiers cheered when they heard of the directive: few mourned Pope's departure. It was almost as if the clock had been turned back over a year to McClellan's arrival after First Bull Run.

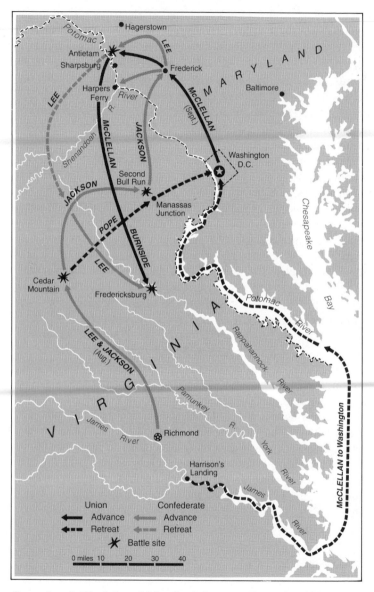

Campaigns in Virginia and Maryland, August to December 1862

Lee had no desire to attack the fortifications around Washington. But it made little sense for him not to follow up his victory. He decided to carry the war into Maryland and Pennsylvania. The enemy was "weakened and demoralized," he told Jefferson Davis, interjecting that his army could use more clothes, shoes, and ammunition. It was time to see whether he could liberate Maryland. His army could feed itself, partaking of the rich harvests of farms north of the Potomac; perhaps it might even sever the Baltimore and Ohio Railroad, a major east-west link. It was worth the gamble. On September 4 lead elements of the Army of Northern Virginia set foot in Maryland.

As his soldiers forded the Potomac, Lee adduced additional reasons for the move. Understanding the link between military operations and national policy, he did not shy from pressing his views upon Davis. Another success might well bolster the chances of European intervention; it might also dishearten Northerners and erode support for the Lincoln administration, to the point that Lee wondered whether it might not then be time to offer to open peace negotiations based upon Confederate independence. These reasons replaced any notion of wooing Marylanders, for as Lee's army marched into western Maryland, it soon became apparent that this area's residents did not share Baltimore's enthusiasm for the Confederate cause.

British leaders were watching and waiting as Lee moved northward. When news arrived of Pope's defeat, Lord Palmerston, the prime minister, anticipating the possible fall of Washington, thought that it would be best if the British prepared for that eventuality by offering the services of England and France for mediation upon the basis of Confederate independence. But much would depend on exactly what happened in Maryland. "If the Federals sustain a great defeat," Palmerston observed, "they may be at once ready for mediation, and the iron should be struck while it is hot. If, on the other hand, they should have the best of it, we may wait awhile and see what may follow."

Thus there was much at stake during the last days of the summer of 1862. As Lee moved westward he set his eyes upon the Union garrison at Harpers Ferry, which effectively blocked Confederate efforts to open a line of supply through the Shenandoah Valley. Using Longstreet's corps as a shield against any possible Union advance from Washington, Lee arranged for three separate columns to surround and capture the garrison. Once this was achieved, he would turn north toward Pennsylvania. McClellan did not concern him. "He is a very able general but a very cautious one," Lee told an officer. "His army is in a very demoralized and chaotic condition, and will not be prepared for offensive operations—or he will not think so—for three or four weeks. Before that time I hope to be on the Susquehanna." Out went Special Orders No. 191, outlining the next week's operations.

For once Lee had underestimated McClellan. For as the Confederate commander issued his instructions, his Union counterpart was taking the field with a reinvigorated and reorganized Army of the Potomac. To be sure, there were for Lee some reassuring continuities in Little Mac's operating procedure. McClellan thought that Lee had at least 120,000 men, when in reality Lee had about 40,000. Nor was he quite sure where Lee's forces were located. But at least McClellan was advancing at a reasonable pace. Then fortune smiled on the Union general when an Indiana corporal came upon an envelope containing three cigars—and a copy of Lee's Special Orders No. 191. "I have all the plans of the Rebels and will catch them in their own trap if my men are equal to the emergency," McClellan excitedly telegraphed Lincoln. Displaying the document that night at headquarters, he declared, "Here is a paper with which if I cannot whip Bobbie Lee, I will be willing to go home."

McClellan would have the chance to make good on his promise. Learning by nightfall of his opponent's good fortune, Lee nevertheless decided to continue his offensive against Harpers Ferry while detaching columns to block the Army of the Potomac's passage through South Mountain, the major obstacle protecting the main Confederate forces from attack. On September 14 the Confederates checked the Yankee advance at Turner's Gap to the north; to the south the Federals forced their way through Crampton's Gap in a half-hearted effort to save the garrison at Harpers Ferry, which fell the next day. Lee then decided to rescind his initial decision to retreat across the Potomac and offer battle to McClellan along Antietam Creek, several miles east of Sharpsburg, Maryland. Although a sizable portion of the Army of the Potomac was ready to assail the small force Lee had gathered—totalling less than 20,000—on September 16, McClellan waited for additional troops to arrive, giving the Rebels another day to prepare much-needed defenses against their numerically superior opponent. They also welcomed the arrival of Stonewall Jackson's men, who were deployed on Lee's left without time to prepare defensive earthworks. Now Lee had 35,000 men—with more to come—to fend off McClellan's 72,000 effectives, although more Yankees were within a day's march. McClellan, however, once more employing his unusual mathematical talents, doggedly clung to the notion that Lee's force was nearly three times its actual size. Given this assessment, the miracle is not that he failed to crush Lee on the 16th, but that he was willing to defy the odds by attacking the next day.

On the morning of September 17, McClellan launched the first of a series of sequential, uncoordinated attacks against Lee's position. The initial blows fell on Jackson's men. Lee's left then his center buckled, gave way, but finally reformed to hold off the Union advance in some of the most heated combat yet seen in the war. McClellan refused to commit his reserve to exploit Confederate weakness, deeming it necessary to contain Lee in case of a Federal setback. Of particular note was the stubborn Confederate defense along a sunken road, which thereafter bore the name Bloody Lane. Lee's lines were stretched to the breaking point: James Longstreet's staff found themselves manning an artillery battery to fill a gap. By midafternoon the action shifted southward to Lee's right, where Ambrose Burnside, finding Antietam Creek swollen by recent rains and unable to discover the location of several fords, launched an assault column across a bridge that today bears his name. The outnumbered Confederates inflicted fearful casualties on the attackers, but eventually Burnside's men forced a crossing and rolled back the Rebel flank. The timely appearance of A. P. Hill's division, marching north from Harpers Ferry, possibly saved Lee's army from a crushing blow. Although the Army of Northern Virginia had lost nearly a third of its 39,000 soldiers, Lee, confident that McClellan would procrastinate rather than pursue, held his ground on the 18th. He knew his foe all too well: McClellan, despite the presence of fresh reinforcements, refused to renew the battle, and nightfall shielded the Confederates' escape across the Potomac.

In later years McClellan would point to the Antietam campaign with pride. His supporters would cite Lee's statements of admiration for his Union counterpart as proof of Little Mac's greatness. In reality, however, the entire campaign proved that Lee held McClellan in justifiable contempt. No commander would have divided an inferior force into five columns without the assurance that his opponent would be unable to take advantage of the situation. And even after Lee had found out that McClellan possessed a copy of his orders, he deliberately modified his plan only to hold off the sluggish Army of the Potomac until Harpers Ferry fell before reuniting his forces. The Confederate commander then not only chose to give battle on September 17, but remained on the battlefield the following day, daring his foe to try again. As if to rub salt in McClellan's wounds, the following month Lee dispatched Jeb Stuart on yet another ride around the Army of the Potomac, highlighting his counterpart's incompetence with the ridicule inherent in such a raid.

Despite this, the Antietam campaign represented a setback for the Confederate cause. Marylanders had not, as Lee had expected, embraced the advancing butternut columns as they crossed the Potomac, and Lee's men never seriously threatened Pennsylvania: at most Lee had taken the war out of Virginia for a few weeks. However gutsy his waging of the battle itself had been, the fact remained that most people, North and South, American and European, interpreted a pitched battle followed by a Confederate withdrawal as a defeat. Chances for foreign intervention declined when news of Antietam reached London and Paris. "These last battles in Maryland have rather set the

North up again," Palmerston concluded. "The whole matter is full of difficulty, and can only be cleared up by some more decided events between the contending armies." Not all of his fellow Englishmen agreed. Chancellor of the Exchequer William E. Gladstone declared at Newcastle that the Confederates "have made an army; they are making, it appears, a navy [with, one might note, British assistance]; and they have made what is more than either; they have made a nation." But this proved to be a minority position when the British cabinet met to discuss the issue. Indeed, one might speculate that, had Lee not decided to press his luck, an offer of European mediation would have been more likely in the absence of Antietam.

Just as significant was the impact of the battle upon Lincoln's decision to make public his decision for emancipation. McClellan, who remained opposed to the measure, had nonetheless given Lincoln something on the battlefield that looked enough like a victory to allow him to issue the Preliminary Emancipation Proclamation—transforming the contours of the conflict into the very shape of revolutionary war McClellan abhorred. However, had McClellan pressed his advantage at any time during the three days he confronted Lee east of Sharpsburg, he might have crushed his opponent and made major strides toward ending the war, rendering emancipation needless as a war measure.

Confederate Counteroffensives: Perryville, Iuka, and Corinth

The Antietam offensive was only one of three major Confederate drives northward that fall, and for all the focus placed on the contest between Lee and McClellan, the Confederacy's chances for victory seemed brighter in Kentucky and Tennessee. As summer began, Union general Don Carlos Buell had hoped to march across northern Alabama and capture the critical rail junction of Chattanooga, Tennessee. But Confederate cavalry raids interrupted his supply lines and eventually forced him to abandon his advance. Confederate commander Braxton Bragg responded to this opportunity by moving half his command of 66,000 men from

Mississippi to Chattanooga via rail and then marching them northward with the aim of reclaiming Kentucky for the Confederacy. The remainder of Bragg's force, left behind under the joint command of Earl Van Dorn and Sterling Price, would at least keep a watchful eye on Grant along the border between Tennessee and Mississippi and perhaps have a chance to drive him out of West Tennessee.

Confederate hopes were high as the campaign commenced. Once in Tennessee, Bragg hoped to cooperate with Edmund Kirby Smith's invading column, some 18,000 strong, and he anticipated picking up even more recruits as he crossed into Kentucky. By late August, Smith had penetrated deep into eastern Kentucky, arousing fears that he was headed for the Ohio River. Bragg moved his army into the central part of the Bluegrass State, but he failed to elicit substantial Confederate support. "The people here have too many fat cattle and are too well off to fight," Bragg growled. Still he persisted in arranging for the inauguration of a Confederate governor in Frankfort on October 4.

While Bragg was moving into Kentucky, Van Dorn and Price prepared to unite their armies for their offensive in northern Mississippi, but they squabbled over exactly how to do so. Grant sought to take advantage of the opportunity to deal Price a crippling blow before Van Dorn arrived to join him, but confusion and poor coordination thwarted his plan to surround Price's force at Iuka, Mississippi, on September 19. Once united, Van Dorn and Price advanced to strike part of Grant's command, under William S. Rosecrans, at Corinth. In two days of battle (October 3–4), the Confederates failed to drive Rosecrans away, but Grant's efforts at pursuit proved unsuccessful.

Up in Kentucky, Bragg was now on his own. Lead elements of Buell's army had reached the outskirts of Frankfort on October 4, and the inaugural ceremony Bragg had arranged was disrupted by the sound of Union cannon fire. Days later parts of the contending armies collided at Perryville, thirty miles south of Frankfort. Although Buell failed to achieve a decisive victory, Bragg and Smith decided to abandon their offensive. Buell did not pursue, much to Lincoln's disgust.

Emancipation and Elections

On September 22, 1862, five days after Antietam, Abraham Lincoln issued the Preliminary Emancipation Proclamation. It was a revolutionary document cloaked in conservative terms. Asserting that the primary aim of the conflict remained reunion, Lincoln revived notions of gradual, compensated emancipation followed by the colonization of black Americans. However, he pledged to declare free all slaves in areas still under Confederate control as of January 1, 1863, and to employ the armed forces of the United States to "recognize and maintain the freedom of such persons." Citing congressional legislation forbidding the military from returning fugitives as well as the Second Confiscation Act, Lincoln also promised to propose compensation for loyal slaveholders upon the achievement of reunion.

The Preliminary Emancipation Proclamation was as much a document of reconstruction as it was a promise of emancipation. Areas under control of the United States as of January 1 would not be affected by the terms of the Proclamation: should certain Confederate states or areas entertain second thoughts about the wisdom of secession, they now had an incentive to return to the Union shortly. To persist in resisting reunion, however, would now cost them. Loyal as well as secessionist slaveholders would be affected (although the former could expect compensation). And, to reuse Lincoln's analogy about broken eggs, it would be nearly impossible to reenslave large numbers of emancipated blacks. Two days after officially issuing the Preliminary Emancipation Proclamation, the president again demonstrated that he would use all his powers to win the war when he declared that martial law would operate in cases concerning overt resistance to the war effort (such as encouraging resistance to enlistment): he suspended the writ of habeas corpus in such cases.

Blacks may have welcomed the Preliminary Proclamation, but in general reaction to it in the North was mixed. Lincoln expressed dissatisfaction with its initial reception. Noting the decline in stock prices and enlistments, he told Vice President

Hannibal Hamlin: "The North responds to the proclamation sufficiently in breath; but breath alone kills no rebels." Democrats scored significant victories in the October elections. In November, New York went Democratic, electing as governor Horatio Seymour, who in his campaign had denounced the Lincoln administration. Just as damaging (and perhaps more so) as the administration's overt commitment to emancipation to Republican electoral hopes was the suspension of the writ of habeas corpus, giving rise to charges of administration tyranny enforced through arbitrary arrests. As New Yorker George Templeton Strong watched Democrats parade down Fifth Avenue, he shuddered "as if a Southern Army had got into New York." But maybe, as James McPherson points out in *Battle Cry of Freedom* (1988), the Northern public's reaction to the Preliminary Proclamation was less serious than Strong perceived, for after the elections the Republicans continued to control seventeen governorships and sixteen state legislatures in the free states and had picked up a net total of five seats in the Senate. Even the Democratic gain of thirty-four House seats left the Republicans with a twenty-five-vote majority in that body—and the smallest net loss of House seats in an off-year election in the past two decades. The returns probably were more an expression of dissatisfaction with the administration's emancipation policy and the lack of substantial military success than they were an endorsement of the Democratic alternative. However, the results did raise questions: as Strong put it, "Have we ... resolution and steadiness enough to fight on through five years of taxation, corruption, and discouragement?"

Nor was the impact of the Preliminary Proclamation on the prospects for British and French intervention quite as clear as one might think. It had been news of Antietam, not of the Proclamation, that had dampened the chance of that step. Indeed, as Howard Jones has pointed out in *Union in Peril: The Crisis over British Intervention in the Civil War* (1992), the release of the Proclamation actually revived calls for intervention, this time to quash anticipated slave rebellions. Eventually the British rejected a French proposal for joint intervention with Russia, but only after some debate. In the end intervention never occurred because it could not gain majority support in the British government until Confederate independence seemed certain. Over time the antislavery thrust of the Proclamation sparked sentiment for the Union cause in England, especially among political liberals and a large segment of the working class.

Finally, the Proclamation failed as a document of reconstruction. Attempts to hold congressional elections in occupied areas of Tennessee and North Carolina failed, although in Louisiana, Arkansas, and Virginia voters protected by the Union army selected a handful of representatives. If anything, the Proclamation enabled the Davis administration to declare that its characterization of Union war aims had been right all along. Sentiment for reunion declined in North Carolina, and Andrew Johnson scrambled to have all of Tennessee exempted from the document.

Meanwhile Union soldiers and officers debated the Proclamation. Rumors reached Washington that some members of the Army of the Potomac's officer corps were even suggesting that McClellan march, not on Lee, but on Washington. Given McClellan's natural sluggishness, such a campaign might well have taken years, but Lincoln, for once in no mood for a joke, ordered the dismissal of one of the discussion's ringleaders. Elsewhere in the military opinions were divided. Advocates of abolition predictably welcomed the news, while a good number of Democrats protested having to fight to free the slaves. Although he applauded the principle at stake, one Massachusetts officer, Robert Gould Shaw, pondered its practicality. "For my part, I can't see what practical good it will do," he told his mother. "Wherever our army has been, there remain no slaves, and the Proclamation will not free them where we don't go."

In October Lincoln visited McClellan's headquarters. The Union commander refrained from composing a sequel to the Harrison's Landing letter and promised to take the offensive soon. But he did not. A frustrated president pointed out that "if we never try, we shall never succeed." Merely to maneuver Lee back toward Richmond again was not enough. Nor was Lincoln in the mood to accept any more of the general's excuses. He was moved to sarcasm when he heard that McClellan had forwarded reports on the exhausted state of his force's cavalry mounts: "Will you pardon me for asking what the horses of your army have done since the battle of Antietam that fatigue anything?"

By the fall of 1862 Lincoln had had enough of generals like Buell and McClellan. Their style of warfare continued to reflect their notions about the limited aims of the war. But the time had passed when waging a conservative war was acceptable. Had McClellan, Buell, or Halleck executed their carefully laid plans with skill and triumphed over their foe, the war already would have come to an end, thus forestalling the implementation of the very measures they so vigorously opposed. But the persistence of Confederate forces in the field and the difficulty of securing loyalty to the Union in occupied areas, combined with the halting advances of Union generals, pointed to a prolonged conflict. With that in mind, Lincoln pushed for a more aggressive prosecution of the war even as he moved to widen its scope through emancipation. "The army, like the nation, has become demoralized by the ideas that the war is to be ended, the nation reunited, and peace restored, by *strategy*, and not by hard desperate fighting," he remarked.

But new ways of war would require new generals. In the field, Halleck's conduct had reflected his conservative notions of limited war—although in Missouri he had demonstrated a willingness to respond vigorously to the onset of guerrilla operations. However, once he came to Washington to assume the office of general-in-chief, he came to view his prime responsibility as facilitating communication between civilian policymakers and generals in the field—not the shaping of policy goals. The same could not be said of McClellan and Buell. The latter was the first to go. Republican governors in the Midwest pushed for his removal, and their complaints received reinforcement when Buell failed to pursue Bragg after Perryville. As October drew to a close, William S. Rosecrans replaced Buell as commander of what soon became known as the Army of the Cumberland, now encamped near Nashville.

Buell's removal revealed the interplay of politics and war in the appointment of commanders. That he was a Democrat in his sympathies won him no favors among Republicans, but it would be wrong to conclude that he was removed simply because of his partisan preferences. Rather, Buell's failure to achieve success on the battlefield and his overly cautious plan of campaign—probably influenced more by his stylized notions of the proper way to conduct warfare than by his conservative political beliefs—led to his dismissal. For partisan sympathies did not ensure military success—as even Lincoln realized. The president reacted sharply to Republican politician-turned-general Carl Schurz's suggestion that the unsatisfactory progress of the war effort was due to Democratic generals. Republican generals, the president fairly pointed out, had enjoyed no more success: furthermore, "be assured, my dear sir, there are men who have 'heart in it' that think you are performing your part as poorly as you think I am performing mine."

The advent of the 1862 election had presented Lincoln with one opportunity for satisfaction. George McClellan had long outlived his usefulness as commander of the Army of the Potomac. On the evening of November 7, a special courier arrived from Washington with sealed orders directing Ambrose Burnside to supersede McClellan as army commander. Several times in the past Burnside had protested against such an appointment, arguing that he was not fit for such responsibility; now he agreed to the change. Many soldiers wept when they heard the news; others swore, and a few contemplated more serious action against the government. In the end, McClellan left, although not before saying farewell in a final review.

No one regretted McClellan's removal more than did Robert E. Lee. The Confederate commander's audacity had meshed perfectly with Little Mac's preference for procrastination. "I fear they may continue to make these changes," he told Longstreet, "until they find someone whom I don't understand."

Union Battlefield Standoffs and Rebuffs

Burnside now devised a plan to bring Lee to battle on terms favorable to the Army of the Potomac. He would march his army to the Rappahannock River opposite Fredericksburg, some fifty miles due north of Richmond, where pontoons would be waiting to permit a crossing. Once across the river, Burnside would head for Richmond: Lee would have no choice but to attack the larger enemy forces if he was to prevent the capture of his capital. The first step of the plan went well: lead elements of the Army of the Potomac reached the crossing area on November 17. But the pontoons, crucial to a crossing of the Rappahannock, were nowhere to be found. Halleck had failed to order them forward, effectively sabotaging Burnside's plan. By the time the pontoons arrived, so had the rest of Lee's army.

Burnside, despite the grumbling of his subordinates, persisted in his desire to bridge the river and attack the waiting Confederates. He outlined a two-pronged offensive, with one thrust to come south of Fredericksburg while a second one assaulted the heights due west of the town. His orders placing this plan in motion, however, were vague; their implementation was further delayed when Union engineers laying the pontoon bridge opposite Fredericksburg came under fire from Confederates in the town. In response, Union artillery bombarded the town, and several regiments were ferried across the river to oust the Rebels and allow the bridges to be completed. But it was not until the evening of December 12 that enough soldiers had crossed the river to prepare an attack for the following day.

On December 13, as the fog lifted west of Fredericksburg, the Army of the Potomac advanced. The assault against Lee's right achieved some success, but it stalled when it was not properly supported. More tragic were the assaults against Lee's left. West of Fredericksburg, James Longstreet had deployed his corps along Marye's Heights; enhancing the defensive properties of this position was a sunken road with a stone retaining wall that served as a premade entrenchment against the advancing Union lines. Some thirteen times during the day bluecoats marched through the town and up the slope leading to the sunken road; thirteen times they were cut down by rifle fire. Lee, watching the slaughter, remarked, "It is well that war is so terrible—we should grow too fond of it!" Incredibly, Burnside continued to order assaults up the bluff long after his subordinates warned him of the position's impregnability. Lee contemplated but did not order a counterattack, despite the urgings of Stonewall Jackson to strike a blow. By nightfall the field below the Sunken Road was blue with the bodies of fallen Yankees. Burnside wanted to resume the offensive the next day, personally leading an attack column, but his subordinates dissuaded him. Instead, the two sides simply eyed each other for the next two days, and on the evening of December 15 Burnside withdrew his men back across the Rappahannock.

Fredericksburg had been a costly defeat for the Union: the Army of the Potomac suffered 12,653 casualties, over 10 percent of its strength, while their opponents lost approximately 5,000 men of a force numbering nearly 75,000. Yet Lee was not satisfied with the victory. The next month, Burnside commenced another offensive, but snow and rain turned the roads into mud; soon wagons, horses, and men were mired in muck. This only added to the popular derision now directed at Burnside, and Lincoln, forced to choose between removing the commander or his subordinates, chose the former, naming Joseph Hooker to replace Burnside as head of the Army of the Potomac.

The impact of the defeat at Fredericksburg was most heavily felt in Washington. "If there is a worse place than Hell," Lincoln reportedly remarked, "I am in it." Congressional Republicans, bitterly dissatisfied with the conduct of the war effort, called for the renovation of Lincoln's cabinet, starting with Secretary of State Seward, who was blamed for advocating a conservative course. Treasury Secretary Salmon P. Chase encouraged this revolt, hoping to destroy his political rival while further promoting abolitionist approaches to waging the war. Lincoln deftly responded to this challenge to his presidency by convening a meeting of the dissident Republicans and the cabinet (minus Seward), in which he forced Chase to admit to all that the cabinet as a body had supported the president's major decisions throughout the conflict. Thus chastened, Chase offered his resignation; Lincoln refused to accept either his or Seward's, and the cabinet remained intact.

Politics also played a role in shaping the course of events in the Mississippi Valley. Having fended off the Confederate attack at Corinth, Grant now turned his attention to the capture of Vicksburg, Mississippi, a major river crossing point and rail terminus. Along with Port Hudson, Louisiana, Vicksburg offered the only remaining link between Texas, Arkansas, and much of Louisiana and the rest of the Confederacy. As a good deal of Confederate supplies came from trade along the Texas-Mexico border, it was important to keep Vicksburg in Confederate hands in order to transport those goods across the Mississippi. Union attempts to capture Vicksburg in the spring and summer of 1862 had failed. But Grant was not the only Union general who eyed this prize. In August, John A. McClernand had travelled to Washington to present his own plan for the capture of the river citadel. He proposed to raise an army in the Midwest and lead it southward, acting independently of Grant. Lincoln embraced the plan, in part because of McClernand's political value as a War Democrat; the president's confidence in Grant was not then established. Grant got wind of the project. Distrustful of McClernand's political ambitions and affinity for intrigue, Grant also suspected his erstwhile subordinate's capabilities as a commander in the field. Assured by Halleck that he could command whatever forces he needed, Grant decided to advance on Vicksburg before McClernand arrived at Memphis to take command of his independent expedition.

But Grant's initial sally against Vicksburg's defenses turned into a disaster. The Union general ordered Sherman to take his troops down the Mississippi River to land at Chickasaw Bluffs, north of Vicksburg, while Grant led the main body of his forces down across central Mississippi to link up with Sherman and hopefully force the fall of Vicksburg. But Confederate cavalry broke Grant's supply line, forcing him to retreat, while Sherman, unaware of this setback, carried out his part of the plan only to be repulsed rather easily by Vicksburg's defenders on December 29. McClernand arrived at year's end, assumed command of Sherman's men, and, acting upon a plan conceived by Sherman, attacked and captured a Confederate garrison near the mouth of the Arkansas River. Grant then decided to concentrate his forces on the west bank of the Mississippi and take charge. From there he went to work on solving the problem of taking Vicksburg, well aware that if he failed to come up with a solution, he might well lose his command for good.

In light of the setbacks at Fredericksburg and Vicksburg, a third battle which did not seem to be a decisive Union victory was celebrated as one by Northerners simply because it had not resulted in a Union defeat. By the end of December 1862, Rosecrans had marched his army from Nashville into middle Tennessee, just northwest of Murfreesboro. Waiting along the banks of Stones River, which runs past Murfreesboro, was Braxton Bragg and the Army of Tennessee. Both commanders planned to attack their opponent's right flank on New Year's Eve, but the Confederates struck first, on the morning of December 31, bending back the Union line until it resembled a horseshoe. Only the fierce fighting of a division under Philip Sheridan averted a complete disaster for the Union. Bragg, believing that he had secured a complete victory, discovered on the morning of January 1 that the Yankees had decided to hold their ground. On January 2 Bragg ordered another assault, this time against Rosecrans's left, but the Confederates were driven back with high losses. Rosecrans refused to retreat, so Bragg, worried by recent reports of the arrival of Union reinforcements, withdrew southward.

At first glance, Stones River seemed to be anything but a Union victory. Each side had lost over 30 percent of its force: the battle ranked as the war's bloodiest clash in proportion to the number of men engaged. But in holding his ground and surviving, Rosecrans claimed victory, and Northerners dispirited by bad news elsewhere decided not to question such claims. "I can never forget, whilst I remember anything," Lincoln later told Rosecrans, "that . . . you gave us a hard earned victory which, had there been a defeat instead, the nation could hardly have lived over." It may not have been a spectacular triumph, but under the circumstances, it was good enough.

As battle raged northwest of Murfreesboro, Abraham Lincoln made good on a promise. On January 1, 1863, he signed the Emancipation Proclamation. In so doing he permanently changed the nature and scope of the Civil War. Yet he still sought to soften his proclamation's impact. Several weeks earlier in his annual message he had called for three constitutional amendments: the first provided for the compensated abolition of slavery by 1900; the second provided for compensation to loyal masters who had lost slaves during the war; the third authorized federal funding for the voluntary colonization of free blacks outside the United States. He argued that the adoption of his plan would bring about a quicker end to the war "than can be done by force alone" and prove cheaper in both money and lives than waging war. It was in support of this plan that he declared: "The dogmas of the quiet past, are inadequate to the stormy present. The occasion is piled high with difficulty, and we must rise with the occasion. As our case is new, so we must think anew, and act anew. . . . Fellow-citizens, *we* cannot escape history. We of this Congress and this administration, will be remembered in spite of ourselves. . . . In *giving* freedom to the *slave*, we *assure* freedom to the *free*—honorable alike in what we give, and what we preserve. We shall nobly save, or meanly lose, the last best, hope of earth." In light of this argument, abolitionists and blacks could be forgiven if they temporarily wondered whether Old Abe was harboring second thoughts. But as the news of the Proclamation's signing came over the wire on New Year's Day, gatherings in Boston and New York exploded in celebration. The pattern was repeated on a lesser scale throughout the nation.

But it was left to a gathering at Beaufort, South Carolina, near Port Royal, to remind everyone of the true meaning of the day's event. Whites and blacks had gathered at the camp of the First South Carolina Volunteers—a regiment composed of former slaves under white officers—to mark the occasion. As the regiment's commander, Colonel Thomas W. Higginson, stepped forward to receive the colors of the regiment, someone sang out:

> My country, 'tis of thee
> Sweet land of liberty
> Of thee I sing

All at once, the assembled blacks joined in. "It made all other words cheap," Higginson recalled, "it seemed the choked voice of a race at last unloosed."

Thus 1863 opened with a new commitment for freedom. Whether it would be made good remained an open question. Union prospects appeared uncertain. In the East and in the West, Federal armies had just suffered decisive setbacks in their assaults on major objectives, although Stones River and Arkansas Post had taken the bitter edge off these defeats. Nevertheless, they remained poised to strike at the Confederacy. In the East, the Army of the Potomac, under Hooker, confronted its old foe, Bobby Lee and the Army of Northern Virginia. In the center, Rosecrans and the Army of the Cumberland still faced Bragg's Army of Tennessee. And in the West, Grant and the Army of the Tennessee worked to push through the dense swamps and cross the Mississippi River to get at Vicksburg and its Confederate defenders, John C. Pemberton's Army of Mississippi. As the new year dawned, the outcome of the military campaigns in these three areas promised to go a long way towards determining whether the Confederacy would win its independence.

CHAPTER FIVE

Gambles Won and Lost

As 1863 began, both the Union and the Confederacy sought once more to bring the conflict to a decisive climax. Lincoln's issuance of the Emancipation Proclamation promised to transform the nature of the war as it broadened its scope. "The character of the war has very much changed within the last year," Union general-in-chief Henry W. Halleck observed. "There now is no possible hope of a reconciliation with the rebels. The union party in the south is virtually destroyed. There can be no peace but that which is enforced by the sword. We must conquer the rebels, or be conquered by them." Should Confederate armies continue to beat back Yankee invaders, independence might not be that far off, especially if the Rebels could score a few triumphs of their own. "At no previous period of the war have our forces been so numerous, so well organized, and so thoroughly disciplined, as at present," Jefferson Davis told his countrymen. "We must not forget, however, that the war is not yet ended, and that we are still confronted by powerful armies and threatened by numerous fleets."

Both sides busily prepared for battle. Yet it was becoming increasingly clear that the war would not end with one climactic clash. So far the outcome of battles had been important but not decisive: a sustained and continuous effort was necessary to prevail, as the struggle tested each side's endurance and will. Each side also had discovered a commander willing to gamble and risk defeat to gain victory. In the East, Robert E. Lee contemplated how best to inflict an overwhelming defeat on the Army of the Potomac, believing that if he failed to do so the preponderance of Union resources would enable the enemy to win a protracted war of attrition. In the West, Ulysses S. Grant pondered his options as he looked to strike deep into the Confederate heartland to deprive the enemy of the resources and morale needed to wage war.

Chancellorsville

When Abraham Lincoln gave Joseph Hooker command of the Army of the Potomac, he also handed the general a letter. The president knew about the general's willingness to connive for the position he now held; he had heard of Hooker's brash pronouncements about the need for a dictator. "Of course it was not *for* this, but in spite of it, that I have given you the command," wrote Lincoln. "Only those generals who gain successes, can set up dictators. What I ask of you now is military success, and I will risk the dictatorship."

Known to soldiers and newspaper reporters as "Fighting Joe," Hooker went to work to revitalize the sagging Army of the Potomac. He granted leaves to his men, reestablished discipline in camp, and took measures that generally improved the men's health and morale. Badges designating a soldier's division and corps fostered unit pride. Only in one area did Hooker not heed Lincoln's heartfelt advice. "Beware of rashness," the president had warned, but Hooker arrogantly bragged, "May God have mercy on General Lee, for I will have none." He planned to destroy his opponent. First, he would send his cavalry—organized, for the first time, in one concentrated force—west and south toward Lee's rear. Once the horsemen were in position along the railroads to Richmond, Hooker planned to take three infantry corps westward to cross the Rappahannock and Rapidan rivers—to be followed by another two, held in reserve—while two other corps, under John Sedgwick, menaced Fredericksburg. Lee would find himself caught between the two columns, forcing him to come out and fight on ground of Hooker's choosing. The plan looked promising, in part because two of Lee's battle-hardened divisions under James Longstreet currently were off in southeast Virginia. At the end of April, the blue-clad columns were in motion, and before long the three corps had forded the rivers and were advancing confidently to battle. "Hurrah for old Joe," celebrated corps commander George G. Meade, "we are on Lee's flank, and he does not know it."

Lee responded to Hooker's movements with audacity and skill. Leaving some 10,000 soldiers under Jubal Early at Fredericksburg, he marched the remainder of his command, 50,000 strong, to challenge Hooker at Chancellorsville, a crossroads marked by a tavern in the woods south of the Rapidan and Rappahannock rivers. On May 1 his men encountered lead elements of the Army of the Potomac. Hooker froze upon hearing the news that Lee was near. Over the protests of his subordinates, he ordered his men to dig in around the crossroads in the woods. Having checked the Yankees, Lee pondered his next move. Stuart's horsemen had discovered that Hooker's right flank, three miles west of Chancellorsville at Wilderness Church, was vulnerable to attack—if Lee could somehow move enough men around on a wide sweep without being detected by the bluecoats. Stonewall Jackson thought that he could lead that column, and he and Lee mapped out the rather daring move. Jackson would take three divisions—approximately 27,000 infantrymen—on the march, leaving Lee with just two divisions with which to face Hooker. If Hooker attacked either column, disaster might ensue, for if Sedgwick simultaneously broke through Early's position at Fredericksburg, it might all be over for the Army of Northern Virginia. Lee, ever the gambler, bet on his foe's inability to respond in time as he ordered Jackson to move out.

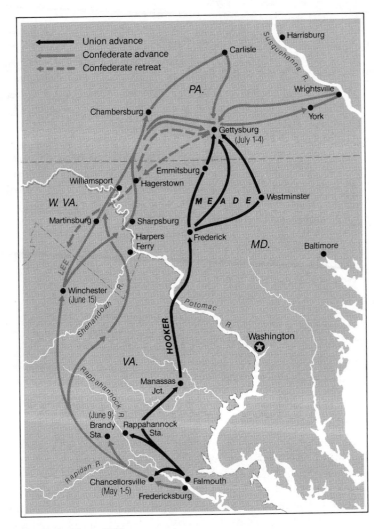

War in the East, 1863

Throughout the morning and afternoon of May 2, Lee waited as Jackson's men marched west and deployed nearly perpendicular to Hooker's right, held by the men of the Eleventh Corps, new to the Army of the Potomac and with several of its regiments filled by recent German-American immigrants. Hooker also waited. He ordered Oliver O. Howard, commander of the Eleventh Corps, to be alert to the possibility of a flank attack, but he failed to act aggressively in response to reports that Confederate forces were in fact moving across his front. Union cavalry, off on a raid against Lee's rear, were unavailable for further reconnaissance. One Yankee corps did sweep southward toward Jackson's line of march, but it failed to cut off the Confederates and lost touch with Howard's men, who were left by themselves on what had quickly become Hooker's rear.

They were not alone for long. Late in the afternoon Jackson's brigades came crashing out of the woods and smashed into Howard's men, many of whom were just settling down to dinner. The Yankees stampeded, despite isolated efforts to offer resistance. Eventually Hooker hurried reinforcements to stem the Confederate assault, which by evening was losing its momentum. Jackson, not satisfied with a half-victory, tried to reorganize his regiments for one final push. As he rode through the woods a North Carolina regiment, mistaking the general and his escort for Union cavalry, fired a volley. Jackson was hit three times, two bullets shattering his left arm. The attack was over for the night.

If parts of the Union army were shaken by Jackson's assault, several fresh units were ready for action. Hooker still outnumbered Lee, and the Confederate forces remained divided; moreover, Sedgwick's men had broken through Early's position at Fredericksburg on May 3 and were marching westward. The battle was far from won—or lost. However, the Union commander continued to collapse under the pressure, abandoning valuable positions and allowing the Confederates to join forces and bombard the contracted Yankee fortifications south of the Rappahannock. Leaving 25,000 men under Jeb Stuart to keep an eye on the still stationary Hooker, Lee directed the remainder of his army east to beat back Sedgwick. Hooker, dazed by Lee's attacks and shaken by a near brush with death, pulled back across the river on May 6—just before Lee would have attacked the rather formidable Federal defensive position. In later years Hooker admitted that he had quickly lost the very self-confidence that was so visible before the battle.

Lee had lost something else. The Army of Northern Virginia suffered nearly 13,000 casualties at Chancellorsville, compared to Hooker's 17,300. This increased Lee's casualty count in battle to some 64,000 men in just under a year—more men than he had present at Chancellorsville. He also lost Stonewall Jackson. Surgeons amputated the wounded general's arm on May 3, prompting Lee to comment, "He has lost his left arm, but I have lost my right." Seven days later Jackson died, depriving Lee of a most trustworthy subordinate and forcing him to redesign the entire command structure of the Army of Northern Virginia. Yet the magnitude of the victory also left Lee with the feeling that his men were invincible. "There never were such men in an army before," he remarked. "They will go anywhere and do anything if properly led."

Vicksburg and Gettysburg

Lee's next move depended in part on events far away along the Mississippi River. For months Grant had been working away at the problem of taking Vicksburg. He tried several times to approach the city by digging canals to divert the course of the Mississippi or open new waterways for his transports and gunboats. High waters, rain, and the obstacles posed by the marshy terrain north of the city thwarted these enterprises. Meanwhile, Grant suffered growing public criticism. Newspapers printed exaggerated reports that his men were plagued by disease, and McClernand lobbied Lincoln to let him take over for Grant. Sherman advised Grant to abandon the entire enterprise, return north to Memphis, and from there move south across Mississippi to Vicksburg. Grant rejected this advice, for he knew that public opinion would interpret such a maneuver as a retreat—

this might well cost him his command. Night after night, aboard a steamboat on the Mississippi, the general puffed away at his cigar as he perused maps and reports, looking for a good way to take the river citadel.

By the beginning of spring he hit upon a solution—one that held great risk but also the potential for great rewards. He would cross the Mississippi south of Vicksburg, at an area devoid of the swamps that dominated the terrain north of the city; once on dry land on the east bank of the river, he could strike at either Vicksburg to the north or Port Hudson, Louisiana, to the south. But in order to ferry his men across the river, a flotilla of transports and gunboats under the direction of David D. Porter would first have to pass under Vicksburg's batteries (to get south of the city). On the night of April 16 a first wave of Union vessels ran past the Vicksburg batteries, losing only one ship; six days later several transports and barges also squeezed through. To conceal his true intentions, Grant left Sherman opposite Vicksburg while a column of cavalry swept south from Memphis into central Mississippi to disrupt supply lines and confuse Pemberton. Marching southward, Grant and his men crossed the Mississippi on May 1 and defeated a Confederate garrison at Grand Gulf. At last Grant could breathe a sigh of relief: he was now across the river on dry land.

At this point Grant's skill for improvisation took over. Originally he had hoped to join up with a second Union column, under the command of Nathaniel P. Banks, and pick off Port Hudson before moving on Vicksburg. As he waited for Sherman to join him, however, he decided to move directly upon Vicksburg, sensing that a lightning strike might capture the city. For this campaign to succeed, Grant's men would have to live off the land, with wagon trains carrying other needed supplies, so that the Confederates could not cut off his supply line. He would also have to move quickly, for already a Confederate force was forming in central Mississippi under the command of Joseph E. Johnston to assist Pemberton and the defenders of Vicksburg. At the end of the first week in May, Grant made his way toward Jackson, the state capital and a railroad hub, with the aim of driving Johnston off and tearing up railroads to impede the ability of a defending Confederate force to supply itself. After a series of clashes Jackson fell on May 14. Grant then turned west to thrash Pemberton, who was moving out from Vicksburg to contest his advance and with an eye toward joining up with Johnston. On May 16, in a pitched battle at Champion's Hill, Grant turned the Confederates back; the next day, the pursuing Yankees caught up to and demolished the Rebel rearguard at Big Black River. Pemberton, who had received contradictory instructions on whether to hold Vicksburg or to abandon it, retreated into the city itself. Grant's men followed and, after failing to dent Vicksburg's defenses in two assaults on May 19 and 22, settled down for a siege, all the while keeping an eye on Johnston's men to the east.

Grant's Vicksburg campaign was a model of military leadership. It reflected his persistence and determination as well as his ability to innovate and improvise in response to changing circumstances. It also established him as a true military genius. Karl von Clausewitz argued that truly great commanders made their own rules of war; Grant observed that those generals who waged war "in slavish observance of rules must fail." In less than a month he had crossed the Mississippi, won five battles against a divided force, which, if united, would have nearly equalled his own, and invested Vicksburg at a cost of less than 9,000 casualties—nearly half of which were incurred only during the two mid-May assaults on Vicksburg. But the Confederates still held on to Vicksburg. Would the Confederate high command shake Grant's hold on the city?

Confederate commanders and civil leaders conferred in Richmond. James Longstreet suggested that he lead a detachment from Lee's army to reinforce Braxton Bragg in Tennessee, with the intent of attacking Rosecrans's Army of the Cumberland; surely Grant then would have to abandon the siege to save Rosecrans. Lee, fresh from Chancellorsville, demurred. Better, he said, for the Army of Northern Virginia to advance northward into Maryland and Pennsylvania. Taking the war into the North (and shifting attention away from Grant) once more might

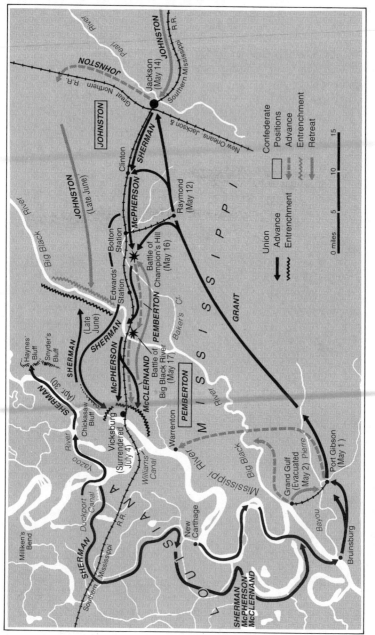

The Vicksburg Campaign, April to July 1863

shake Union resolve. It even might revive the chances of foreign recognition and intervention, play on Lincoln's concern for Washington's safety, and take the war out of Virginia for a season, allowing farmers there to grow some food for his army while his men lived off the land in Pennsylvania. In the meantime, perhaps Grant would have to give up the siege anyway; it was more than likely, Lee reasoned, that the sickly summers along the Mississippi would drive the Yankees away. (Fear of summer diseases had contributed to Grant's decision to order his second assault against Vicksburg.) In any event, Lee currently was more worried about Virginia than Vicksburg. His comments about the impact of his proposal on Grant were designed to fend off other options. He got his way. As May ended he prepared for his second invasion of the North.

But events were moving so quickly at Vicksburg that it is doubtful that they would have been affected much by whatever the Confederates proposed. Throughout June, Yankee artillery and gunboats shelled the town. Grant's men dug mines and exploded holes in the Confederate fortifications, and reinforcements arrived to solidify Grant's hold and keep Johnston in check. By early July it was obvious that the 30,000 starving Confederates must either surrender or be overwhelmed by one last assault. On July 3, Pemberton met with Grant to discuss terms of capitulation. He rejected Grant's initial demand of unconditional surrender; then Grant, who had begun to contemplate the logistical difficulties inherent in moving such a large body of prisoners north, decided to parole the men and allow them to go home, not to take up arms until exchanged for captured Union soldiers. He reasoned that few of these demoralized men would actually return to the Confederate army, and that their despair in the aftermath of defeat might prove contagious to their homefolk. He insisted, however, that any slaves accompanying paroled officers or men be promptly notified of their freedom.

On July 4, Grant entered Vicksburg. Five days later the Confederate garrison at Port Hudson surrendered. "The Father of Waters again goes unvexed to the sea," Lincoln observed: the Union now controlled the entire Mississippi River. At least as important was that Lincoln had finally found a general. Grant had silenced all doubters, including the president. "He doesn't worry and bother me," Lincoln remarked. "He isn't shrieking for reinforcements all the time. He takes what troops we can safely give him . . . and does the best he can with what he had got. And if Grant only does this thing right down there . . . why, Grant is my man and I am his the rest of the war." Upon hearing of Vicksburg's capitulation, the president did a most unusual and gracious thing, telling Grant in a letter of congratulations that he had wanted the general to unite his forces with Banks instead of proceeding as he had: "I now wish to make the personal acknowledgment that you were right, and I was wrong."

As Grant and Pemberton met to discuss surrender terms, Lee's invasion into the North was reaching a dramatic climax. The Army of Northern Virginia crossed the Potomac into Maryland and fanned out across southern Pennsylvania in June. However, this time Lee was operating without the valuable assistance of Jeb Stuart's cavalry. At the outset of the campaign, Stuart's troopers had clashed with Union cavalry at Brandy Station, Virginia, and had been roughly handled. Still smarting over this setback at the hands of the improving Yankee horsemen, Stuart liberally interpreted Lee's orders for a raid and launched yet another ride around the Army of the Potomac. This time the loop had not been so easy, consuming far more time and energy than either Stuart or Lee had anticipated, and it deprived Lee for quite some time of his primary means of acquiring information about the location and strength of Union forces, leaving him uncertain.

At first, Hooker had proposed to respond to Lee's advance by marching south toward Richmond. Lincoln sharply rejected this plan: "I think Lee's army, and not Richmond, is your true objective point," he reminded his general. As Hooker moved north, using the Army of the Potomac as a shield to defend Washington from Lee's columns, he squabbled with General-in-Chief Halleck about the disposition of other bluecoat detachments. Exacerbated, Lincoln removed Hooker on June 28, replacing him with George G. Meade. Not only was Meade dependable, he was also from Pennsylvania, Lincoln remarking that perhaps Meade would fight better "on his own dung hill." Meade quickly prepared a defensive position, then dispatched his cavalry north to locate Lee. Two Union brigades, under the capable John Buford, arrived at the crossroads town of Gettysburg, Pennsylvania, on the last day of June.

On July 1, Confederate infantry marching towards Gettysburg in search of shoes collided with Buford's troopers. Both sides fed the fight with reinforcements. In the afternoon a Rebel assault struck and outflanked the ill-fated Eleventh Corps once more; by dusk the Yankees had been driven south through Gettysburg to a chain of hills resembling a fishhook. Lee's subordinates, claiming that their victorious troops were too exhausted to assault the position, refrained from pressing their advance. Meade, hurrying north, decided to stand and fight; during the night more divisions arrived, as both sides prepared for battle.

On the morning of July 2, Lee, with memories of Chancellorsville still strong, ordered an assault by both wings of the Army of Northern Virginia on the flanks of the Union position. Longstreet, whose experience on Marye's Heights at Fredericksburg had led him to question the wisdom of frontal assaults, disagreed, urging instead a southward movement designed to flank the Union position, threaten Washington, and force the Yankees to attack on ground of Lee's choosing. Lee prevailed; the resulting offensives, mired in a breakdown of command, were poorly coordinated. Longstreet's assault against the Union left was delayed until midafternoon, but when it moved out at last, it crashed through a poorly positioned Union corps. Several Rebel brigades swung east toward Little Round Top; if they took it, Meade's left flank would lose its anchor and his entire position would be endangered. Two Union infantry brigades hurried to the summit just in time to turn back the attackers. Other advancing Confederates also nearly made their way to the Union center before faltering in the face of countercharges and a stiff defense; for years to come Americans would read of the Peach Orchard, the Wheatfield, and Devil's Den. The second assault, against the Union right on Culp's Hill and Cemetery Hill, did not get underway until dusk: although the attackers made some headway at Culp's Hill, they were unable to exploit early successes at Cemetery Hill. The day closed with tremendous casualties, little progress, and the Army of the Potomac holding firm. Both Lee and Meade determined to continue the fight the next day. However, a Union counterattack early on the morning of July 3 drove the Confederates off Culp's Hill, disrupting Lee's original plan to continue to press home the attacks of July 2.

Having attacked both flanks of the Union position, Lee, over Longstreet's renewed objections, now aimed to breach Meade's center on July 3 with a massive frontal advance preceded by a tremendous artillery bombardment. George Pickett's division, which had arrived on the evening of July 2, was chosen to spearhead the three-division assault. Meanwhile, Stuart, who had finally arrived on the scene, was to circle behind the Union right and cut off the retreating Yankees. Meade, anticipating a blow against his center, prepared his defensive position on a low-rising slope called Cemetery Ridge. At 1 PM the Confederate bombardment opened up, blasting away at the Union lines over a mile away. For all the fearsome racket, there was very little damage; when the Union artillery ceased returning fire in order to conserve ammunition, the Confederates, believing that they had silenced the Yankee cannon, advanced. Some 13,000 men, mostly Virginians and North Carolinians, moved forward across open fields; when they were less than 400 yards away, the Union artillery reopened its fire, tearing gaping holes in the gray lines. Still the Rebels advanced, finally breaking into a charge. The Union line wavered, then held; reinforcements moved out on each side of the assaulting column, which soon found itself boxed in on and under fire from three sides. It proved too much. Less than half of the attacking force made it back to Confederate lines, where they met Lee, who, riding out to meet them, declared, "It's all my fault."

The repulse of Pickett's Charge, one of the most dramatic incidents of the war, proved the battle's climax, for Stuart's men were intercepted and then repulsed yet again by Union cavalry east of Gettysburg. Although Lee prepared for a counterattack, none was forthcoming, as Meade preferred not to risk what had been gained. On the afternoon of July 4 the Confederates began to retreat south toward Virginia. Meade followed cautiously, failing to take advantage of Lee's difficulties in crossing the Potomac to deliver another blow. "We had them within our grasp," Lincoln bitterly remarked. "We had only to stretch forth our hands and they were ours." As the president later told Meade, "to have closed upon [Lee] would, in connection with our other late successes, have ended the war." While Lincoln may well have been far too optimistic in making such predictions—there was no assurance that an attack by a pursuing Meade would have succeeded—his dissatisfaction with Meade indicated that he believed that he had not yet found the man who could beat Lee.

In later years it would become fashionable to debate the question why the Confederacy lost at Gettysburg. In postwar memoirs and recollections Confederate commanders took turns blaming each other for the defeat. Such disputes reflect the fact that at Gettysburg the Confederate command system, from Lee on down, faltered; it also overlooks the fact that, finally, the Army of the Potomac overcame its previous missteps to emerge victorious. Nor is it quite certain what a Confederate victory at Gettysburg would have achieved. A triumph on July 1 would have involved but a small portion of the Army of the Potomac; a later victory certainly would have come at significant cost to Lee's remaining men. The Rebel commander would have found it quite difficult if not impossible to destroy the Union army. Even had he claimed victory, he would have had to continue to move on with his severely battered army to forage for food. Nevertheless, any of these alternatives seem more promising than what did happen, for Lee lost at least 23,000 of the 75,000 men he brought to Gettysburg—bringing his total losses for the last thirteen months to nearly 90,000—while some 23,000 of Meade's 85,000 became casualties at Gettysburg.

Whether Gettysburg was the turning point of the war, as has been frequently asserted, is debatable. If the Army of the

Potomac had beaten Lee, it had done so only on the defensive inside a Northern state; it remained unclear whether it could attack and beat Lee in Virginia, and the reluctance to deal Lee one more blow before he escaped across the Potomac suggested that Marse Robert still haunted the Yankees. Confederate victory was still quite possible, although it was now far less likely. And, in a sense, Lee had achieved his primary objective of taking the war away from Virginia. However, the Army of Northern Virginia never fully recovered from the losses it sustained those three July days, and the impact of the Battle of Gettysburg would become evident in the spring of 1864, when Lee could no longer replace his losses.

Chickamauga and Chattanooga

As the campaigns in Virginia and Mississippi reached their climax, the logjam in middle Tennessee finally gave way. Bragg's army remained in place south and west of Murfreesboro throughout the spring, with Rosecrans taking months to refit his command after Stones River. Telegrams from Lincoln, Stanton, and Halleck urging him to do something elicited at best vague promises of future movements and at worst curt replies. Finally, during the last week of June, Rosecrans began to move. Through skillful maneuver he succeeded in driving Bragg first to Tullahoma and then to Chattanooga with minimal loss of life. There Rosecrans regrouped, refitted, and resupplied his men, while another Union force in Kentucky, under the command of the ill-fated Ambrose Burnside, prepared to advance on Knoxville, Tennessee. The authorities in Washington were elated with Rosecrans's success; however, when Stanton urged him to press forward to meet Bragg in battle, Rosecrans, pointing to the Confederate departure from Middle Tennessee, churlishly replied, "I beg in behalf of this army that the War Department may not overlook so great an event because it is not written in letters of blood." He resumed his flanking movements in the middle of August. Once again the Confederates withdrew; Burnside entered Knoxville on September 3, and Rosecrans's men occupied Chattanooga six days later.

As Rosecrans advanced into northern Georgia, his columns dispersed, presenting ripe targets for a Confederate counterattack. Bragg was more than ready to respond—in part because he knew that he was about to be reinforced by two divisions from the Army of Northern Virginia under Longstreet. The Davis administration would try in September what Lee's insistence had prevented it from attempting in the spring of the year: the shifting of forces westward with the goal of pushing back the advancing enemy. Between ramshackle railroad cars and a patchwork rail network, it took nearly two weeks to effect the transfer, but enough of Longstreet's men arrived in time to make a difference. For Rosecrans had finally figured out that Bragg, far from engaging in a headlong retreat toward Atlanta, was simply drawing Rosecrans further away from Chattanooga in the hope of nabbing one of his dispersed columns. Twice the Confederates missed opportunities to do so. Rosecrans now ordered his subordinates to rendezvous just west of a creek whose Cherokee name, Chickamauga, meant "river of death." Bragg responded by making plans to strike Rosecrans's left with an eye to once more trapping the extended Union forces.

The two armies met on September 19, with George Thomas smashing into Bragg's right; by nightfall both commanders had committed reinforcements to the fight, which took place on fairly level but heavily wooded terrain, with only small meadows breaking up the forest, making it very difficult for generals to exercise much command over the movement and actions of their troops— or to understand exactly what was going on. The next day fierce fighting opened on the Union left, where Thomas drove back several attacks. In shifting reinforcements to Thomas, Rosecrans mismanaged his right flank, removing a division from a spot already vulnerable to attack. Longstreet's arriving forces advanced through the resulting gap and shattered the Yankee position. One of Longstreet's division commanders, John Bell Hood, who had just returned to the field after suffering a serious wound at

Gettysburg that left his left arm limp, reeled in the saddle, his right thigh shredded by rifle fire, but his men pushed forward. Longstreet planned to swing northward and crush Thomas; elsewhere the Union right also crumbled, and Rosecrans made his way back to Chattanooga. Thomas sought to stem the rout (and protect the routed) by making a stand at Snodgrass Hill. Repeated Rebel assaults failed to break the position: Thomas earned the nickname of "the Rock of Chickamauga" for his actions that day. As dusk came, the remaining Federals began to withdraw from the hill and make their way back to Chattanooga.

"My report today is of deplorable importance," a War Department official wired Washington from Chattanooga. "Chickamauga is as fatal a name in our history as Bull Run." The Confederate triumph seemed overwhelming, if costly. Each side had lost approximately one-third of its men in battle (about 35,000 casualties between the two armies). However, Rosecrans was now shut up in Chattanooga, and as Confederate forces seized the high ground to the south and the east of the city, they trained their cannon on the few possible escape routes that crossed the winding Tennessee River, which wraps itself around the western and northern edges of Chattanooga. The Army of the Cumberland found itself besieged. Instead of driving out the Yankees, Bragg proposed to starve them out. Rosecrans seemed a bit dazed. Meanwhile Burnside fell back upon Knoxville, abandoning any notion of coming to the relief of the defeated and trapped Union command.

The Lincoln administration had already made plans to send Rosecrans reinforcements before Chickamauga, but the news of the defeat sparked more action. Meade, who was on the point of launching an attack against Lee in Virginia, instead dispatched two infantry corps westward under the command of Joseph Hooker, while Sherman's corps made its way east from Mississippi. However, it soon became apparent that something more would be needed to salvage the situation. Telegrams to Washington portrayed Rosecrans as on the verge of a nervous breakdown, an impression confirmed by his own pitiful despatches alternating between anguish and melodrama. Lincoln remarked that the Union commander seemed "confused and stunned like a duck hit on the head."

It was time to make a change. In early October, Grant—bedridden for nearly a month after suffering a nasty injury when his horse shied, then fell, crushing his left leg—received a telegram ordering him to travel to Cairo, Illinois: when he arrived there another dispatch directed him to go to Louisville, Kentucky, to meet with an official from the War Department. The hero of Vicksburg took the next train to Indianapolis, where he encountered none other than Edwin M. Stanton himself. The war secretary strode forward, announcing that he recognized the general from his photographs—and then vigorously shook the hand of Grant's medical director.

Proper introductions having been made, Stanton informed Grant that the general was to take command of a newly created military division extending from the Appalachians to the Mississippi. Given the option to retain Rosecrans or to replace him with Thomas, Grant chose the latter. Then he slowly made his way by rail and horse to Chattanooga, arriving on the evening of October 23. Immediately things began to change. Grant ordered the implementation of an existing plan to secure a supply line to the besieged force and moved Sherman and Hooker into position to break Bragg's hold on the city. "We began to see things move," a Union officer remarked of Grant's arrival. "He began the campaign the moment he reached the field."

This task was made far easier by Bragg and Jefferson Davis. In the aftermath of victory Bragg had commenced quarreling with his commanders once more. This time he found a ready sparring partner in Longstreet, who informed the secretary of war that "nothing but the hand of God can save us or help us as long as we have our present commander." Davis arrived at Bragg's headquarters to resolve the dispute. He decided to send some of the dissatisfied subordinates elsewhere, and directed Bragg to detach Longstreet and some 15,000 men to drive Burnside out of Knoxville. Thus, as Grant was getting stronger Bragg was growing weaker, and the main Confederate army could do little more than look down from its fortified positions on Missionary Ridge and Lookout Mountain upon the Yankees in Chattanooga. The Union commander drew up a plan of battle whereby Hooker would strike the Confederate left, anchored on Lookout Mountain, while Sherman assaulted the Rebel right on the northern part of Missionary Ridge. Thomas and the Army of the Cumberland would be used in support of these flank assaults, in part because they were still recovering from their ordeal at Chickamauga and in part because Grant did not trust Thomas to act vigorously on the offensive.

On November 23, the battle of Chattanooga opened as Thomas's men seized Orchard Knob to the west of Missionary Ridge. The following day Hooker led three divisions against the lightly defended Confederate position on Lookout Mountain and in the legendary "Battle Above the Clouds" swept to victory, while Sherman's men moved into position. Finally, on November 25, Grant ordered Sherman forward. Sherman, misunderstanding the terrain, found the attack tough going. Grant, convinced that Bragg had withdrawn troops from his center to reinforce his right against Sherman, ordered Thomas's men to advance to the base of Missionary Ridge, capture the first row of rifle pits, and force Bragg to reinforce his center, weakening the force opposite Sherman. Thomas's brigades were then to await orders before moving up the steep face of the ridge itself—although that was apparently part of Grant's plan.

Thomas's men overran the rifle pits with relative ease, but they then found themselves subject to a rain of heavy fire from the Rebels at the top of the ridge. Deciding not to wait for orders to advance, the blue lines surged forward and scampered up the slope, much to the shock of its defenders, who found that their cannons could not be brought to bear on the charging Yankees due to a mislaid line of entrenchments. As the Cumberland boys reached the crest of the ridge, the Rebels broke, and Bragg's position collapsed. Union control of Chattanooga was assured. Grant entertained notions of a pursuit, but repeated telegrams from Lincoln made clear the president's concern about Burnside. A relief column marched to Knoxville, only to find that Longstreet, having failed to take the city, had slipped away towards Virginia. At long last, Lincoln had realized his desire to rescue the Unionist stronghold of East Tennessee from Confederate control.

Chattanooga capped the case for Grant's ascension to high command. His campaigns had been instrumental in seizing the Mississippi Valley and Tennessee for the Union. They also more than made up for the continuing stalemate in Virginia. For all the blood spilled at Chancellorsville and Gettysburg, things were little different along the Rapidan and Rappahannock then they had been after Fredericksburg the previous year. Lee and Meade had spent the last months of 1863 moving back and forth across northern and central Virginia, achieving little. As November drew to a close, Meade crossed the Rapidan but decided not to attack Lee's prepared position along Mine Run. Lincoln grew more disappointed. That Lee's losses were becoming much harder to replace seemed minor in light of the Army of the Potomac's continued failure to win a victory on Virginia soil.

However, the Union's successes on the battlefield were matched by its triumphs in diplomacy. In the aftermath of Fredericksburg, Napoleon III offered to mediate a settlement; Lincoln and Seward quickly rejected the idea. Then the British public's reaction to the issuance of the formal Emancipation Proclamation eroded support for intervention in Britain. Though voices for recognition of the Confederacy rose once more in the aftermath of Chancellorsville, with Napoleon III renewing his offer of Anglo-French arbitration, Gettysburg and Vicksburg, along with an incautious mention of the French offer on the floor of Parliament, put an end to such discussions for good.

There remained, however, the serious issue of British-built Confederate ships. In the summer of 1863 it was well known that British shipbuilders were constructing a pair of ram-equipped ironclads designed to pierce the Union blockade. These Laird rams (named after their builder) provoked great protest from Charles Francis Adams, the U.S. minister in London, who finally told Foreign Secretary Lord John Russell that in case the Laird rams made their way into Confederate hands, "it would be superfluous in me to point out to your Lordship that this is war." Adams's warning was indeed superfluous, for Russell had already decided to detain the rams, acknowledging at last that the evidence that they were intended for Confederate hands was overwhelming—although the announcement that he was doing so came the day after Adams penned his ultimatum.

When Jefferson Davis learned of Russell's decision, he decided to take action. He ordered the expulsion of British consuls from the Confederacy, while chief Confederate diplomat James Mason was told to leave London. Negotiations with the French seemed more promising, for the French had something more concrete to gain in diplomatic negotiations: Confederate recognition of Maximilian's regime in Mexico in exchange for French recognition of the Confederacy. However, Napoleon III feared taking on the United States without Great Britain at his side, making an agreement with the Confederates unlikely. Soon affairs in Europe began to demand far more attention from both Great Britain and France. And by year's end, Davis had abandoned any hope for foreign intervention: "We now know that the only reliable hope for peace is in the vigor of our resistance."

The Impact of Emancipation

As Union armies penetrated deeper into the Confederate interior, more slaves flocked to Yankee camps and columns. Commanders put them to work in support of military operations: blacks helped rebuild railroads, drive wagons, prepare food, dig entrenchments, and bury the dead, freeing a higher percentage of white soldiers for duty on the front lines. In some areas commanders gathered black refugees in so-called contraband camps in order to make sure that they did not interfere with military operations. In other cases they simply impressed blacks into service and paid them wages—although after their salaries had been reduced to cover various expenses such as clothes, food, and health care, many black workers understandably pondered whether the differences between slavery and freedom were all that significant.

Still, not all of the former slaves could be put into military service of one sort or another. The problem of what to do with these people—a question raised with military considerations foremost in the minds of many whites—also held implications for what sort of life blacks would live after emancipation, and thus shed light on the visions of black freedom held by both blacks and whites. Perhaps the primary issue was black labor. Most blacks and whites assumed that the vast majority of ex-slaves would continue to engage in agricultural work. But would blacks work the land for themselves as independent farmers, or would they work for somebody else—and under what conditions? The answers varied according to the local circumstances. At Port Royal, South Carolina, there was some effort to establish black homesteads, although speculators often bought up the best land. In the Mississippi Valley, several alternatives appeared. Some planters continued to run their plantations much as they had before, except that now they paid their black workers wages. Blacks could contract with whomever they chose, but they had to work for someone or else face working for the army or unionist governments. These annual contracts, enforced by occupation army personnel, often forced freedpeople into working relationships that were not all that different from slavery; certainly these arrangements did not approach the full definition of "free labor." Conditions for blacks on government-run plantations were often an improvement over slave-work conditions, and in exceptional cases blacks were able to manage their own plantations, as was the case on the captured lands of Jefferson Davis's brother, Joseph, at Davis Bend, Mississippi, just south of Vicksburg. Grant, endorsing the new enterprise, hoped to establish "a negro paradise" in the area. Elsewhere the government allowed private relief societies to manage the plantations in Union-occupied territory, thus allowing administrators to test their theories about how best to help blacks make the transition to freedom.

A good number of these arrangements reflected paternalistic assumptions about the newly freed people. Only in a few cases were blacks allowed to decide for themselves what they wanted. But it was too much to ask the army and other federal agencies to conduct a war and oversee a social revolution at the same time. So much time was being spent on the act of securing freedom for blacks that few people had time to think through exactly what freedom for blacks meant. Moreover, as James McPherson has pointed out in *Ordeal By Fire*, the presence of so many black male workers in the Union army meant that something had to be done for the black women, children, aged, and infirm who were often left behind. Perhaps the solutions raised did reflect paternalistic assumptions, but, as McPherson argues, "The alternative would have been neglect and an appalling death rate that would have been cause for greater condemnation."

The issues of the confiscation and redistribution of conquered lands complicated the discussion. If blacks ever were to become free landholders, they must have their own land. But the chances for large-scale land reform in the South were never good. The United States Constitution (Article III, Section 3) limited property forfeiture to the lifetime of the owner convicted of treason; after that, said land would revert to the owner's descendants. Efforts to confiscate land due to Confederate owners' failure to pay U.S. taxes fell short. Eventually, Lincoln's Amnesty Proclamation of December 1863 promised to restore all property (except slaves) to all those Confederates who swore an oath of future allegiance to the United States. Even the two most significant postwar efforts to make land redistribution a reality—the Freedmen's Bureau Act of March 1865 and William T. Sherman's Special Field Order No. 15, issued in January 1865 (which set aside a strip of land from Charleston, South Carolina, to Jacksonville, Florida, some thirty miles wide, for black settlement)—made the establishment of permanent titles contingent on government action. Thus everyone would have to wait for the war to end to see what would happen. For now, all arrangements were temporary.

Short-term solutions devised elsewhere in response to immediate circumstances forecasted what was to come. The majority of blacks became farm workers, not farmers of their own land.

In a sense, this reflected a larger shift in American society at the time from independent farmer and artisan to wage earner, challenging the Republican ethos of free labor by redefining it. The president himself, whose life exemplified the fruits of free labor, did not rule out some form of apprenticeship as an appropriate transition for the ex-slaves. Such a notion conformed with his preference for a gradual process of emancipation. Nevertheless, neither the Lincoln administration nor the United States army adopted a uniform approach to this issue, leaving solutions to be improvised by different agencies with various priorities in mind. By promising planters a compliant and affordable work force, for example, some Union commanders hoped to present large slaveholders with evidence that the disruption of emancipation might well be minimized, thus further eroding support for the Confederacy. Voluntary societies wanted to educate and assist the freedpeople, but in ways that conformed to the white volunteers' beliefs of what blacks' freedom meant. Emancipation, then, did not necessarily result in autonomy for blacks, but it was certainly a big step in the right direction.

Of greater immediate importance to many people was the issue of blacks serving in the armed forces of the United States. Blacks had served in the Union Navy from the beginning of the war, and there had been scattered black regiments in existence in Louisiana, South Carolina, and Kansas. In July 1862, Congress, in the Militia Act, provided for the enlistment of blacks. Even then Abraham Lincoln was reluctant to implement the policy. In August he rejected the offer to raise two black regiments in Indiana, remarking that to do so would cause 50,000 Kentuckians to switch sides. Not until the release of the Emancipation Proclamation on January 1, 1863, did he publicly embrace the idea. Once he had done so, however, he revised his calculations about the impact of the policy. "The colored population is the great *available* and yet *unavailed* of, force for restoring the Union," he told Andrew Johnson, the military governor of Tennessee. "The bare sight of fifty thousand armed, and drilled black soldiers on the banks of the Mississippi, would end the rebellion at once."

Other observers saw even more clearly the possible revolutionary impact of enlisting blacks. Frederick Douglass had been advocating it for some time. "Once let the black man get upon his person the brass letters, *U. S.*; let him get an eagle on his button, and a musket on his shoulder, and bullets in his pocket, and there is no power on earth which can deny that he has earned the right to citizenship in the United States," he declared. Grant agreed, arguing that enlistment would be one in a series of steps in which blacks' actions would disabuse whites of notions of racial prejudice and stereotypes.

Union soldiers differed over the new policy. Some protested so loudly that they were expelled from the service; a number more followed William T. Sherman's example of private dissatisfaction coupled with public compliance. Generals, officers, and soldiers sympathetic to abolition from the beginning of the war welcomed it; so did others, like Grant, who believed that the time had come to mobilize all available resources to achieve victory. White officers and enlisted men sought commissions in the new black regiments that were forming. Yet the primary purpose of these units was to serve on garrison duty in occupied areas and perform manual labor, freeing white soldiers for the battlefront. This purpose was reflected in their pay, for initially black soldiers earned $10 a month, while white privates were paid $13 plus a clothing allowance of $3.50.

The new units soon saw combat. In May two black Louisiana regiments assaulted Port Hudson; on June 7, Confederates attacked a training camp for black recruits at Milliken's Bend, Louisiana. When the black soldiers learned that the Rebels were executing their black prisoners, they rose up and counterattacked fiercely. Grant noted that while the black recruits "had but little experience in the use of fire arms" they had been "most gallant and I doubt not but with good officers they will make good troops." The most famous of the early battles involving black soldiers took place at Fort Wagner, South Carolina. For months the Union high command had tried to gain a foothold near Charleston Harbor. Efforts to secure a beachhead or to force a way into the harbor had failed. As July came, a joint army-navy expedition commenced, in which the army would overwhelm several outlying forts, then watch as the navy steamed into the harbor itself.

Essential to the success of this operation was the capture of Fort Wagner, located south of the harbor. When it did not fall to heavy naval bombardment, Union commanders planned a ground attack at night. The assault column would be spearheaded by the Fifty-fourth Massachusetts Infantry, a regiment composed of free blacks and some former slaves under the command of Colonel Robert Gould Shaw. The young colonel was a model of New England's elite, with his Harvard education and impeccable pedigree. Although his parents were fierce abolitionists, Shaw was slow to develop a passionate commitment to his (abstract) antislavery beliefs. Now, however, he knew that the only way to silence critics of emancipation was to show the world that American blacks would indeed fight for their freedom. On the night of July 18, he led his men forward; in the bloody assault that followed, the Fifty-fourth failed to gain the fort and suffered heavy casualties. Among the dead was Shaw. The Confederates, in an effort to mock the colonel, buried him alongside his men in a mass grave; Shaw's father later resisted efforts to remove his body elsewhere, saying that there was "no holier place" for his son to be buried than with his men.

Port Hudson, Milliken's Bend, Fort Wagner—the evidence was mounting that black men would fight for their freedom. Some white soldiers began to treat blacks as true comrades in arms, although no one should exaggerate the degree to which black performance in combat eradicated racial prejudice. Of equal interest was whether Confederate authorities would distinguish Union soldiers by the color of their skin rather than the color of their uniform: to arm former slaves was, after all, to encourage insurrection. The Confederate Congress ruled that captured bluecoats who were former slaves were to be treated as escaped slaves, not as prisoners of war; moreover, their white officers, if captured, were subject to execution on the grounds of inciting a slave insurrection. Some Confederate soldiers went even further, killing black soldiers on the spot instead of taking them prisoner. Reports of such behavior appeared during the summer of 1863; Grant, responding to one rumor, reminded a Confederate general that when it came to black soldiers Union authorities "are bound to give the same protection to these troops that they do to any other troops." The Lincoln administration promised to retaliate.

By far the most infamous incident involving black soldiers occurred at Fort Pillow, Tennessee, along the Mississippi. On April 12, 1864, a Confederate force under the command of Nathan Bedford Forrest attacked the fort, which was garrisoned by black soldiers as well as a contingent of Tennessee whites. What happened next is still open to controversy, but it seems apparent that Rebel cavalrymen gunned down many blacks attempting to surrender. It is doubtful that Forrest actually ordered this action, but it is a fact that he was not disturbed by it and was well aware that such acts might occur. Indeed, he hoped that the battle "will demonstrate to the Northern people that negro soldiers cannot cope with Southerners." Although Grant favored retaliation in the form of executing one Confederate prisoner for each Union soldier (white or black) thus killed, the Lincoln administration declined to authorize it: it would be left to black soldiers to take their own vengeance on Confederate soldiers, accompanied by the cry, "Remember Fort Pillow."

Fort Pillow overshadowed other instances in which black prisoners of war suffered mistreatment. In October 1864, Confederates put black prisoners of war to work on fortifications within range of Union fire. Grant approved Benjamin F. Butler's decision to respond by putting Confederate prisoners to work under similar conditions. Robert E. Lee, who had earlier refused to exchange any black prisoners, protested this act—but removed the black prisoners from the front, claiming an administrative mix-up. Grant, refusing to discuss Lee's lengthy justification of Confederate policy, simply replied that it was his duty "to protect all persons received into the Army of the United States, regardless of color or Nationality." He never backed down from that position.

Black regiments fought well when they had the opportunity to do so. Still, most black soldiers were frequently assigned to menial tasks, digging trenches, doing garrison duty, and patrolling rear areas. Some commanders justified this by claiming that blacks supposedly possessed a special resilience to the diseases prevalent on the coast and along rivers and swamps. Lincoln approved such assignments, for he worried about the fate of blacks taken prisoner in combat. Not surprisingly, a good number of black soldiers died of disease; some whites dismissed this, claiming that the high mortality rates were due to poor sanitary practices.

Nevertheless, the 180,000 blacks who eventually served in the Union army—free as well as newly freed—proved invaluable. At a time when approximately half of the "boys of '61," who had signed up for three years of service, had decided that they would not remain in the service beyond their original term of enlistment, it was of great importance that new sources of manpower be found. Lincoln argued that blacks' service could not be spared: "This is not a question of sentiment or taste, but one of physical force which may be measured and estimated as horse-power and Steam-power are measured and estimated. Keep it, and you can save the Union. Throw it away, and the Union goes with it." And, unlike conscripts, substitutes, and bounty hunters, black soldiers had a reason to fight. Grant believed that emancipation followed by the arming of blacks "is the heaviest blow yet given the Confederacy," because "they will make good soldiers and taking them from the enemy weaken him in the same proportion they strengthen us." It was useless, he thought, to speak of a peace without the destruction of slavery, for "slavery is already dead and cannot be resurrected."

Slavery dead beyond resurrection. . . . It was no longer a war simply to preserve the Union. The war itself had changed what the war was about. Yet certain goals remained constant. It was worth reminding Americans of that, and it was left to Abraham Lincoln to do so. He travelled to Gettysburg in November 1863 to offer a few appropriate remarks at the dedication of a national soldiers' cemetery adjacent to the town cemetery. The assembled crowd listened for hours as the famed orator Edward Everett (who had run as the vice presidential candidate on the Constitutional Union ticket in 1860) replayed the three days of battle. Then the president stood up and began to speak.

Four score and seven years ago our fathers brought forth on this continent, a new nation, conceived in liberty, and dedicated to the proposition that all men are created equal. Now we are engaged in a great civil war, testing whether that nation, or any nation so conceived and so dedicated, can long endure. We are met in a great battle-field of that war. We have come to dedicate a portion of that field, as a final resting place for those who here gave their lives that that nation might live. It is altogether fitting and proper that we should do this. But, in a larger sense, we can not dedicate—we can not consecrate—we can not hallow—this ground. The brave men, living and dead, who struggled here, have consecrated it, far above our poor power to add or detract. The world will little note, nor long remember what we say here, but it can never forget what they did here. It is for us the living, rather, to be dedicated here to the unfinished work which they who fought here have thus far so nobly advanced. It is rather for us to be here dedicated to the great task remaining before us—that from these honored dead we take increased devotion to that cause for which they gave the last full measure of devotion—that we here highly resolve that these dead shall not have died in vain—that this nation, under God, shall have a new birth of freedom—and that government of the people, by the people, for the people, shall not perish from the earth.

That was all the president said. It was over almost before it began. Contrary to the author's expectations, the world thereafter did note what was said that autumn afternoon. One of the first people to grasp that truth was none other than Everett. "I should be glad," he wrote Lincoln the following day, "if I could flatter myself that I came as near to the central idea of the occasion, in two hours, as you did in two minutes."

At the end of 1863 the North could look back on a series of military successes that had transformed the contours of the conflict. In capturing Vicksburg and repelling the Confederate threat against Chattanooga, Grant had secured control of the Mississippi River and East Tennessee for the Union. He had gambled and won, exploiting opportunities and making the best of fortuitous circumstances. In contrast, although Robert E. Lee had played for high stakes and won at Chancellorsville, his luck ran out at Gettysburg. It now seemed unlikely that the Confederacy could win its independence by assuming the offensive and overwhelming Yankee armies on the field of battle. But Confederate independence was not yet lost, for if the Rebels could frustrate their foe long enough, a war-weary North might well turn away from the Lincoln administration and let the South go its separate way. It was not yet clear whether the Union dead at Gettysburg—and elsewhere, from Vicksburg to Fort Wagner—had died in vain.

CHAPTER SIX

The Home Front

The impact of the American Civil War transcended the battle-field. As Abraham Lincoln reminded Northerners in 1861, the war was "a people's contest"; Jefferson Davis would have agreed. An English newspaper correspondent noted that everywhere he looked, Southern whites "were anxious to do or sacrifice something for the general weal." Indeed, at times the conflict took on aspects of a religious crusade. Northerners and Southerners alike explained defeat on the battlefield as the verdict of Providence, a punishment for their sins; they celebrated victory as the ratification of the righteousness of their cause. The war became more than simply a clash of armies: it pitted North against South in a massive struggle in which only one could triumph. Both sides mobilized their resources as they never had before in order to meet the challenge. At the same time, divisions within both North and South threatened to sap the strength of the antagonists at home. The ability and will of both sides to wage war would be determined as much by what happened on the home front as by what happened on the front lines.

The Folks Back Home

If soldiers saw the face of battle first hand, the people who remained at home experienced it in several ways. For some people, of course, the war literally came to their front yard. Residents of Sharpsburg, Gettysburg, and other small towns found their lives forever altered by what happened in the surrounding fields; so did the inhabitants of larger towns and cities such as Fredericksburg, Petersburg, Chattanooga, Charleston, Atlanta, Nashville, and Vicksburg. No one felt the hard hand of war more than residents who lived in the Shenandoah Valley, throughout the contested regions of Middle Tennessee, along the line of the march of Sherman's men in Georgia, or in Chambersburg, Pennsylvania, burned by Confederate soldiers in 1864. Occasionally civilians died in battle: Mrs. Judith Henry, bedridden, was fatally hit as Union and Confederate forces battled around her house during First Bull Run, while a bullet killed Jennie Wade of Gettysburg as she was baking bread for Union soldiers in a house on the northern slope of Cemetery Hill. Occasionally civilians fought, from the erstwhile irregulars in West Tennessee to the aged John Burns, a resident of Gettysburg who shouldered a musket for the Union army. For these people, the war at home changed when the war came home to them.

Civilians in the border and some Confederate states found that living in a war zone—whether in an occupied region or simply in an area in the wake of conflict—changed one's life in substantial ways. In some regions, notably Missouri and Tennessee, guerrillas and armed citizens joined with soldiers in fighting long after the focus of operations had moved elsewhere. Many blacks—some emancipated by Union arms, others asserting their own independence—formed their own communities, found themselves herded into contraband camps, or returned to work on the plantation under the supervision of the army or government officials. Across the South, plantations were abandoned, seized, or transformed from slave to free labor as the Union armies advanced; slaves still on Confederate-owned plantations slowed the pace of their work, became more assertive in the absence of white overseers, or left altogether. The behavior of occupation forces and their commanders toward occupied populations varied considerably, although some of this variation may be attributed to how local civilians responded to occupation. In such cases, the distinction between home front and battlefront was not easy to make.

Even in those areas far removed from the battlefield—including the vast majority of homes above the Ohio and Potomac rivers—civilians eagerly sought news of the battles being waged. They turned to a variety of sources. Newspapers presented extensive but often inaccurate accounts of battle. Government efforts to affect the flow and content of news reports proved largely ineffective or counterproductive, as when Northern readers became overly excited by the prospect of immediate victory in the spring of 1864 after Secretary of War Stanton issued a series of optimistic reports to the press, only to acknowledge later that the end remained a long way off. Early declarations of victory were dashed by subsequent sober accounts of defeat. Throughout the war, editorials praised heroes, searched for scapegoats, or offered various rationales to explain away events. Quarterlies and magazines offered an ongoing analysis of the war; an occasional account sought to bring the battlefront and field hospital home to the reader, as when Oliver Wendell Holmes, Sr., contributed to the *Atlantic Monthly* the story of his search for his wounded son (the future Supreme Court justice) after Antietam. More compelling were the illustrated weeklies such as *Harper's Weekly* and *Frank Leslie's Illustrated*, whose artists, such as Winslow Homer, rendered visions of camp and combat for their readers.

Newspaper editors were not always shy about injecting themselves into the policy process. Joseph Medill of the Chicago *Tribune* shared his opinions in personal correspondence with politicians; Horace Greeley of the New York *Tribune* actually tried to become a player in peace negotiations, while his rival, Henry J. Raymond of the New York *Times*, privately offered Lincoln advice on how to deal with Jefferson Davis. The Confederate president also confronted trial by editorial. The Charleston *Mercury*, edited by fire-eater Robert Barnwell Rhett, Jr., made clear its dissatisfaction, as did the Richmond *Examiner*. Occasionally editors were duped by pranks, as when two New York papers printed a bogus proclamation in 1864 calling for a day of prayer in the aftermath of an alleged military disaster—for which the Lincoln administration arrested the editors and briefly shut down the papers.

Another way for civilians to experience the war was through contact with the soldiers at the front—usually through personal correspondence. These rich lodes of letters that scholars assiduously mine tell us as much about American society as they do about the war at any given time. For the letters exchanged between soldiers and civilians in themselves represent an active, if subjective, shaping of images. Soldiers did not always share their full feelings with their readers and presented different accounts to different correspondents. Male associates might hear more graphic descriptions of wounds suffered and the chaos of battle than might parents, wives, or girlfriends; indeed, audience was all important, for soldiers soon discovered (if they did not already know) that what they said to one person might well become the talk of their hometown.

Finally, there was the photograph. Mathew Brady was only the most famous of the war's cameramen; from studio portraits of generals to carte de vistes of enlisted men, his work provided images of the living—and the dead. Although there are only a handful of photographs that claim to be of combat action (none are terribly revealing, for there was no way to capture combat itself on the medium's glass plates, which only registered static subjects well and required long exposure times in order to render a good image), as armies moved away, photographers scrambled over battlefields to capture pictures of landmarks and dead bodies—sometimes even moving and posing the latter for effect as they stayed one step ahead of burial parties. If some of the resulting photographs seemed almost pastoral in their portrayal of the sleep of the dead, others were quite graphic, revealing severed limbs and gaping wounds.

If there was something morbid in all of this, it reflected contemporary American society's preoccupation with death. At the time it was not uncommon for grieving parents to have photographs taken of dead children to preserve their images forever. Moreover, Americans even experimented with the supernatural. President Lincoln himself attended a seance in which a spiritualist attempted to assuage Mary Lincoln's grief by contacting her two dead sons, including one, Willie, who had died in the White House in 1862. But the blows of loss and death suffered by all Americans as a direct result of the nation's civil war led to another fascination—a desire to experience battle, or at least its residue, vicariously. A reporter for the New York *Times*, examining a exhibition of photographs taken at Antietam by Brady and his associates, observed in October 1862: "Mr. Brady has done something to bring home to us the terrible reality and earnestness of war. If he has not brought bodies and laid them in our dooryards and along the streets, he has done something very like it." Those who had experienced the reality of combat, like Ulysses S. Grant, were pained by what they saw and heard away from the battlefront; Grant later remarked that he never wanted to see another painting of a battle. But, lacking the real thing, civilians thought that they could approach it through viewing these photographs: "Let him who wishes to know what war is look at this series of illustrations," the elder Holmes remarked in reviewing Brady's Antietam series.

If the experience of war had a significant impact on the lives of soldiers and their families, it also reshaped the communities that the soldiers had left behind. Community ties were strongest at the beginning of the war for both sides. At first, companies often were raised in the same town, ward, or adjoining localities, and soldiers often elected their captains and lieutenants. Townswomen often sewed uniforms and flags for their local regiment. Indeed, flags assumed an importance far beyond their use in identifying units and assisting their movement in battle, for the flags—one national, one state—were usually produced by the community, tying the soldiers to their homes as well as to their states and nation. Soldiers wrote home about camp life and the battlefield, sharing news about their fellow soldiers to family, loved ones, and neighbors. As Reid Mitchell points out in *The Vacant Chair: The Northern Soldier Leaves Home* (1993), soldiers knew that their comrades would not only scrutinize each other's behavior but also share it with the home folks; at times letters back and forth commented on the contents of other correspondence in an effort to counter reports of cowardice or immoral behavior. In light of the disproportionate burden of battle on various regiments, communities felt the impact of each battle differently: a particularly bloody engagement could shatter a community by killing or crippling a good number of its young men at one blow.

However, the bonds between home front and battlefront changed during the conflict as conscripts, substitutes, replacements, and bounty-hunters, as well as subsequent waves of volunteers, replaced members of the original boys of '61. Many of the newer soldiers cared less about what was said about them, for the restraint of community did not operate on these outsiders. Just as important was the reciprocal tug of home. When things got tough, wives might make it clear to their husbands that they had served long enough. Letters from home could have a decisive impact on morale at the front. One Alabama newspaper reminded women in 1863 that desertion was punishable by death. "When you write to soldiers," the columnist concluded, "speak words of encouragement; cheer their hearts, fire their souls, and arouse their patriotism. Say nothing that will embitter their thoughts or swerve them from the path of duty." The link between the morale of women at home and that of the men at the front was especially evident in the South, due to the increasing threat or the very presence of an invading army. Letters from home begging men to return made it honorable for those men to desert or refuse to reenlist. If notions of honor and manliness underlined the original urge to volunteer—any man who would stay home at a time like this was a coward and certainly no "real man"—now, as General Joseph E. Johnston noted, many soldiers who were not planters or wealthy members of the elite "were compelled to choose between their military service and the strongest obligations men know—their duties to their wives and children."

The morale of soldiers and civilians played off each other. "With such noble women at home, and such heroic soldiers in the field, we are invincible!" Jefferson Davis declared as 1863 began. But it was not clear that this would always be the case. "Defeats, retreats, sufferings, dangers, magnified by the spiritless helplessness and an unchangeable conviction that our army is in the hands of ignorant and feeble commanders, are rapidly producing a sense of settled despair, from which, if not speedily dissipated by 'some bright event or happy change,' the most disastrous consequences may be apprehended," one Mississippi senator predicted. Mary Chesnut, wife of a prominent South Carolinian, put it more bluntly: "Is anything worth it? This fearful sacrifice, this awful penalty we pay for war."

Critical to the strength of the popular support for the war on both sides was the position of the women the men left behind. As farmers left for war, their wives took over the responsibilities of managing the business affairs and the production of the farms (in some cases also working the fields themselves). Wives of slaveowners, especially planters' wives, found themselves saddled with new responsibilities and new vulnerabilities, for they were never certain that slaves would respond to their orders as they had to those issued by their husbands, which had carried with them the threat of force. Factories needed workers regardless of gender. More women became teachers; some even entered the government bureaucracy. But one should not exaggerate either the quantity or quality of these opportunities, many of which would fade away at war's end. As armies moved through the South, sizable numbers of Southern women became refugees, stranded in unfamiliar places with few if any means of support. And then there was the tragedy of loss. Fathers, husbands, brothers, sons, and other men never came back—or returned maimed, sometimes in body, sometimes in soul, sometimes in both. Surely grieving mothers, widows, sisters, and children would have looked askance at the argument that war offered women an opportunity to advance.

The impact of the link between the home front and the battlefront was not lost on military commanders and political leaders. During the Vicksburg campaign Grant had not returned to Memphis to restart his campaign because he knew that such a movement would have looked like a retreat once Northern newspapers got wind of it; a year later he observed that Confederate victory depended upon the demoralization of the Northern public. The mere thought of newspapers seemed to raise William T. Sherman's temper to alarming heights, for he argued that reporters leaked valuable information about military operations while misleading readers about the true state of affairs at the front. After Gettysburg, Robert E. Lee complained that his army "ought not to have been expected to have performed impossibilities or to have fulfilled the anticipations of the thoughtless & unreasonable." Responding to a critical newspaper column, he lashed back at the "unreasonable expectations of the public." Nevertheless, generals grasped the reciprocal relationship between public opinion and military policy and acknowledged the former's importance in determining the conflict's ultimate outcome.

The Northern Economy and War Effort

Neither the Union nor the Confederacy had been prepared to wage war on the scale required by the Civil War. Each side had to work very hard to mobilize its warmaking resources; as the conflict intensified, expanded in scope, and turned into a prolonged struggle, this continued, high-level mobilization of resources promised to transform America whatever the outcome of the war.

In order to wage war, the Union had to find ways to pay for it. Its own financial structure was feeble, still reflecting the policies of the Jacksonian era, in which payments to or by the federal government had to be made in specie, while a patchwork of state and local banks issued notes of varying value. In 1861 Congress levied an income tax of 3 percent on incomes exceeding $800, but it would be a year before this act generated any revenue. Initial efforts to float a war-bond issue proved disappointing, and before long banks could no longer loan specie to the federal government without threatening their own solvency—a situation exacerbated when the *Trent* crisis led to the hoarding of silver and gold. At year's end both the Treasury and the banks suspended specie payments. The Union was going broke.

The Republican-controlled Congress responded to the crisis by passing on February 25, 1862, the Legal Tender Act, authorizing the issuance of $150 million in government notes—the first of what were to become known as greenbacks. These could be used in all transactions, except to pay import duties and interest on the national debt (which included interest on government bonds), as if they were specie—although before long they spurred inflation and the creation of a gold market in which the price of gold was measured in its worth in greenbacks. At the same time Congress adopted new revenue measures, increasing the income tax, imposing a series of excise taxes, and raising tariffs. Such measures, in tandem with the bond issues, prevented runaway inflation.

Treasury Secretary Chase was not enamored with the Legal Tender Act. He supported the issuing of bonds and the creation of a new national banking system. In appointing Jay Cooke of Philadelphia to market government bonds, Chase made a wise choice, for Cooke skillfully promoted bond sales and encouraged large numbers of Northerners to invest in the war effort (making Cooke a wealthy financier). The following year Congress passed the National Bank Act, providing for the chartering of federal banks through the purchase of government bonds and the issuance of federal banknotes, whose total value could not exceed 90 percent of the chartering bonds. This represented a first step toward a uniform national currency: additional legislation passed in the next two years eventually eliminated state banknotes from circulation. In the end, bond sales financed nearly two-thirds of the Union war effort, taxes accounted for a fifth, while the greenbacks contributed 13 percent.

At this time, Lincoln's selection of Edwin M. Stanton as his new secretary of war proved most fortunate. Simon Cameron, the initial occupant of that office, had been overwhelmed by the responsibilities of raising, training, and supplying the largest army in American history. Stanton, despite some early slips—as when he suspended recruiting for a short period in 1862—proved equal to the task. He brought the department's various staff positions together as a war board and coordinated the operations of the adjutant general and the quartermaster. He also coordinated the ordnance, commissary, and engineering departments and formed advisory committees to help procure supplies for Union armies. Finally, he oversaw the cooperative military operations of northern railroads. Quartermaster General Montgomery Meigs proved a skillful bargainer when it came to purchasing contracts, and he efficiently moved supplies to the front, as did his counterparts in the commissary and ordnance departments. Secretary of the Navy Gideon Welles and his assistant, Gustavus V. Fox, also performed in commendable fashion, building a blockade fleet and a riverline navy in remarkably short order.

Recruiting proved to be a more challenging task. In the summer of 1862 Lincoln persuaded Northern governors to issue a new call for volunteers; Congress augmented the president's powers by passing a Militia Act authorizing him to conscript militia to fulfill recruiting quotas and providing for the enlistment of blacks. The promise of conscription spurred volunteering, but the following year revealed the need for yet more soldiers, especially in light of expiring enlistments. In response, Congress in March 1863 passed legislation providing for conscription if congressional districts failed to meet recruiting quotas set by the War Department. Drafted men could evade service by paying $300 or by hiring a substitute. State and local governments offered men bounties to volunteer; eventually the federal government followed suit. The system thus created opportunities for certain types of fraud and the occasion for protest. "Bounty jumpers" enlisted, collected their money, then deserted at the first opportunity, some with the intention of repeating the entire process. Meanwhile, poor workers denounced the policies of commutation and substitution, claiming that they allowed the rich to avoid service. Finally, substitutes deserted at a higher rate than did volunteers. Nonetheless the new system of recruitment, on the whole, induced more men to volunteer.

Contracts for munitions and supplies bolstered manufacturing on both sides during the war. Northern industry boomed: after initial slumps, coal and iron production surpassed prewar levels. Railroads also prospered as soldiers and supplies frequently moved by rail to the front. But some sectors of industry suffered: for example, textile mills slowed for lack of raw cotton. Wartime production on a mass scale also led to innovation: standard sizes for uniforms and shoes became commonplace, an idea that carried over into postwar retailing. Northern agriculture thrived during the war, due in part to European crop failures that opened new markets for American foodstuffs abroad. Some farmers away on the battlefront were replaced by mowers and reapers as agriculture moved toward mechanization.

Between stocks, bonds, and forms of speculation afforded by various commodities and the appearance of the greenback (with its fluctuating value) finance capitalists found many avenues to enrichment. One of the more sordid enterprises conducted during the war was cotton trading, which afforded many opportunities for government representatives and army officers, as well as private citizens, to make money in ways that would not bear the light of day. Most workers did not share in such prosperity. During the war their wages did not keep up with inflation, leading to occasional unrest and widespread dissatisfaction. In some cases workers, especially skilled laborers, decided to unite to advance their cause; they soon discovered, however, that strikes irritated the government as much as they did management, especially when the war effort was involved. Union army soldiers were dispatched to break up some strikes, and in several instances they arrested strikers. As workers were also vulnerable to conscription—most of them lacking the money to pay the $300 commutation fee—they understandably agreed with their Southern counterparts that it was indeed a rich man's war and a poor man's fight.

One source of economic change and development in the Union during these years was the federal government policy. Wartime majorities in Congress passed and Lincoln signed into law a series of measures that had hitherto been blocked by Southern votes and presidential vetoes. The Homestead Act (1862) offered 160-acre plots of public land to anyone who would reside on them for five years (veterans received more generous allotments of acreage and terms of ownership), promoting the settlement of the West. The Morrill Land Grant Act (1862) helped establish state universities "to teach such branches of learning as are related to agriculture and the mechanical arts." Tariff legislation also promoted the development of Northern industry, while the Pacific Railroad Act provided for the construction of a transcontinental line.

However, the cumulative impact of the war on economic growth and development is more difficult to assess. Once generally accepted claims that the war launched the industrial revolution in the United States have faded in the face of evidence that industrialization had been well underway by 1860 and that the pace of U.S. economic growth actually slackened during the conflict. Of course, these aggregate statistical measures include data from the South, where the economy, especially its industrial sector, suffered significant (physical) wartime damage. But the war did alter the direction of economic growth. Federal legislation reshaped the national political economy by injecting the government more explicitly into the process as an agent fostering growth. The Homestead Act, the Morrill Land Grant Act, and the construction of the transcontinental railroad bolstered national agricultural development and expansion. Tariff, tax, and banking legislation reshaped fiscal policy, and the Legal Tender Act represented the first of several steps in the realm of governmental monetary policy.

Even before the war the North's economic might was considerable: this helped conceal some weaknesses in Union leadership during the early years of the conflict. It would not be until 1864 that the Union high command under Grant mobilized these resources in an effective and telling manner against the Confederacy. Nevertheless, as Lincoln noted, after nearly four years of war, "The national resources . . . are unexhausted, and, as we believe, inexhaustible."

The Southern Economy and War Effort

Ironically, the Confederacy took more extreme measures to centralize its economic planning—out of necessity. Before the war it lacked the financial resources and the fiscal institutions of the Union. The King Cotton strategy of 1861 only exacerbated matters, for the cotton embargo cut short a substantial source of money. To make things worse still, Secretary of the Treasury Christopher Memminger could not get the Confederate Congress to impose taxes—after all, such a move would have given the central government more power and clashed with notions of limited governance—until August 1861. When it did come, the measure, which looked to contributions from the member states of the Confederacy, was in most cases satisfied not through taxation but loans. Confederate bond issues were too small to raise sufficient funds, yet those that were sold drained the economy of specie. Efforts to sell bonds to planters in exchange for the proceeds from crop sales proved even less successful. Creating paper money in the form of treasury notes was the only alternative. In 1861 and 1862 the Confederate Congress authorized the printing of a total of over half a billion dollars. Inflation resulted: as prices went up, the printing presses churned out even more money, driving prices still higher. State governments and banks added to the flood of paper with their own issues.

Confederate authorities soon realized the consequences of the course they had chosen to pursue. In 1863 the Confederate Congress passed a broad revenue measure, levying taxes on consumer goods, wholesale profits, professional and business licenses, and personal income. Farmers could pay their tax with agricultural products. (In later legislation land and slaves became subject to taxes as well.) But it was too late: by this time sizable areas of the Confederacy were already under Union occupation; citizens chafed at paying the taxes when they did not manage to evade the levies; and crops gathered as part of the tax-in-kind sometimes spoiled while in storage. With insufficient revenue a fact of life for the would-be nation, inflation spiraled upwards at astonishing rates: what cost $1 in 1861 cost $46 three years later and $92 by the spring of 1865. Imported goods cost even more. Its fiscal policy cost the Confederacy popular support as well as money. An occasional triumph—such as the securing of a $14.5 million loan from the French in 1863—mitigated the impact of their failure, but only temporarily. Some 60 percent of the income for the Confederate war effort was financed through the issuance of paper money; only 5 percent came from tax revenue. Neither Memminger nor his successor, the South Carolina banker George Trenholm, ever managed to right the problems of Confederate finance, despite their best efforts.

A succession of five men served Jefferson Davis as secretary of war. Davis's insistence on his close supervision of military affairs made it difficult for anyone else to manage that department. Secretary of the Navy Stephen Mallory faced the even more daunting task of building a navy from scratch. He pushed for the purchase of ships built abroad and the building of ironclads to overcome the quantitative inferiority under which the Confederacy would labor at sea. The Confederacy also pushed ahead with the development of mines and submarines to protect harbors and break the blockade, although the submarines they came up with proved primitive and as dangerous to friend as to foe. However, Confederate commerce raiders did devastate the U.S. merchant marine; Union newspapers cheered in June 1864 when one of the most famous Rebel raiders, the *C. S. S. Alabama*, fell victim to a Yankee frigate off the French coast.

Having adopted conscription in the spring of 1862, the Confederate government gradually closed loopholes as it broadened the number of whites liable to the draft. Eventually the hiring of substitutes was eliminated, as were several categories of exemptions from service. Between volunteering and conscription, the Confederacy mobilized approximately 80 percent of its available white manpower for military service, although what at first seems a rather remarkable figure is explained in part by the fact that much of its labor force was composed of black slaves. And nearly a fifth of the total force mobilized was obtained as a direct result of conscription.

As the war commenced, Southern farms and plantations shifted production from cotton to foodstuffs, although yields declined as more farmers (and livestock) went to the army, and total production declined as Union armies swept southward. When farmers withheld produce from market in the hope that prices would go up, the Confederate Congress responded by passing legislation authorizing the government to impress goods at set prices; when this proved only a partial solution to agricultural hoarding, the Confederate government cracked down on recalcitrant farmers, thus increasing the conviction of many citizens that their government had turned tyrannical. But even with the general shift toward growing food, Confederate planters continued to grow cotton: the 1862 crop was the second-largest on record. In short, as much as Southern farmers did, they could have done more to feed their armies. Meanwhile, the successful campaigns of Grant, Sherman, and Sheridan in 1863 and 1864 severed rail links (disrupting the distribution of food), deprived the Confederacy of prime farmland, and either destroyed crops in the field or reaped them to feed Union soldiers and livestock. Finally, Commissary General Lucius B. Northrop proved an unfortunate choice of administrator: Mary Chesnut labelled him "the best-abused man in Richmond."

Despite evident disadvantages, the Confederacy worked long and hard with some success to secure weapons and ammunition for the war. Ordnance Department head Josiah Gorgas worked diligently to build an industrial base to supply Johnny Reb. Munitions factories appeared across the South; the government supervised the production of nitre, essential in the manufacture of gunpowder. In Richmond, the Tredegar Iron Works expanded, producing cannon, plating for ironclads, and machinery necessary for other foundries. Weapons and munitions captured from Yankee arsenals or collected from battlefields contributed to the arming of Rebel soldiers. The Confederates were far less successful when it came to clothing their soldiers, in part because of the increasing difficulty of transporting goods to the front, and in furnishing their armies with adequate numbers of horses and mules. Quartermaster General Abraham C. Myers was unable to surmount the difficulties he faced.

The success of the Union blockade and the capture of major Southern ports forced the Confederacy to look even further within to supply its war effort. Blockade runners found it increasingly difficult to make their way into port; some of these sailor-merchants gave up on the enterprise altogether, while the blockade runners that still operated tended to do so with smaller and lighter vessels, which, of course, had less cargo space. When blockade runners looked to increase their profits by carrying luxury goods instead of war matériel, the Confederate government stepped in yet again, in February 1864, mandating that one-half of the cargo space of each vessel be reserved for its own goods. The sale of cotton, both abroad and across enemy lines, financed luxury purchases, and the combination of supply and inflation meant that the staple could still command a good price.

Indeed, although both sides were at war, each found reasons to trade with the other. Northern speculators and the government wanted Southern cotton: the former hoping to use it get rich quick, the latter hoping to obtain enough of it to feed textile mills at home, satisfy foreign demand in order to reduce pressure for intervention, and revive Southern loyalty to the Union by an appeal to the pocketbook. Grant and Sherman protested the government's cotton policy, pointing out that it sustained the enemy forces. But other generals had fewer qualms about the ethics and impact of such trade, most notably General Benjamin F. Butler, who oversaw a thriving trade between enemies at New Orleans and Norfolk—and made sure that his brother (and perhaps he himself) prospered. Lincoln argued that it was better for the North to buy the South's cotton than to force the Confederates to sell it at even higher prices abroad—where they would reap even larger amounts of cash with which to procure war matériel. For his part, Jefferson Davis also sanctioned North-South trade over the objections of several of his generals, noting that the survival of the Confederate army depended on it. In such transactions prescient observers saw the roots of postwar corruption in business and politics.

Politics and Society: The North

If the Prussian military theorist Karl von Clausewitz was correct in claiming that war was politics through other means, politics remained an essential part of the war effort for both sides. Politics shaped policy and governance. It influenced military appointments and operations, and it provided Americans North and South a forum in which to debate the issues of the war. Nor was political participation limited to voting and holding office: other people also claimed their right to be heard and to shape their own lives.

In the North, the Republican party, despite internal disagreements over how to approach the issues of slavery and the reconstruction of occupied areas, rarely allowed such differences to shake their control of the political agenda or the prosecution of the war. Radicals such as Charles Sumner of Massachusetts and Benjamin Wade of Ohio in the Senate and Pennsylvania's Thaddeus Stevens in the House pressed Lincoln to wage war in earnest and to take aim at slavery. Lincoln kept a careful eye on this Radical wing of the party, for some of its more frustrated leaders were interested in securing a new Republican presidential nominee in 1864. Moderate Republicans usually found themselves in step with the president, although few of them displayed deep loyalty to the chief executive.

Lincoln proved a superb politician precisely because he was able to navigate the troubled waters within his own party. He was aided by Republicans' realization that whatever divided them, those differences paled in comparison to their opposition to the Democrats. The president played a key role in the transformation of the Republicans from a coalition seeking power to a party exercising it. He balanced contending interests where possible, and he knew how to use patronage to mobilize support for himself and his policies (and to damage the chances of his major rival for the 1864 Republican nomination, Salmon P. Chase). Although he found some members of his party frustrating as colleagues, he rarely let personal resentments get in the way of achieving his political ends. Great as these skills were, however, Lincoln truly excelled in assessing and shaping public opinion. In public letters, formal addresses, interviews, and occasional speeches, he explained his policies, prepared the public for new measures, and continually sought its support. Lincoln may have asserted, "I claim not to have controlled events, but confess plainly that events have controlled me," but no one accepted that as the whole truth. As one Republican appreciatively noted, "he always moves in conjunction with propitious circumstances, not waiting to be dragged by the force of events or wasting strength in premature struggles with them."

Where Lincoln was a bit more shaky was in his capacity as commander-in-chief of the Union's armed forces. Although he proved an apt student of the fundamentals of military science, he experienced a great deal of friction and bad feelings with several generals. Politics necessarily shaped several of his military appointments, especially in the war's early stages, with mixed results on the battlefield. If John A. Logan and Frank P. Blair proved successful politician-generals, they were overshadowed by the far more mixed records of Nathaniel P. Banks, John A. McClernand, Benjamin F. Butler, and Franz Sigel. Contrary to historical myth, Lincoln did not spot Grant early on as the coming man of the war; rather, he remained unsure and ambivalent about the general until Grant besieged Vicksburg. That in the end the two men established a warm working relationship owed much to Grant's understanding of the nature of civil-military relations and the political dimensions of the war effort, although by 1864 Lincoln had also learned much about military administration through trial and error.

If Lincoln proved a skilled leader, he was not always a popular one. Abolitionists denounced him for moving at what they considered a glacial pace against slavery, although some of them, led by William Lloyd Garrison and Frederick Douglass, became the president's warm supporters as he embraced the destruction of slavery. Northern blacks, somewhat lukewarm at first in their support of the war, later saw to it that the struggle for freedom might also become a struggle for equality. Of the 180,000 blacks who served in the Union army, 34,000 came from the free black population. At home, blacks pushed for more rights, and in some cases scored gains. For example, streetcar service in several Northern cities was integrated. Opposition to black enfranchisement eroded but did not crumble.

Northern Democrats faced difficult choices, well aware that to oppose the war outright risked political oblivion for their party (as it had for the Federalist party after the War of 1812). Some decided to become supporters of the administration as well as of the war; these Democrats, led by Massachusetts's Butler and Illinois's McClernand, were richly rewarded by Lincoln for their support, with Butler and McClernand receiving commissions as generals. A second group of Democrats supported the war effort but broke with the administration over its approach to emancipation, reconstruction, conscription, and the suspension of the writ of habeas corpus. A third group of Democrats went even further to question the war itself: they became known as the Copperheads, likened to the poisonous snake by their foes.

Copperheads argued that the war and the actions of the Lincoln administration made reunion impossible, and they urged compromise through a negotiated settlement. Like other Democrats, they spoke out against emancipation, conscription, and Lincoln's extreme uses of executive power. Confederate agents encouraged such sentiments, believing that a Copperhead political triumph would result in Confederate independence. Distressed as the Lincoln administration might have been by their direct criticism, what moved Republicans to question the loyalty of Copperheads to the Union itself was evidence that some Copperhead activity went beyond the legitimate channels of political debate to talk of taking up arms against the federal government. Copperhead contact with Confederate agents also called into question the former's claims of serving as a loyal opposition. Republicans surely exaggerated but did not fabricate such reports.

In such circumstances Lincoln had to distinguish between legitimate political opposition and treason, a challenge made all the more important by his insistence that the war was a test of American political institutions. Early in the war he had suspended the writ of habeas corpus to help unionist forces secure control of wavering border states and to guarantee the safe passage of soldiers to Washington. Such measures may have warned dissenters of the consequences of their speech and acts, but they did not end dissension. Moreover, the majority of such arrests took place in occupied Confederate territory or the border states, where the line between dissent and treason was not always clear. Few of these cases actually made it to trial: in most of them, suspects were released after taking an oath of loyalty. Nevertheless, reports that Seward and Stanton had bragged about exercising the power to imprison anyone simply by ringing a bell sounded ominously like arbitrary and unaccountable behavior.

Lincoln's decision in September 1862 to suspend the writ again and impose martial law in cases involving resistance to recruiting proved even more controversial. Coming just two days after the issuance of the Preliminary Emancipation Proclamation, Lincoln's announcement spurred Democrats to cite both measures as evidence that Republicans were bent on transforming the Union under the guise of saving it. But it was the arrest of Copperhead Clement Vallandigham that sparked a crisis. While running for governor of Ohio in 1863, Vallandigham fiercely attacked the Lincoln administration's conduct of the war. General Ambrose Burnside, who had been given a rear-area command after Fredericksburg, judged Vallandigham's comments as treasonous and arrested him in the early morning hours of May 5. The arrest posed a serious dilemma for the Lincoln administration. Although the president would have preferred that the incident never occurred, he upheld Burnside and reminded Democrats that the encouragement of desertion was as much a violation of the Constitution as the act of desertion itself. As he posed the matter in responding to a Democratic protest, "Must I shoot a simple-minded soldier who deserts, while I must not touch a hair of a wily agitator who induces him to desert?" But to keep Vallandigham imprisoned would raise charges that Republicans would incarcerate opponents to secure victory at the polls. Lincoln decided to banish Vallandigham to the Confederacy. Before long the Copperhead agitator made his way to Canada, where he completed his campaign in exile. When he returned to the United States in 1864, Lincoln ignored him.

The decision to embrace emancipation as a war aim sparked new criticism of the administration. Many Democrats claimed that they would not fight to free the black man. The advent of conscription in 1863 fueled these protests, as did Lincoln's willingness to enforce the draft and take action against its leading opponents. The most vivid of these protests occurred in New

York City in July 1863, when rioters, mainly Irish immigrants, expressed their resentment by attacking pro-Union enterprises such as newspapers before turning their wrath directly upon the city's black residents. The riots backfired: reports of the courage of black soldiers under fire, especially at Fort Wagner, blunted the force of blatant racist appeals by Democrats to voters, while the rioters came under heavy public criticism for having resorted to violence. Elsewhere resistance to the draft revealed class as well as political and racial divisions.

The Northern electorate would have a chance to pass judgment on the administration at the polls in 1863. Seats in several state legislatures (which selected U.S. Senators) and governorships were up for grabs. Democrats renewed their attack on emancipation, conscription, and the suspension of the writ as evidence of Lincoln's revolutionary intentions. The president confronted these criticisms in a series of public letters. Defending emancipation as a necessary war measure, he also highlighted the accomplishments of black soldiers. Should the war vindicate the strength of representative institutions, he remarked, "there will be some black men who can remember that, with silent tongue, and clenched teeth, and steady eye, and well-poised bayonet, they have helped mankind on to this great consummation; while, I fear, there will be some white ones, unable to forget that, with malignant heart, and deceitful speech, they have strove to hinder it." When November came, the Republicans claimed victory. Vallandigham lost, as did other prominent Copperheads: neither emancipation nor conscription had turned a majority of Northern voters against the administration. "The crisis which threatened to divide the friends of the Union is past," the president observed at year's end.

But there were ways other than the exercise of the franchise to express support of or opposition to the government and its conduct of the war. Many women became involved in the war effort through their involvement in various charitable and relief operations designed to offer assistance to soldiers and their families. The most noteworthy examples of these were the sanitary commissions. In 1861 the Reverend Henry Bellows organized the United States Sanitary Commission, which provided soldiers with food and other items and investigated the state of military hospitals and medical care. The commission organized fairs and ran lotteries to supplement private donations to fund its operations. The United States Christian Commission looked after soldiers' spiritual well-being by distributing tracts and making visits to the front. Other relief efforts included the operation of homes for invalid soldiers or children whom the war had orphaned. Various volunteer efforts sewed socks and underwear for the boys in blue. The writer Louisa May Alcott summarized the prevailing attitude for many women when she declared, "As I can't fight, I will content myself with working for those who can."

Women also sought to contribute to the war effort through serving as nurses—as Alcott herself eventually did. Clara Barton's exploits in caring for the wounded Union soldiers at Antietam and elsewhere remain well-known, but many soldiers in the West recalled with fondness Mary Ann Bickerdyke, an Ohio widow who soon became known to all, from Grant and Sherman down to the lowest private, as Mother Bickerdyke, a nurse who brooked no opposition to getting her way. Mary Livermore, a prewar newspaper editor and reporter and the only woman correspondent present at the Republican presidential convention of 1860, and other women worked under the auspices of various sanitary commissions. Other women chose to express their opinions in the political arena. In 1863 Susan B. Anthony, Elizabeth Cady Stanton, and Lucy Stone, prominent advocates of women's rights, established the Women's Loyal League to press for abolition in the form of a constitutional amendment. Anna Dickinson proved a most outspoken abolitionist speaker, drawing large audiences. From Richmond, Elizabeth Van Lew fed information to Union authorities; Harriet Tubman, an escaped slave herself, worked hard during the war to raise black regiments and promote the erosion of slavery along the Atlantic coast.

Finally, the war energized Northern politics and society, even if it did not always unify it. Vigorous debate over the means and ends of the conflict testified to an awareness that the Civil War promised to transform the Union it sought to preserve. Not everyone embraced these changes; circumstances and what was at stake suggested that the days of politics as usual were through. Nevertheless, the vibrancy of political discussion demonstrated the durability of American political institutions and the persistence of core principles in times of stress.

Politics and Society: The South

Confederate politics and society were shaped in fundamental ways by the circumstances facing the new nation in 1861. Fighting for survival, literally fending off invading armies while trying to establish a new government that embodied the principles enshrined by secession proved a demanding, even impossible task. Strains within the Confederacy dissipated much-needed unity. "We crippled ourselves—blew ourselves up—by intestine strife," Mary Chesnut asserted. Many of these tensions were the result of contradictions between the reasons that Southerners had cited in the justification of secession and the need to secure that independence through war. For once commenced, the war revealed deep societal fissures between large slaveholders and other whites, subverting efforts to preserve unity. In conducting the war, the Davis administration and its supporters in the Confederate Congress embraced measures that smacked of centralized authority, leading opponents to charge the government with the abandonment of states rights.

In his February 1861 inaugural address, Jefferson Davis recited the constitutional justification for secession, arguing that the compact that had created the Constitution had been rent asunder by the triumph of the Republican party, leaving the Southern states free to exercise the right of sovereign entities by severing their association with the Union. He never mentioned slavery. Just over a month later, however, Vice President Alexander H. Stephens told an audience at Savannah that slavery "was the immediate cause of the late rupture and present revolution." As for the new Confederacy, "its foundations are laid, its cornerstone rests, upon the great truth that the negro is not equal to the white man; that slavery, subordination to the white race, is his natural and moral condition." Yet once their government had to assume responsibility for the conduct of the war, debates over states rights and slavery divided Confederates. Ironically, it would be those measures advocated by Davis himself that would cause defenders of states rights to denounce the Confederate president.

The debate over conscription highlighted Confederate divisions. The provision that exempted owners or overseers of twenty or more slaves pitted large planters against small slaveholders and nonslaveholding whites, replacing race with class as the major political division within Confederate society—something many large planters had always dreaded. The concept of conscription in itself appeared to be a violation of the concept of states rights, for it was necessarily the act of a powerful central government. The same themes appeared again in response to legislation authorizing the impressment of slave labor and the establishment of sources of revenue to fund the war. Slaveholders claimed that such government interference with private property was exactly what they had hoped to avoid through secession; so did small farmers and others who resented the new taxation measures. Yet unless the Confederate government mobilized its resources, both human and financial, its chances of securing victory diminished. As General Albert Sidney Johnston sarcastically noted, "These people have given their sons freely enough, but it is folly to talk to them about a negro or a mule."

Other issues reinforced societal divisions. Unlike Lincoln, Davis did not automatically claim that he could suspend the writ of habeas corpus or declare martial law. Instead, he sought and received legislative approval for such powers, and then used them to arrest disloyal citizens and exercise direct control over troublesome areas, including Richmond in 1862. Although his initial authorization to exercise extraexecutive powers was not renewed in 1863, Davis secured a second authorization to do so in 1864. Critical of such legislation and of conscription, Stephens remarked that "our President is aiming at the obtainment of power inconsistent with public liberty." Before long Stephens became a bitter opponent of the president, so did governors Joseph E.

Brown of Georgia and Zebulon Vance of North Carolina. Davis complained that Brown, Vance, and others were "hindering the action of this government, obstructing the execution of its laws, denouncing its necessary policy, impairing its hold on the confidence of the people, and dealing with it rather as if it were the public enemy than the government which they themselves had established for the common defense and which was their only hope of safety from the untold horrors of Yankee despotism." Thus Davis revealed the real impact of the debate over states rights upon Confederate fortunes. Although Brown and Vance provided for the defence of their states and the relief of their citizens, their defiance of the Confederate president wore away at national unity and widened divisions in the Southern society.

Perhaps Davis did face an impossible task, but in his commitment to Confederate independence he was willing to sacrifice just about anything. It is difficult to see who could have done a better job under the circumstances. Yet the Confederate president had his shortcomings as well. His military expertise proved a mixed blessing, for his intervention in the conduct of military affairs was not always wise. Stiff and formal with his associates, Davis made few friends, often impressing observers as cold. Physically ailing throughout the war, the death of his young son Joseph in 1864 added to his personal woes. Impatient with others, quick to engage in disputes, and possessed of a sharp tongue and pen, he took his responsibilities so seriously that he often failed to delegate enough work to subordinates. Such characteristics only swelled his burdens as they intensified his opposition; yet it must be noted that his counterpart in Washington, so much Davis's opposite in many ways, encountered similar obstacles. Davis's iron will and determination were remarkable, and they help explain why the Confederacy lasted as long as it did.

Within the Confederacy, opposition to the Davis administration appeared in areas of prewar Unionist and Whig strength, especially when and if these areas were still under Confederate control. Members of the Confederate Congress from regions already under Union control or imminently threatened by invasion understandably pressed for a more vigorous prosecution of the struggle to liberate their constituents, while the citizens of areas firmly under Confederate control, especially those dominated by poor whites, were not always eager to shoulder the burden of any such measures. In such ways the progress of the conflict pitted white Southerner against white Southerner, creating new fissures in Confederate society even as it widened old ones. With the Confederacy void of political parties, one vehicle for organizing and maintaining support for administration measures, Davis found it difficult to manage such internal conflicts.

The degree of opposition became apparent during the congressional elections of 1863. Forty-one of the 106 representatives returned by the voters were openly hostile to Davis, and the administration clung to a slim and shaky majority in the Senate. More significant was the fact that areas under Confederate control returned an anti-administration majority; those members of Congress representing areas occupied by Union forces asserted their claim to victory based upon a scattering of refugee support. That year a North Carolina newspaper editor, William W. Holden, began calling for a negotiated peace; the following year he ran for governor of his state. Although Holden lost the election, his candidacy and the support it attracted suggested that a growing number of Southern whites were weary of the war.

What had once unified Southern whites now divided them. Debates over slavery and conscription pitted planter against farmer and worker, nationalists against states rights advocates, government against slaveholder and farmer. Conscription and impressment, taken together, alienated both slaveowners and nonslaveowners from the Confederacy. The Confederate government, in testing the meaning of states rights, and those slaveowners who protested its actions, were both seeking the same goal of preserving the independence of a slaveholding republic. Not for some time would it become apparent that the Confederate government and wealthy slaveholders often differed on whether it was more important to preserve the independence of slaveholders or that of the republic they sought to establish. The Confederacy was becoming a victim of its internal contradictions, contradictions revealed in the crucible of war.

Yet one can make too much of these strains upon morale. Through 1864, at least, despite the emergence of some major fissures in Confederate society, most civilians retained faith in the cause. Officials at Wofford College in Spartanburg, South Carolina, used the school's endowment to purchase Confederate bonds in 1864—a patriotic if not exactly a timely or wise investment. That many Southern whites reacted in shock to news of the ultimate defeat suggested that at least some Confederates harbored hopes for victory long after it was virtually impossible.

The spirit of white Southern women proved one barometer of public commitment to the cause. And, in light of the rather high level of mobilization of Southern white males for the war, women's contribution to the war effort was very important. They took pride in making do in austere times, improvising with a sense of humor as well as commitment to the cause. But fulfilling the role of the innovative homemaker left many women unsatisfied. "If I was only a man!" exclaimed Sarah Morgan of Louisiana. "I don't know a woman here who does not groan over her misfortune in being clothed in petticoats; why can't we fight as well as the men?" There were other ways to serve. Belle Boyd and Rose Greenhow gained great renown for their activities as spies; they were successful in part because they could flatter men into confiding military secrets to them, for few men thought women capable of espionage. Other Southern women worked in hospitals, and Richmond's Sally Tompkins actually received a captain's commission to assist her in her endeavors. Nor did Southern white women always quietly accept the authority of occupation forces: in New Orleans, their behavior caused Union general Benjamin F. Butler to issue his so-called "woman order," directing the arrest of protesting women on charges of prostitution.

But it was not always easy to maintain such spirited patriotism. It became harder and harder to make ends meet and manage affairs as the war dragged on: women decried these circumstances, as when a riot broke out over bread prices in Richmond in April 1863. (Jefferson Davis personally intervened to restore order.) As Union armies penetrated into the Confederate heartland, slaves slipped away, food became more expensive and more difficult to obtain, and concern grew in many localities over what the invaders might do to the women should they ever march through the community. Life in occupied regions could be very tough, for Union soldiers did not always treat civilians gently—perhaps because at times those civilians were not above participating in guerrilla operations. Yet it was also true that many Southern civilians complained almost as much about the behavior of Johnny Reb. The destructiveness of the conflict rendered many families homeless; others chose to flee their hometowns rather than suffer through military occupation. In the absence of a relief program, this shifting refugee population imposed new municipal burdens wherever it alighted, and friction between refugees and long-standing residents was not uncommon. Confederate women also complained to the authorities in Richmond about the government's failure to protect them against invasion and its aftermath; many also begged their soldier-husbands to return home to defend loved ones. In such circumstances, it was understandable that ties of loyalty to the Confederacy eroded, for it failed to protect the very homes its soldiers had gone to war to protect. And internal division, as one Confederate administrator put it, "menaces the existence of the Confederacy as fatally as . . . the armies of the United States."

Wartime Reconstruction: Early Steps

Lincoln understood that the Civil War was not a traditional Victorian conflict between rival nation-states. The goal of reunion shaped in fundamental ways how he approached the problem of reconstruction. Conquest by itself would not suffice: in order to truly save the Union, Confederates must someday return to the fold. As was seen, Lincoln stubbornly held on to the notion that in time—or with the appearance of Union armies—Southern unionism would reassert itself. This vision did not remain intact. As Union armies penetrated Confederate territory, the vast majority of the people who welcomed them were not white unionists anxious to reaffirm their loyalty but black slaves seeking their freedom. Although some Southern unionists, including Tennessee's

Andrew Johnson, showed great courage in denouncing the Confederacy, other self-styled Union loyalists proved reluctant to assert themselves, even after they came under the protection of Union arms. Disappointed that he had overestimated the number of Southern unionists, and furious with their failure to come forth, Lincoln snapped that "this class of men will do nothing for themselves, except demanding that the government shall not strike its open enemies, lest they be struck by accident!"

Nevertheless, by 1862 Lincoln had assisted in commencing the process of erecting unionist governments in areas of Virginia (whose main function was to accede to the formation of West Virginia), Tennessee, Louisiana, and North Carolina; the following year Arkansas took its first significant steps in that direction, while in 1864 Lincoln unsuccessfully sought to include Florida. Wartime exigencies explained why these governments were formed: Lincoln wanted to create rallying points for unionists in these areas, and he promised to shield them from the impact of the Emancipation Proclamation. The final document that Lincoln signed enumerated exempted parts of Virginia and Louisiana and did not apply at all to West Virginia or Tennessee.

The effort to reestablish a unionist government in North Carolina floundered, in part due to opposition there to emancipation; elsewhere military conquest determined the sort of materials Lincoln, his generals, and local unionists would use in reestablishing loyal state governments. Thus the taking of New Orleans in April 1862 brought within Union lines a good number of white unionists as well as the city's free black community. In Tennessee the story was much different. Unionist sentiment was quite strong in the eastern third of the state, and during the first year of the war Lincoln had sought to organize an offensive to liberate it. However, Union arms made far more progress in West and Middle Tennessee, where support for the Confederacy had carried the day. Thus until Union victories secured East Tennessee, military governor Andrew Johnson was more concerned about preserving order and suppressing opposition than he was about cultivating support for the new government.

In fostering the growth of these new governments Lincoln proffered suggestions rather than issuing mandates—although he was not above using patronage to assure that these new bodies would be in compliance whenever possible with administration preferences. He insisted that the new governments abolish slavery, sharing his preference for a gradual transition from slavery to freedom. He also pushed for the establishment of some program of public education and apprenticeship to prepare the emancipated for a world without slavery. Nor would he stand for letting the reconstructed state governments fall into the hands of the disloyal. "Let the work of reconstruction be the work of such men only as can be trusted for the Union," he told Tennessee's Johnson. Time was of the essence, for Lincoln realized that he might not win reelection in 1864.

Through the first two years of the war Lincoln held fast to these principles, but he failed to formulate an overall approach to Reconstruction. In December 1863 he remedied that shortcoming when he issued a proclamation of amnesty and reconstruction. To most Southern whites in the ten states covered by the proclamation (Virginia, having always had a unionist regime, was excluded), he offered a full pardon and the restoration of personal property other than slaves—except where confiscation proceedings had not transferred property to a third party—to all people who took an oath of future loyalty to the United States. Excluded from this offer were certain classes of Confederate civil and military leaders, those people who had resigned U.S. civil or military positions to join the Confederacy, and those people who had mistreated Union prisoners of war. Residents of a state in rebellion could commence structuring a new state government once the number of people who had met voter eligibility requirements in 1860 had taken the oath to equal one-tenth of that state's total ballots cast in 1860's presidential election. Such governments then had to be constructed in accordance with the wartime acts of Lincoln and Congress concerning slavery—a wordy way of saying that they had to embrace emancipation if Lincoln was to recognize them.

Lincoln's proposal—which some historians have labelled the Ten Percent Plan—offered one route toward reconstruction. The president remarked that there were alternatives, and he acknowledged that each chamber of Congress retained the right to accept or reject the credentials of its members. In so doing, he simply reiterated what was already contained within the Constitution, but he did so to reassure Congress that it would play a role in the reconstruction process while simultaneously reminding the reconstructed that voices other than his would have to be heard if the process were to prove a complete success. Nor did he care to discuss whether the seceded states were currently in or out of the Union (if one deemed that they had forfeited their status as states, as some Republicans argued, then they had reverted to territories, whereupon they came under the direct control of Congress), terming this concern "a merely metaphysical question."

Nowhere in Lincoln's proposal was there a provision for black participation in the new state governments. In March 1864, he "barely" suggested to Michael Hahn, the newly chosen governor of Louisiana, that it might not be amiss to extend the franchise to "very intelligent" blacks (the president had just met a delegation of free blacks from Louisiana and apparently had been very impressed by them) as well as those blacks who had fought in the Union army or navy. Such voters would augment the unionist electorate: "They would probably help, in some trying time to come, to keep the jewel of liberty within the family of freedom." For the moment, however, with the presidential election only eight months away, it was best to keep such ideas private. He did encourage emancipation in Missouri and Maryland, believing that state-initiated abolition honored notions of federalism. But beyond this he did not go. Although he favored offering blacks opportunities for education and some sort of economic transition whereby "the two races could gradually live themselves out of their own relation to each other, and both come out better prepared for the new," he never elaborated on these inclinations. Understandably, the war remained Lincoln's first priority, fol-

lowed closely by the need to balance the interests and preferences of several constituencies as he looked toward the 1864 elections. "I hope to 'stand firm' enough to not go backward," he
told a Michigan Republican, "and yet not go forward fast enough
to wreck the country's cause."

CHAPTER SEVEN

The Campaigns of 1864

On March 8, 1864, a nondescript major general walked into Willard's Hotel in Washington, D.C., his son by his side. The hotel desk manager took one look at the stranger—although generals were not infrequent guests of the capital's most renowned hotel—and said that perhaps he could find a room up on the top floor for the officer and his boy. The officer accepted the offer and scribbled his name in the guest book. The clerk looked at the signature, sputtered, and hastily offered his guest a suite instead. Ulysses S. Grant had arrived in Washington.

The next day, Grant accepted a lieutenant general's commission—the first officer to hold that full rank since George Washington—and Lincoln named him general-in-chief of all the Union armies. He didn't look the part. Those observers hoping for the pomp and circumstance of another McClellan were disappointed; Grant "had no gait, no station, no manner," noted one New Englander, who somewhat redundantly concluded that the general was an "ordinary, scrubby looking man with a slightly seedy look." Grant even cut Lincoln short by turning down a

White House dinner invitation, explaining, "Really, Mr. President, I have had enough of this show business." But there was an air of earnest determination about the man. "He habitually wears an expression as if he had determined to drive his head through a brick wall," observed a staff officer in the Army of the Potomac, "and was about to do it." Things would be different from now on. As Lincoln put it to one of his private secretaries, "Stoddard, Grant's the first general I've had! He's a general!" Those Confederates who knew Grant from the old days at West Point agreed. "That man," commented James Longstreet, back with Lee's army, "will fight us every day and every hour until the end of this war."

Grant's Grand Design

Before Grant became general-in-chief, he had offered the Washington authorities some ideas on how he thought the campaigns of 1864 should be fought. In the West, he outlined a two-pronged offensive against Atlanta, to commence with the capture of Mobile, followed by thrusts from Chattanooga and Mobile against the Georgia railroad hub. In the East, he thought that enough men could be culled from the Army of the Potomac and other commands to launch an assault at the Confederate heartland from the coast of North Carolina, while the remainder of the Army of the Potomac kept Lee in check. The invading column, living off the land in a grand bushwhacking expedition, would rip up Richmond's rail connections to the Southern heartland, forcing Lee to abandon Virginia or be cut off from the rest of the Confederacy. The Union expedition would also recruit Southern unionists and escaped slaves to strengthen the Union army, while Confederates from the Carolinas would desert the main Rebel forces in order to return to and protect their homes. This proposal revealed Grant's preference for a war of maneuver and movement, as opposed to one of grinding attrition and bloodshed. However, the Washington authorities thought the plan too risky; besides, they told Grant when he came east to accept his commission, his first and foremost order of business

was to defeat Robert E. Lee. Grant, who had originally preferred to stay out west, came to agree that his presence was
needed in the East, in large part to shield the Army of the
Potomac from the political pressures sure to be placed upon it
in the upcoming campaign.

Adjusting to circumstances, Grant developed a new overall
plan, one based upon coordinated, simultaneous movements
against the main Confederate armies in Virginia and Georgia.
In Virginia, he called for a three-pronged attack against Lee's
Army of Northern Virginia and Richmond. A column would
move southward through the Shenandoah Valley, destroying it
as a source of supply to the Confederates while denying them
access to it as a protected avenue of invasion. The Army of the
James would move from Fort Monroe by water toward Richmond in a small-scale replica of McClellan's 1862 offensive, with
orders to threaten not only the Confederate capital but also its
rail connections with the Confederate heartland, most of which
ran through Petersburg, some twenty miles due south. These
moves would strike at Lee's rear and threaten his supply lines: if
they were successful Lee would have to retreat or try to turn the
tables by attacking the Army of the Potomac. While Grant chose
to retain George G. Meade as field commander of that army, the
general-in-chief personally would accompany it as it crossed the
Rapidan and Rappahannock rivers once more in an effort to
bring Lee to battle. In the West, Grant retained the major fea-
tures of his original plan, leaving his trusted lieutenant William
T. Sherman to take the offensive against Joseph E. Johnston's
Army of Tennessee, which shielded Atlanta from invaders. At
the same time he hoped to launch a second offensive from the
Gulf of Mexico aimed at the capture of Mobile and followed by
a drive northeast toward Atlanta and Johnston's rear.

Several political circumstances shaped Grant's planning.
President Lincoln was seeking reelection that year, and his
chances for victory would fluctuate according to the fortunes of
the Union cause on the battlefield. With that political reality in
mind, some military commands had to be reserved for generals
more renowned for their political influence than for their mili-

tary skill. Three such men were placed in charge of key supporting offensives—Nathaniel Banks in Louisiana, Franz Sigel in the
Shenandoah Valley, and Benjamin Butler with the Army of the
James. In the end, none of them proved able to accomplish the
tasks assigned them, and their failures had a major impact on
Grant's plans, posing him and Lincoln with a dilemma: to retain
in command such generals would serve to prolong the war and
add to the casualty list, damaging Lincoln's reelection prospects;
but to remove them would create new political enemies and
strengthen the opposition to Lincoln's renomination and election. Moreover, Banks would not be able to commence operations against Mobile until after he had occupied central
Louisiana and eastern Texas for the Union, for Lincoln wanted
to secure as much of Louisiana as possible as he initiated reconstruction in that state while reminding French forces in Mexico
of Northern military might—operations whose relationship to
the collapse of the Confederacy were more political than military. Banks also had to act as Lincoln's man on the scene in Louisiana, overseeing the process of reconstruction there under
Lincoln's Ten Percent Plan. Finally, the election year calendar
set a series of deadlines for Grant to meet. He had to achieve
military success in time to benefit Lincoln at the polls. Historians who assert that eventually Grant would wear down the Confederacy overlook these considerations of timeliness. The
question was not whether Grant would eventually win the war;
it was whether he could achieve enough success in time to secure Lincoln's reelection.

The Confederacy thus held several advantages in the campaigns to come. It would not have to achieve victory on the
battlefield in order to achieve victory in the war. What Confederate generals had to do was to erode Northern morale by creating a stalemate on the battlefield. If they could inflict heavy
losses on the invaders and manage to launch a few counteroffensives of their own, the resulting anxiety and war-weariness
among Northern voters would do the rest. Few Confederates
doubted that a Democratic triumph in the presidential election
would lead to a negotiated peace settlement and their nation's

independence. Lincoln's reelection, on the other hand, meant at least four more years of war, and it was at this point doubtful that white Southerners possessed the will to continue the fight that long in light of the destruction of their homes and the suffering of their families.

A second advantage the Confederates now had was the changing composition of the Union armies. Many of the veterans in the ranks of the blue armies had signed up for three years of service in the spring of 1861. Those terms of service were quickly coming to an end. Although many veterans, encouraged by pride, determination, or incentives including furloughs and money, decided to sign up again, nearly half decided that it was time for someone else to serve their country. These men, fighting with one eye on the calendar, would not be as effective in combat knowing that they were on the verge of escaping the war alive. Their replacements were bound to be both inexperienced and uninspired, draftees and substitutes as well as volunteers, and the quality of the average combat soldier in a blue uniform would decline, especially in the Army of the Potomac.

The Confederates also possessed one other advantage in Virginia. Robert E. Lee had been in command of the Army of Northern Virginia for almost two years, and he knew the skills and shortcomings of his subordinates, officers, and men. His military successes inspired his men and intimidated many a man in blue. Grant, newly arrived, was unfamiliar with the officers and men of the Army of the Potomac. It would take time for him to learn their strengths and weaknesses, their capabilities and limits, and his education would cost lives. Many veterans, remembering the accolades accorded the Union's past "saviors," looked at the new man with skeptical eyes. His record in the West, many agreed, had come at the expense of inferior opponents. Here and there one could hear the grumble, "He hasn't met Bobby Lee." But he would, and soon enough.

The Wilderness Campaign

On May 4, 1864, the Army of the Potomac (reinforced by a separate corps under the command of Ambrose Burnside) moved by the right flank of the Army of Northern Virginia, crossed the Rapidan River, and marched into the Wilderness, near the site of Stonewall Jackson's flank attack the year before. At the same time the other Union armies also went into motion, marking the opening of the campaigns of 1864. Grant hoped that by advancing he would force Lee either to meet his columns or retreat south to block the way to Richmond. On the morning of May 5, the Union commander had his answer, as Confederates collided with a Union brigade along the Orange Turnpike. The Battle of the Wilderness was soon under way. Over the next two days, as regiments made their way along the heavy undergrowth, the two armies took turns attacking and defending in a seesaw grapple in the woods. The battle grew so hot that the trees and underbrush caught fire, the flames consuming many of the wounded—their anguished cries disturbing many a surviving veteran. Both sides missed opportunities to break open the battle; at one point Lee had to rally his men to stop a Union breakthrough. Grant worked off his frustration and anxiety by whittling and smoking until he had frayed his dress gloves and emptied his pockets of cigars. But when one Union officer, panicked by news of a Confederate success in one area, began to offer the general his opinions on what Lee would do next, Grant abandoned the calm facade he had maintained. "Oh, I am heartily tired of hearing about what Lee is going to do," he exploded. "Some of you always seem to think he is suddenly going to turn a double somersault, and land in our rear and on both flanks at the same time. Go back to your command, and try to think what we are going to do ourselves, instead of what Lee is going to do."

On the morning of May 7, the noise from the battlefield slackened as both sides assessed what had happened. Of some 118,000 men present for duty (with an effective fighting force of just over 100,000), Grant had lost some 17,666 killed, wounded, and missing—a larger loss than that suffered by Hooker the previous year. Lee's army, some 64,000 strong, had also been hit hard, losing just under 12,000 casualties. Neither side had driven its adversary from the field. In such circumstances in the past, Union commanders had withdrawn back north across the Rapidan and Rappahannock. By midmorning Grant had issued orders to

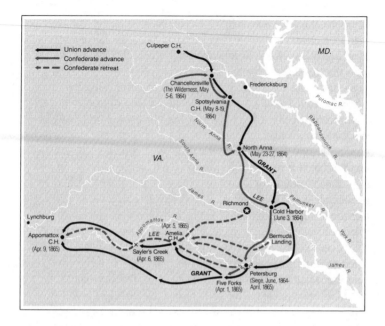

Grant vs. Lee

move; that night the Union soldiers pulled out of their entrenched positions and fell into the line of march. But when they reached the crossroads this time, they turned south, not north. The men realized that they were advancing. When they saw Grant riding along the road they cheered—until Grant, never one for show business, told them to hush lest the Confederates realize what was going on. The war in Virginia would never be the same. Back in Washington, a newspaper correspondent relayed to Lincoln a personal message from his general. "He told me I was to tell you, Mr. President, that there would be no turning back." It may have been the only time a president kissed a reporter.

Lee, unsure at first whether Grant was advancing or retreating, moved his army to Spotsylvania Court House, in a position to block the Federal line of advance. Over the next several days both sides entrenched as Grant probed for weak spots in Lee's line. An attack on May 10 achieved a momentary breakthrough at the Confederate center. Grant ordered a second, more massive assault on May 12. His columns crashed through the Confederate trenches, capturing thousands of prisoners. Once more Lee personally rallied his men; for the remainder of the day the two sides slugged it out at a portion of the line thereafter known as the Bloody Angle, the bullets flying so thick that they cut down an oak tree with a trunk some twenty-three inches in diameter. Grant seemed determined to fulfill his promise "to fight it out on this line if it takes all summer."

As Grant and Lee battled it out at Spotsylvania, news came of a significant Confederate setback north of Richmond. When Grant came east he placed Philip H. Sheridan in command of the cavalry of the Army of the Potomac. Hot-tempered and impatient, the diminutive but jaunty Sheridan argued with Meade over consolidating cavalry units into a single command. When confusion between horsemen and foot soldiers hindered the advance to Spotsylvania, allowing Lee's men to seize that crucial crossroads, Grant resolved the ensuing argument by dispatching Sheridan on a raid towards Richmond to disrupt enemy communications and supplies. Lee sent Jeb Stuart and company to intercept the Yankee cavalry: on May 11 the two forces met at Yellow Tavern, some ten miles north of Richmond. The Union troopers drove the Rebels from the field; Stuart, mortally wounded, died the next day. Although Sheridan achieved little else of lasting value on the raid, Stuart's death deprived Lee of a valuable commander at a time when he could not spare one. Longstreet had been wounded at the Wilderness, Lee's other corps commanders were too ill to exercise command, and Lee himself was not in the best of health. At long last he was paying the price for the risks he had taken in seizing the offensive so many times. He no longer had either the men or the commanders to make up for the losses he had sustained. At Spotsylvania the Confederates suffered another 12,000 casualties, while 18,400 Union soldiers were killed, wounded, or captured. "This army cannot stand a siege," Lee observed. "We must end this business on the battlefield, not in a fortified position."

At Spotsylvania Grant learned of the failure of his other two offensives. Franz Sigel's advance through the Shenandoah Valley had been turned back on May 15 at New Market. Lee would continue to collect supplies and reinforcements from the valley, and Richmond's rail links remained undisturbed. Sigel's removal was perhaps the only bright spot for Grant. The news was no better from the James River. Although Butler successfully landed his forces south of Richmond on May 5, he failed to exploit his initial success by advancing on Richmond, Petersburg, or the railroads linking those two cities. Indeed, Butler and his subordinates seemed more intent on fighting each other than the Rebels before Richmond. By mid-May the Confederates had contained the Army of the James, in Grant's words, "as if it had been in a bottle strongly corked," freeing more reinforcements for Lee. Only Butler's political clout prevented his sharing Sigel's fate.

These setbacks seriously hampered Grant's plan. Lee no longer had to worry about his supply lines, and, far from having to detach elements of the Army of Northern Virginia to meet Butler and Sigel, he actually received reinforcements in the aftermath of the twin Union failures. Grant's pledge "to fight it out on this line if it takes all summer" no longer made sense; he would now have to rely on his own forces alone to pin Lee against Richmond and sever the Confederate capital's links to the south. On May 20 his army moved toward Hanover Junction; Lee, responding with alacrity, countered by establishing a new defensive line across the North Anna River just north of Hanover. For a moment part of the Union army seemed vulnerable to attack by Lee, but the old warrior was incapacitated by illness, depriving him of an opportunity to strike a blow. Grant shifted left and south once more, eventually reaching Cold Harbor, some ten miles east of Richmond, on the site of the opening clashes of the Seven Days Battles nearly two years ago. Here he ordered an all-out assault on the Confederates, but delays and fatigue forced him to delay his plans for twenty-four hours, giving Lee more than enough time to prepare a rather elaborate set of defensive fortifications. When the assault was launched at dawn on June 3, it was obliterated. In less than an hour some 5,500 Union soldiers fell as Lee's men blazed away from their well-built fortifications.

At first glance Cold Harbor was an unmitigated disaster. Yet this bloody exercise in futility, which Grant later admitted was a mistake, failed to shake the Union commander from his goal. It did, however, convince him that Lee's men, if dulled as an offensive force, could still ably defend a position. Grant would not settle for the stalemate of defensive warfare, and he saw little advantage in shifting around Lee's left to the north of Richmond. Only one move was left, although it was a daring one—to cross the James River and strike at Petersburg to Richmond's south. If Lee detected the movement, he could attack a portion of Grant's army while it was strung out on the line of march, with the promise of a brilliant success. But if the movement succeeded, Petersburg might well fall, rendering precarious the Rebels' hold on Richmond. At the least Grant's shift southward would threaten Confederate supply lines and make it difficult for Lee to detach troops to reinforce Joe Johnston.

Grant commenced moving southward on June 12. Lee remained uncertain as to his foe's intention, and for several days it looked as if the Yankees had finally stolen a march on Bobby Lee. Several Union infantry corps crossed the James and advanced on Petersburg, defended by a thin line of Confederates under P. G. T. Beauregard. But battle fatigue, hesitation, a lack of coordination among Union commanders, and just plain bad luck foiled Grant's plan, as Lee belatedly moved enough reinforcements to Petersburg to save the city. It looked as if Grant was going to have to settle for a siege after all.

Grant's drive toward Richmond and then to Petersburg in the spring of 1864 remains one of the war's most misunderstood campaigns. Initially planned as a campaign of maneuver against Lee's flanks and rear, the nature of the campaign changed after Lee chose to engage the Army of the Potomac and the supporting columns under Butler and Sigel failed to achieve their objectives. The failure of these drives did not allow Grant to take advantage of the weakened state of Lee's army after ten days of nearly continuous battle. Thus, the Wilderness and Spotsylvania became less valuable to the Union than they might have been, although in both cases Grant retained the initiative—an accomplishment no other Union general had achieved against Lee. Moreover, Grant transformed the relationship of battles and campaigns. Most generals viewed campaigns as preludes to the climactic event of battle, and they maneuvered to bring their foe to the battlefield. Grant's Wilderness campaign, like the Vicksburg campaign of the preceding year (and, to a lesser extent, Jackson's Valley campaign of 1862), used battles as elements of a larger, ongoing plan of campaign. What other generals would have regarded as a decisive defeat—Cold Harbor—Grant treated as a momentary setback, just as he adjusted to the collapse of Butler's and Sigel's advances. Always able to improvise in response to the changing circumstances of combat, the Union general-in-chief simply adopted new means to achieve the same end of negating Lee.

Although the Wilderness campaign succeeded in pinning down Lee and most of the Army of Northern Virginia, eroding much of that army's offensive potential, it had fallen short of the triumph Grant had hoped to achieve. While Lee had neither regained the initiative nor defeated Grant, his conduct of defensive operations was brilliant, almost flawless. High casualty rates and the stalemate of siege disheartened Northerners, who had anticipated great and immediate results from their new commander. As morale plunged, so did the prospects for Lincoln's reelection. Lee was correct in concluding that once Grant laid siege to Petersburg the fall of Richmond was "only a matter of time," but time was one commodity in short supply for Grant and his president in the summer of 1864.

At the same time Grant sought to break the stalemate outside of Richmond by moving on Petersburg, Lee decided to make a bold move of his own to threaten Washington. Lincoln, always concerned about the safety of the capital, might well order Grant to abandon his offensive; failing that, Lee reasoned, even a quasi-successful advance would serve to embarrass the Lincoln administration. In a reprise of Jackson's 1862 Valley Campaign, Jubal

Early led a force of 14,000 Confederates from Richmond with orders to oust Union forces under David Hunter (Sigel's successor) in the Shenandoah Valley. Deciding not to engage Early at Lynchburg, Hunter unwisely decided to withdraw towards West Virginia, leaving the route northward to Washington clear for the Confederates. Early seized the opportunity to launch a strike into Maryland, and, after scattering a makeshift Federal force at Monocacy on July 9, the Confederates descended on Washington itself. The Union capital was lightly defended, for Grant had drawn upon the garrison forces for reinforcements.

Slow to realize the extent of the threat to Washington, Grant finally dispatched an infantry corps north, with the Union soldiers debarking from steamboats on July 11 and marching through the streets of Washington to the city's outer defenses just in time to meet Early's advance elements. President Lincoln personally observed the resulting clash from the parapet of a fort, his tall lanky profile offering such a tempting target that Union officers ordered him to take cover. Repulsed, Early tested the Washington defenses once more on July 12, and, finding them manned by battle-hardened veterans, withdrew altogether. Union efforts to pursue the retreating Confederates collapsed in confusion as Federal generals failed to cooperate. Finally Grant placed Sheridan in charge of Union forces in the area, with orders to "put himself south of the enemy and follow him to the death." Moreover, Sheridan was to clean out the Shenandoah Valley, leaving it so barren that not even a crow would be able to feed off what was left. Lee's plan to divert Grant's attention from Richmond by employing the Shenandoah Valley diversion succeeded only in persuading the Union commander to eliminate the valley as a Rebel source of food and campaign corridor once and for all.

As Early withdrew from the outskirts of Washington, Grant seized upon an idea to crack the siege at Petersburg. The soldiers of the Forty-eighth Pennsylvania Infantry—coal miners by profession—suggested that perhaps the best way to break through the Confederate lines was by blowing a hole in them— literally—through digging a mine under Confederate entrenchments, filling it with explosives, and detonating it. Grant, who had supported similar projects at Vicksburg, was intrigued, and he allowed Ambrose Burnside, commander of the Ninth Corps, to supervise the mining operation and prepare the assault that was to follow it. Throughout July, the miners dug away; Burnside, thinking that fresh troops were required to mount a spirited attack, decided that his division of black soldiers, which up to this point had guarded supply trains, would take the lead, and for weeks these men enthusiastically rehearsed their attack plan. But George G. Meade, skeptical of both Burnside's ability and the wisdom of using black troops in such an assault, failed to give the operation his full support, convincing Grant that if the black soldiers were slaughtered, Union commanders would be accused of sacrificing them as cannon fodder. Foiled in his original plan, Burnside decided to let his three white commanders draw straws for the assignment. The worst commander, James H. Ledlie, with a reputation for incompetence and intoxication, pulled out the short straw.

All seemed ready before dawn on July 30, the date set for the operation. Grant had laid the foundation by moving against Lee's position north of the James, thereby drawing Rebel reserves away on the eve of the attack. At 4:30 AM the mine exploded, throwing up men, horses, and cannon as it created a huge crater in the Confederate line. But Burnside's men, lacking preassault preparation, bungled the offensive, deciding to enter the crater rather than move around it to roll up the Confederate flanks and break the enemy's rear line. Reinforcements poured into the crater, including the black division, only to become hopelessly confused and disorganized. Before long the surviving Confederates rallied, counterattacked, and drove back the attackers. "It was the saddest affair I have witnessed in the war," Grant later reported. "Such opportunity for carrying fortifications I have never seen and do not expect again to have."

The opposing armies settled down to a long siege. Grant's armies probed for weak points in Lee's lines, as the Union commander stretched his own lines south of Petersburg westward in a continuing effort to sever the city's rail links to the rest of the

South. Though several offensives tested the Confederate left and right, the small gains that were achieved did not constitute a major victory. But Grant had nullified Lee's attempt to shape the outcome of the 1864 election by denying him the opportunity to make another daring offensive thrust. For his part, Lee had deprived Grant of making Richmond, Petersburg, and central Virginia the theater of decision. Both generals would have to look elsewhere for the battles that would decide the fate of both the Lincoln administration and the Confederacy.

The Atlanta Campaign

Grant's grapple with Lee was not the only major Union offensive undertaken in the spring of 1864. The Union general-in-chief had directed William T. Sherman to advance against Joseph E. Johnston's Army of Tennessee and, hopefully, the railroad center of Atlanta. Sherman's force of 98,000 was distributed among three field armies: George H. Thomas's Army of the Cumberland (60,000); the Army of the Tennessee (25,000), led by James B. McPherson; and some 13,000 in the Army of the Ohio, commanded by John M. Schofield. Against this force Johnston had some 50,000 men, with 15,000 more soon to join him, deployed in northern Georgia.

Sherman preferred maneuver to battle, while Johnston preferred retreat to engagement. Thus perfectly matched, the two generals engaged in a campaign of move and countermove, with Sherman using his superior numbers to outflank Johnston's carefully prepared defenses. McPherson's forces usually swung out to bypass Johnston, while the reliable Thomas confronted the enemy directly across fortifications. Slowly but surely Sherman, flanking left and right, forced Johnston to retreat, but the Confederate always found another line to defend, forcing Sherman to try again. By late June, Johnston had deployed his men across Kennesaw Mountain, twenty miles northwest of Atlanta. Increasingly worried about the vulnerability of his lengthening supply line to attack, and concerned that his men were losing their combat readiness, Sherman ordered a frontal assault on June 27. It was Cold Harbor all over again, on a smaller scale, as Sherman lost 3,000 casualties to Johnston's 600. Then it was back to marching and flanking, as Federal columns crossed the Chattahoochee River before a surprised Johnston could react. The Confederates fell back once more behind Peachtree Creek, with Atlanta only five miles away.

Although Johnston had done a good job of preserving his strength and exchanging ground for time, his past record now caught up with him. In 1862 he had conducted a similar withdrawal against McClellan, giving rise to fears that he might retreat right through Richmond. In 1863 he had called for the evacuation of Vicksburg. Jefferson Davis, who distrusted Johnston and was fed up with yet another exhibition of masterly withdrawals, considered replacing him with John Bell Hood, a veteran of the Army of Northern Virginia with a reputation as a fighter. Lee expressed reservations about Hood's fitness for high command, suggesting that it might be better if Johnston abandoned Atlanta, retreated into the interior of Georgia, and then used his cavalry to strike at Sherman's elongated and vulnerable lines of communication and supply along the railroad from Chattanooga to Atlanta. Davis ignored this advice. He favored holding Atlanta and vigorously contesting Sherman's advance. On July 18, Hood replaced Johnston in command of the Army of Tennessee.

Hood wasted little time in preparing to take the offensive. On July 20, as Sherman swung Schofield and McPherson to the east to seize the Decatur Railroad—the closest rail connection between the armies of Hood and Lee—Hood assaulted Thomas's army, only to be driven back with heavy losses. Two days later, Hood turned on McPherson, but after initial successes and the death of McPherson, the Confederates were driven back by a counterattack, which moved Sherman ever closer to Atlanta. Finally, on July 28, Hood's men collided with the Army of the Tennessee once more at Ezra Church, west of Atlanta; once again the Union defenders beat back the Confederate attack with heavy losses. In just over a week Hood had lost over 13,000 men to Sherman's 6,000, and he found his position somewhat eroded.

But he had held on to Atlanta, and he had secured his supply line to the south. Sherman was forced to commence siege operations.

As military exercises, the campaigns of Grant and Sherman were clear-cut successes. In each case the opposing army had been driven back to the defense of a critical city, and in time the besieging forces would most probably attain their goal. By pinning down the major Rebel armies, Grant and Sherman foreclosed any opportunity for the Confederates to shift reinforcements from one to the other. Grant had taken the initiative away from Lee; he had also made his mark on his own men, helping them overcome their fear of their famous opponent. The end result already seemed inevitable to Edward Porter Alexander, a Confederate artillery commander: "However bold we might be, however desperately we might fight, we were sure in the end to be worn out. It was only a question of a few months, more or less."

But this was not enough. War-weary Northerners saw their side's mounting casualties as evidence of futility and judged the sieges as signs of stalemate. Impatient for victory and tired of seemingly endless fighting, the Northern electorate might well turn against Lincoln. By fighting tenaciously to defend Richmond and Atlanta, the Confederates had added much to the symbolic value of these cities. While it remained true that only by eliminating Confederate armies could the Union secure a final victory, civilians (and thus voters) in the North became transfixed by these twin sieges, and they were prepared to mark the fall of either city as a great victory. But whether either would fall in time to help Lincoln's reelection prospects remained an open question. "We must win if not defeated at home," Grant told Sherman; to another friend he remarked, "We will peg away, however, and end this matter, if our people at home will be but true to themselves."

Lincoln's Bid for Reelection

As 1864 opened, Abraham Lincoln set his eyes upon obtaining reelection. The president, despite his nonchalant manner and his ability to dismiss criticism with a shrug and a story, wanted a chance to complete the job of saving the Union. Not all Republicans shared Lincoln's desire. For several months rumors had circulated that perhaps Grant would be a far more suitable candidate, despite his response that becoming president would be "highly unfortunate for myself, if not for the country." And Lincoln had secured assurances of Grant's lack of interest in the job before appointing him general-in-chief. But others hungered to replace Lincoln, most notably his secretary of the treasury, Salmon P. Chase, who was far less modest than Grant about his qualifications for high office. Some Radical Republicans, believing that Lincoln was too lenient toward white Southerners and not fully committed to emancipation, supported a Chase candidacy.

However, the Chase movement collapsed before it got underway. His supporters prematurely began circulating calls for his candidacy in early 1864. But the treasury secretary, intent on building a movement through his use of the patronage power of his office, soon discovered that the president already had done the same thing in other departments. Republicans, speaking through state party conventions or legislatures, endorsed Lincoln's reelection bid. Even Ohio, Chase's home state, fell in line behind the administration. Lincoln refused to accept Chase's resignation for the moment; in July, after he had won the party's renomination, he accepted the secretary's resignation in a dispute over patronage matters.

Even more abortive was the splinter candidacy of John C. Frémont, who was nominated at the end of May by disgruntled Radicals who still refused to accept Lincoln as the Republican standard bearer. Some Democrats seized upon this movement as a way to weaken support for the president, but the clear signs of Democratic influence in the naming of Frémont's running mate and in the adoption of a platform defending civil liberties from executive encroachment discredited the movement in the minds of nearly all Republicans.

By the time the Republican convention met in June at Baltimore, Lincoln had secured renomination. Only the determination of the Missouri delegation to vote for Grant spoiled a unanimous vote on the first ballot. At the same time, Republicans endeavored to broaden their appeal to the Northern electorate. They restyled the party, calling it the National Union Party, and nominated as Lincoln's running mate Andrew Johnson of Tennessee, a former Democrat who was currently the military governor of his home state. The nomination was also an implicit endorsement of Lincoln's reconstruction policy.

Obviously, not all Republicans were delighted with Lincoln's renomination. Radicals grumbled that the president was not as committed as they to the eradication of slavery, the protection of the freedmen, and the need for a firm policy toward the postwar South. To secure these goals, congressional Republicans framed their own plan of reconstruction. Called the Wade-Davis Bill after its cosponsors, Senator Benjamin F. Wade of Ohio and Congressman Henry Winter Davis of Maryland, it provided that only after the cessation of all resistance to U.S. authority could a state commence the process of reconstruction. A majority of a state's eligible electorate (as opposed to Lincoln's ten percent) had to support the move to reestablish civil government by taking an oath of allegiance; in turn, only those southern whites who could swear that they had always been loyal to the Union—the so-called ironclad oath—could vote for delegates to a reconstructed state constitutional convention, and only those southern whites who could and did take the oath could win election as delegates. It was then incumbent upon said conventions to declare slavery illegal, pass legislation providing for the protection of blacks' civil rights, nullify the ordinance of secession, and repudiate the Confederate war debt as part of their state's new constitution. Then, and only then, would Congress consider seating the state's new and duly elected senators and representatives.

In framing the Wade-Davis Bill, Republicans had reacted to events in Louisiana, where unionists were acting in compliance with Lincoln's Ten Percent Plan. The president, worried that efforts to secure emancipation would fail if he did not win reelection, wanted Louisianans to adopt a free-state constitution as soon as possible, thus accepting emancipation through state (and not federal) action. In his eagerness, he overlooked procedural irregularities and excused Banks's decision to establish a state contract labor system for its freedmen. While Lincoln privately urged Louisiana unionists to consider some form of black suffrage, perhaps limited to veterans and "the very intelligent," no such clause appeared in reconstructed Louisiana's final constitution. Congressional Republicans worried that conservative Louisiana unionists would do all they could to minimize change; they also dwelled on the small base of support for the new government, arguing that it provided an inadequate foundation for the freedom of the state's black citizens. "Majorities must rule," Wade declared, "and until majorities can be found loyal and trustworthy for state government they must be governed by a stronger hand."

Yet the Wade-Davis Bill was as significant for what it omitted as for what it included. It did not mandate black suffrage, a concession to political pragmatism, for otherwise the bill would have failed to pass Congress. Nor did it provide for either land or education for the freedpeople, much to the disappointment of many abolitionists and Radicals. "The negro has earned land, education, rights," Wendell Phillips had declared several months before. "Before we leave him, we ought to leave him on his own soil, in his own house, with the ballot and the school-house within reach. Unless we have done it, the North has let the cunning of politics filch the fruits of war." However admirable this program of social revolution might sound, it was beyond the boundaries of what was either politically possible or acceptable in 1864, with Democrats charging that it was a black man's war and a white man's fight and Republicans divided over exactly what emancipation and reconstruction meant.

Congress passed the Wade-Davis Bill on July 2. Lincoln decided not to sign it, arguing that Congress could not demand emancipation by legislative enactment outside of the grounds of military necessity—the very justification he had used on behalf of his Emancipation Proclamation. The veto infuriated Radicals. So had his decision to accept Chase's resignation as treasury secretary only days before. On August 5, the New York *Tribune* published a scathing attack on the president, written at white heat by Wade and Davis. They reminded him that "if he wishes our support, he must confine himself to his executive duties—to obey and to execute, not to make the laws—to suppress by arms armed rebellion, and leave political reorganization to Congress." This ill-tempered outburst went too far to suit most Republicans, but it did suggest that not all was well within party ranks.

For months to come some Radicals continued to contemplate alternatives to Lincoln. The slow progress of affairs at the front proved their biggest help. So did increasing complaints about the refusal of Stanton and Grant to prevent the suffering of Union prisoners of war in Confederate prison camps by exchanging them for Confederate prisoners—a decision reached at the beginning of the year in response to problems in regulating paroles and the refusal of Confederate authorities to exchange any black prisoners. Grant held fast to his position, citing these concerns. Of increasing importance to the Union commander, however, was the need to drain the Confederacy of all available manpower. "It is hard on our men held in Southern prisons not to exchange them," he admitted, "but it is humanity to those left in the ranks to fight our battles." Confederates would return to their armies; Union soldiers, their enlistments up or too ill to serve, would go home. "We have got to fight until the military power of the South is exhausted, and if we release or exchange prisoners captured it simply becomes a war of extermination." So captured Yankees continued to waste away at Andersonville, the most notorious of the Confederate prison camps, and prisoners on both sides continued to suffer at camps elsewhere. It had become a very hard war indeed.

A naval victory brightened Lincoln's prospects slightly in August, when at long last Grant's delayed offensive against Mobile commenced. The first step had been to knock out several forts at the mouth of Mobile Bay, a task complicated by the presence of mines and several Confederate gunboats, including the ironclad *C.S.S. Tennessee*. On August 5, Admiral David G. Farragut, aboard his flagship *U.S.S. Hartford*, led a fleet of fourteen wooden ships and four ironclads into battle. When the leading Union ironclad struck a mine and sank almost instantaneously, the attack force wavered as the Confederate cannon on shore and ships blasted away. "Damn the torpedoes! Full speed ahead!" Farragut reportedly declared, as he rallied his fleet and led it past the forts into Mobile Bay, in which it defeated the Confederate naval force and accepted the surrender of the *Tennessee*.

If the victory at Mobile Bay offered a glimmer of optimism to Republican partisans, the stalemates outside Richmond/Petersburg and Atlanta still daunted the administration. Many Northerners were growing more than tired of the conflict, as the mercurial newspaper editor Horace Greeley told Lincoln, "our bleeding, bankrupt, almost dying country . . . shudders at the prospect of fresh conscriptions, of further wholesale devastations, and of new rivers of human blood." Several covert attempts to test the waters for a negotiated peace, however, revealed only that no common ground existed for such negotiations to proceed. In late August, Lincoln, concerned with charges that abolition was the only sticking point preventing negotiations aimed at reunion, even toyed with the notion of abandoning it as a precondition for peace. Ultimately he rejected this idea on the political grounds that it would anger antislavery Republicans who would question anew the president's commitment to emancipation, and on the grounds of a principle, for he characterized the Emancipation Proclamation as a "solemn promise" that he would and could not retract. Still, he remained skeptical of his chances for reelection. He urged Frederick Douglass to do what he could to assist the escape of as many slaves as possible in the months before the election, in order to secure their freedom no matter what the result; then he had his cabinet sign a sealed envelope containing a memorandum pledging cooperation with the president-elect "as to save the Union between the election and the inauguration, as he will have secured his election on such ground that he cannot possibly save it afterwards."

Nearly a week later the Democrats convened in Chicago to nominate their candidate. Peace Democrats held fast to their preference for an armistice followed by negotiations; realizing that they alone could not nominate a candidate, however, they swung a deal with the War Democrats whereby the former would get to compose the platform (and name George Pendleton of Ohio as the vice presidential candidate) in exchange for the War Democrats agreeing to select George B. McClellan to head the fall ticket. McClellan's opposition to emancipation was as strong as ever, but he still supported a war for reunion and insisted that reunion be a precondition for peace. Therefore he struggled to prepare a letter of acceptance that might bridge the gap between his beliefs and the platform he was bound to extol, finally composing a statement that in effect repudiated the Peace Democrats' insistence on an unconditional and immediate armistice. Still, Democrats moved into the election contest confident of victory.

Victory on the Battlefield and at the Ballot Box

Events on the battlefield cut short the Democrats' euphoria, for even as delegates gathered in Chicago to declare the war a failure, Grant's grand strategy began to reap dividends. Sherman took the first step. On August 25, his army moved in a great counterclockwise arc south of Atlanta and headed for Jonesboro, Georgia, intent on severing Hood's supply line. At first the Confederate commander thought that Sherman was withdrawing altogether, and he notified Richmond that he had triumphed at last. But celebration ceased when news came that Sherman's men were in fact busily ripping up and twisting rails. Hood attempted to drive the Yankees away, only to end up retreating in the face of a counterattack. Realizing that if he did not give up Atlanta he might face encirclement, he and his force pulled out of the city after dark on September 1, setting fire to anything of military value as they left. "So Atlanta is ours, and fairly won," Sherman telegraphed Washington as his soldiers entered the city on September 2.

The fall of Atlanta proved to be the turning point in the 1864 presidential contest. Coming on the heels of the Democratic convention, it made a mockery of Democratic claims that the war was a failure. Parades and hundred-gun salutes heralded the news throughout the North. At last Grant's overall strategic conception had realized a political as well as military payoff. As one Southern newspaper noted in despair, "All of us perceive the intimate connection existing between the armies of the Confederacy and the peace men in the United States. . . . Our success in battle assures the success of McClellan. Our failure will inevitably lead to his defeat." The reaction to Atlanta's fall in the North suggested that the public still measured victory in terms of cities taken as well as in armies destroyed. The spirit of "On to Richmond!" never quite died. Indeed, Sherman's triumph resembled McClellan's way of making war by taking cities, yet it was the capture of Atlanta that would doom McClellan's bid for the presidency. Ironically, Sherman, the man who despised politics and politicians, played a major role in the outcome of the 1864 presidential contest.

Indeed, the capture of Atlanta was far more important for its political than its military significance. Hood's army, though on the move, still remained intact, capable of inflicting significant damage. During September and October it threatened to sever Sherman's rail link to Chattanooga. Sherman shielded his supply lines, but he was unable to bring the Confederates to bay. It slowly became clear that holding Atlanta might well prove an albatross around Sherman's neck, so he began to contemplate a campaign that would leave him free to move at will into the interior of the Confederate heartland.

As Hood thrust and Sherman parried, attention shifted to the Shenandoah Valley, where Sheridan had spent over a month in organizing his men to carry out Grant's instructions to defeat Early and devastate the valley. Lincoln began to squirm at Sheridan's inaction; finally Grant travelled to the cavalryman's headquarters to prod him, only to find Sheridan putting the finishing touches on a plan to defeat Early at Winchester, Virginia. On September 19, after a slow start, he did just that; by late afternoon the Confederates had fled southward. The Yankees followed, and three days later Sheridan struck again at Fisher's Hill. Early's men hastily retreated through the valley, apparently eliminated as a fighting force. Once more cannonades and cheers echoed throughout the North. Sheridan's columns then moved southward and torched the valley, carrying out his promise to ensure that when he was done it would "have little in it for man or beast." While Early's broken force stayed out of range, Sheridan's troopers engaged in a rather ruthless war to the throat against Confederate guerrillas and partisan rangers under John S. Mosby, deterring Sheridan from complying with Grant's original instructions to complete his campaign by coming up on Petersburg from the west—a maneuver which would have brought a quick if perhaps bloody end to the siege of that city.

Sheridan, convinced that Early no longer posed a serious threat, returned northward in mid-October, encamping his army at Cedar Creek while he travelled to Washington. But the redoubtable Rebel commander was not yet licked; he had simply bided his time, lulling Sheridan and his men into a false sense of security as a prelude to combat of his own making. On the morning of October 19, Early struck the Union position at Cedar Creek. The unprepared Federals broke, although some rallied to contest the Rebel advance, and began retreating north toward Winchester. Looking up the Valley Turnpike, the disheartened men saw a cloud of dust and a horseman galloping southward. It was Sheridan. Returning to Winchester from Washington on the night of October 18, the general was on his way back to join his army when he heard the faint echoes of battle. Sheridan rallied the retreaters, cajoled them into rejoining their comrades, and by midafternoon launched a counterattack. This time it was the Confederates' turn to be surprised; the Rebels had been so sure that their work was done for the day that they had broken ranks to search for food and booty in the captured Yankee camps. They reeled in the face of the assaulting bluecoat lines, and by nightfall Sheridan's men had recaptured their camps and dealt Early's force a defeat from which it would never recover.

News of the dramatic victory electrified the Northern electorate, putting to rest whatever hopes remained for a Democratic victory. Grant's strategic plan, punctuated by the triumphs at Atlanta, Winchester, and now Cedar Creek, had convinced a majority of voters that the war effort was finally moving in the right direction, towards ultimate victory. The October elections in Ohio, Indiana, and Pennsylvania confirmed their confidence. Nonetheless, all along Lincoln had been taking steps to increase his margin of victory. He wooed disgruntled Radicals by accepting the resignation of the conservative Montgomery Blair as postmaster general, then dropped hints that he would nominate Chase to fill the position of Chief Justice after the post fell vacant upon the death of Roger B. Taney. This put an end to Radical efforts to replace Lincoln or to run an independent candidate, as Frémont withdrew from the race.

Union soldiers would have their say about the next president at the ballot box as well as on the battlefield. Americans had held presidential elections in wartime (1812), but never before had such a large portion of the population been in uniform. Nineteen states provided for voting in the field, although Democrats had managed to block such proposals in the key states of Indiana and Illinois. However, for the soldiers to vote against Lincoln would be to admit that their own endeavors had failed and that their sacrifices had been in vain.

On November 8, voters decided to try Long Abe a little longer. The president won reelection, securing 55 percent of the popular vote and 212 electoral votes. McClellan carried only Delaware, Kentucky, and New Jersey, giving him a mere 21 electoral votes. Most reassuring to the president was the soldier vote; Union soldiers voting in the field overwhelmingly endorsed the president's reelection bid, giving him 78 percent of their votes. McClellan did not even secure 30 percent of the vote in his old command, the Army of the Potomac. Other soldiers returned home on furlough to cast their ballots, and Grant and other Union commanders released troops to vote in several critical contests. Lincoln celebrated the process as well as the results: "We can not have free government without elections; and if the rebellion could force us to forego, or postpone a national election, it might fairly claim to have already conquered and ruined us." Instead, events had "demonstrated that a people's government can sustain a national election, in the midst of a great civil war."

Yet the election results deserve closer scrutiny. In light of Union battlefield triumphs, that the Democratic candidate, running on a platform that overtly declared the war a failure, could still garner 45 percent of the popular vote should give one pause—especially when one considers that the Confederate states had not participated in the election. One might think that military victory necessarily would rebound to the credit of the Republican party, but the reintegration of the ex-Confederate states into the Union would augment the Democratic electorate unless the Republicans either barred former Rebels from the polls or enfranchised all of the freed blacks. Either policy would carry with it political liabilities in the North. Lincoln's landslide committed the North to carry on the war to a victorious conclusion, but it was far from clear what the political fortunes of peace would be.

CHAPTER EIGHT

Victory and Defeat

With the reelection of Abraham Lincoln as President of the United States on November 8, 1864, America's Civil War entered its final stage. Gone were whatever hopes the Confederacy had of ousting the Lincoln administration by fostering war-weariness in the Northern electorate. But the war was not yet over, and the Union high command knew it. No sooner had Atlanta fallen in September than Ulysses S. Grant wanted more. "We want to keep the enemy constantly pressed to the end of the war," he told William T. Sherman. "If we give him no peace whilst the war lasts, the end cannot be distant." If the Confederacy was doomed, its leaders showed no sign that they recognized it. "Our cause is not lost," Jefferson Davis, on a visit to John Bell Hood's Army of Tennessee, declared in late September. "Sherman cannot keep up his long line of communication; and retreat sooner or later he must. And when that day comes, the fate that befell the army of the French Empire in its retreat from Moscow will be reenacted." A month later, the Confederate chief executive asserted, "There are no vital points on which the preservation of the Confederacy depends. There is no military success of the enemy which can accomplish its destruction." As long as Confederates believed their president, the war would continue. To crush the Confederacy, Union armies would have to destroy both its ability and will to keep the fight alive.

Lincoln and Grant were well aware that it was just as important how the war was won as that victory was achieved. The end of formal hostilities in itself would not mark the end of the process of reunion, nor would it necessarily denote an acceptance of the changes wrought by the war. Bands of guerrillas might prolong the struggle and transform it into an even more embittering process, further complicating the prospects for peace. Even as they exerted themselves to the utmost to destroy the Confederacy's ability to resist, Lincoln and Grant looked for ways to erode the enemy's will to keep on fighting and to secure their foe's acquiescence in defeat.

Sherman's March to the Sea

Although Sherman's occupation of Atlanta had led to massive celebrations throughout the North and provided a major boost to Lincoln's bid for reelection, the Army of Tennessee remained a threat to his army. During October, Hood struck at the railroad between Chattanooga and Atlanta in an effort to sever the Yankee army's lifeline. Although Sherman fended off these blows, he was unable to bring the Confederates to decisive battle. Realizing the futility of such operations, the Union commander began formulating an alternative approach. The Georgia piedmont was rich with grain and livestock. Why not cut loose from Atlanta altogether and strike into the state's interior? Why not take the war directly to the Southern people? It was time that they learned what war was all about. "War is cruelty and you cannot refine it," Sherman believed. Now he intended to show Southern whites exactly what he meant. To march an army through the Confederate heartland, he told Grant, would demonstrate the irresistible power of Union military might to all observers: "This may not be war, but rather statesmanship."

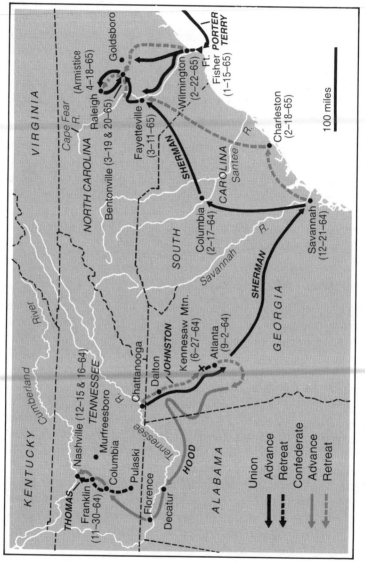

Campaigns in the West, 1864–65

Initially Grant preferred that Sherman first eliminate Hood's army; when Sherman countered that he would leave enough men behind under the command of George H. Thomas to keep an eye on Hood's Confederates, the general-in-chief acceded to his lieutenant's plan. Sherman celebrated the good news: "I can make the march, and make Georgia howl!"

In mid-November, Sherman's men carried out his order to destroy everything of military value left in Atlanta. Then, as smoke filled the air, he led his column, 60,000 strong, out of the city and into the heartland of Georgia. The aim of the march was simple: the sight of a Union army, marching virtually unopposed through the South, would shatter Confederate morale. The mere idea of Yankee soldiers living off the land, threatening by their very presence the safety of Southern civilians, including women whose fathers, husbands, lovers, and sons were away at the front, terrified Southern whites. As one of Sherman's staff officers noted, "If that terror and grief and even want shall help to paralyze their husbands and fathers who are fighting us," the Confederacy would collapse. Sherman declared that his target was enemy morale: "I propose to demonstrate the vulnerability of the South and make its inhabitants feel that war and individual ruin are synonymous terms."

As Sherman's men headed south, Hood turned his army north. Unable to cut his opponent's supply lines, the Confederate commander decided instead to advance into Tennessee, although his ultimate objective remained unclear. He missed an opportunity to inflict a serious blow on two Union corps that were withdrawing northward through central Tennessee at Spring Hill, thus allowing John M. Schofield to set up a defensive perimeter on the outskirts of Franklin, some twenty miles south of Nashville. Angry at his failure to trap Schofield, Hood on November 30 ordered a series of frontal assaults against the Union position. Federal fire proved so heavy that one Confederate private remarked that as his regiment advanced, "we instinctively pulled our hat brims down as though to protect our faces." Still the Rebels came on, meeting their foes in hand-to-hand combat. "Blood actually ran in the ditch and in places saturated our clothing where we were lying down," one private remembered. Some 6,000 Confederates fell killed or wounded. Six Rebel generals were killed; five more were wounded; one fell prisoner. Fifty-five of Hood's regimental commanders were among the casualties.

Schofield managed to withdraw across the Tennessee under cover of darkness. Hood followed him to the outskirts of Nashville, where Thomas was waiting. Too weak to attack, too weary to go anyplace else, the Rebels waited. Thomas carefully readied his forces to drive off Hood. But his preparations were so methodical and his reputation for slowness so fixed in Grant's mind that the general-in-chief first pestered Thomas with telegrams directing him to attack and then made plans to relieve him from command. The general-in-chief worried, as did administration officials, lest Hood slip away and head toward the Ohio River. "Thomas seems unwilling to attack because it is hazardous," scoffed Secretary of War Stanton, "as if all war was anything but hazardous." In fact, weather conditions made it difficult if not impossible for Thomas to mount an assault. When he finally did strike (on December 15) however, the Confederate position first bent, then crumbled in the face of a flank attack; the next day, the Yankees launched an overwhelming frontal assault followed by a pursuit that sliced through the disarray of the retreating Rebels. Hood's army disintegrated, its shattered remnants finally gathering in northern Mississippi.

With Hood eliminated, Sherman could rest easy about the results of his march. The second week of December found his army on the outskirts of Savannah (on the Georgia coast); the garrisoned Confederate soldiers left the city on December 21. "I beg to present to you, as a Christmas gift, the city of Savannah," Sherman telegraphed Lincoln. Following immediately upon the news of Thomas's victory at Nashville, the occupation of Savannah made Christmas 1864 a most rewarding one for the Union cause.

Although in later years Confederate sympathizers would wax eloquent about the destruction caused by Sherman's march to the sea, the fact is that the blue columns actually inflicted little lasting damage on the Georgia countryside they traversed. However, deserters from both armies, some fugitive slaves, Confederate cavalry, and the so-called "bummers" of Sherman's army were less than scrupulous in their behavior toward the region's white civilians. In any event, the resulting chaos did bring the war home to supporters of the Confederacy, achieving Sherman's goal of shattering their will to persist in rebellion. Nor did the advancing Yankees feel much sympathy for Confederate civilians when they came across the shrunken bodies of comrades who had escaped from Andersonville prison. "These people made war on us, defied and dared us to come south to their country, where they boasted they would kill us and do all manner of horrible things," Sherman later remarked. "We accepted their challenge, and now for them to whine and complain of the natural and necessary results is beneath contempt." Nor were Confederates exactly exempt from vindictive behavior. John McCausland's burning of Chambersburg, Pennsylvania, in retaliation for David Hunter's incineration of the Virginia Military Institute suggested that neither side had a monopoly on arson; far more disturbing was an effort by Confederate spies to set fire to ten hotels and P. T. Barnum's museum in New York City on November 25. Coming a month after a group of Confederate raiders fell short in their efforts to burn and loot several Vermont towns, the plot to burn down the Union's most populous city suggested how desperate the Confederacy had become, and it gave the lie to their pretensions of conducting a more "civilized" war than their enemy.

Although Sherman's march to the sea inflicted serious damage on the Confederacy's ability to wage war, what it did to Confederate morale was far more devastating. The march accomplished what Sherman had predicted it would. For a Union army of some 60,000 men to march virtually unmolested through the Confederate heartland was indeed a telling blow to Southern whites' hopes for independence. Women, afraid of facing Yankees, wrote their soldier-husbands that if they had signed up to defend their home, now was the time to do it by heading home. Desertion eroded Confederate regiments. As Richard H. Sewell put it in *A House Divided*, soldiers and civilians alike increasingly were placing defense of the homestead above defense of the homeland.

Fort Fisher and the March through the Carolinas

As Sherman refitted his army in Savannah, he contemplated his next move. Grant initially urged him to ship his men north to Virginia to help close out Lee. Sherman countered with the proposal of yet another march, this one through the Carolinas toward Virginia. He won his point when Grant realized the difficulties and delays involved in transporting Sherman's command north via water. Instead, the general-in-chief decided to assist his subordinate's advance by ordering the seizure of Wilmington, North Carolina, the last functioning Confederate port. In December an initial attempt to capture Fort Fisher, which guarded the approaches to the city, failed, due in large part to the failure of Admiral David Porter and General Benjamin Butler to coordinate their respective sea and land operations. Grant promptly secured Butler's removal—in the aftermath of Lincoln's reelection, Butler's political leverage was not the threat it once was—and authorized a second expedition, with General Alfred Terry in charge of the land forces. On January 13, 1865, Terry's men landed on the beaches outside of Fort Fisher, supported by a continuous bombardment from Porter's ships; two days later the Yankees overran the fort. Although it took until February 22 for Union forces to enter Wilmington, the Confederacy was now completely sealed off from Europe, rendering the supply situation of the Rebel armies even more precarious.

Four days after the fall of Fort Fisher, Sherman commenced his march northward. By the beginning of February his columns had reached South Carolina. Feinting toward Charleston, Sherman instead drove toward Columbia, the capital of the Palmetto State. Confederate general Wade Hampton's small force offered but token resistance. On February 16, Yankee cannon bounced artillery shells off the walls of the state house; the next day the bluecoats entered the city. In their haste to evacuate the city, Hampton's men set fire to bales of cotton to prevent their capture by the invaders. In the chaotic situation that followed, these burning bales helped set fire to a significant portion of Columbia. Some of the arriving Yankees did what they could to contain the blaze, but others helped spread it: many Union soldiers showed little concern for the conflagration, deeming it just revenge. To this day the image of Sherman as a wanton destroyer is rooted in large part in the myth that he torched Columbia, igniting a controversy that still smolders in many a Southern heart. That he had not set fire to other cities, such as Savannah, when Confederate forces abandoned them rather than contest their occupation, is often overlooked; Sherman always calibrated his acts according to the purpose he wished to achieve and the behavior of his foe. As Confederate forces retreated toward North Carolina, they also evacuated Charleston, and on February 18, Union infantry finally entered the city whose militia had fired the first shot of the conflict. "Everything looks like dissolution in the South," Grant observed.

The Confederate high command looked on helplessly as Union forces advanced into what remained of the Confederate heartland. Two decisions, one reflecting what might have been, the other accepting what was once thought to be unthinkable, reflected desperation rather than hope. On February 6, Jefferson Davis formally named Robert E. Lee general-in-chief of the armies of the Confederacy. Lee for some time had been consulted on military operations and appointments outside of Virginia, and he had been Davis's military adviser in 1862 and had not abandoned that post when he took over the Army of Northern Virginia. Yet it was difficult to see what difference such an appointment would make at this stage of the conflict.

If many observers viewed this as a step long overdue, the other significant measure taken by the Confederacy in the winter of 1865 was one that nearly everyone would have agreed was inconceivable in 1861. Throughout the conflict proposals had periodically surfaced calling for the enrollment of slaves in the Confederate army. "The day you make soldiers of them is the beginning of the end of the revolution," Howell Cobb of Georgia reminded his colleagues in the Confederate Senate. "If slaves will make good soldiers our whole theory of slavery is wrong." That, of course, would be revolutionary itself. There was also rich irony in the proposal. As R. M. T. Hunter pointed out, "If we are right in passing this measure we were wrong in denying to the old government the right to interfere with the institution of slavery and to emancipate slaves." But Lee, scrambling for more men and more food, endorsed the idea. Although he had long believed that "the relationship of master and slave, controlled by humane laws and influenced by Christianity and an enlightened public sentiment, as the best that can exist between the white and black races while intermingled as at present in this country," it was time to enlist slaves: if the Union prevailed, emancipation was a certainty anyway. On March 13, 1865, the measure became law. It was too little, too late, and it remained an open question whether racist Confederate commanders truly would rely upon blacks soldiers to hold a position or spearhead an assault.

The proposal to arm the slaves and to give these black Confederates their freedom reflected the degree of Dixie's desperation and the erosion of the original purposes of the Confederate experiment. The cornerstone of Confederate identity was turning into quicksand. Understandably, those Southern whites who had flocked to the banners of the Confederacy in 1861 wondered what purpose their sacrifices still served. States rights, the Southern way of life, slavery—all had come under attack by the very government established to protect them. For Davis, Lee, and others the Confederate army had taken on a life and rationale of its own, forged in the crucible of war; but for most white Southerners, especially those not in uniform, there seemed no reason to continue the struggle. "Naturally, the wives & mothers left at home wrote longingly for the return of the husbands & sons who were in the ranks in Virginia," recalled Confederate artillery commander Edward Porter Alexander. "And naturally, many of them could not resist these appeals, & deserted in order to return & care for their families." Lee noted the growing desperation when he remarked in January about "the alarming frequency of desertions in this army"; a month later, he added, "It seems that the men are influenced very much by the representations of their friends at home, who appear to have become very despondent as to our success." Literally thousands of soldiers faded away from Confederate ranks in February and March 1865. Both the ability and will of white southerners to achieve independence was dissipating—and the spring campaign season was only a few weeks away.

Emancipation, Reconstruction, and Peace Proposals

With military victory finally in sight, Abraham Lincoln began to contemplate the peace that was to follow. He believed that only a policy that mixed justice with leniency would lead to a reconstruction of the Republic that would justify the sacrifices of the last four years. During the winter of 1864–1865 he had struggled with congressional Republicans over the fate of his governments in Arkansas and especially Louisiana. Radical Republicans, led by Charles Sumner, joined with Democrats to frustrate Lincoln's desire to secure congressional recognition for these regimes by refusing to seat their elected representatives. The president had even sought a compromise whereby in exchange for recognition of these governments he would accede to congressional Republicans' terms concerning the reconstruction of the governments of other Southern states.

If Lincoln and Radical Republicans clashed over Reconstruction, they found common ground on emancipation. For years Lincoln had insisted that the only way to secure abolition would be by constitutional amendment or state action, for the impact of the Emancipation Proclamation would end with the conclusion of the war, while congressional legislation on the matter was subject to later repeal. Thus he supported passing a constitutional amendment abolishing slavery that would expand the scope of emancipation, freeing slaves in areas left unaffected by the Emancipation Proclamation and in those states that had failed to end slavery on their own. The Senate had overwhelmingly passed the amendment in the spring of 1864, but it had failed to win House approval. With the fall elections over, Lincoln renewed his effort to secure House approval, reminding Democrats and others that the next Congress, with its increased Republican majorities, would make short work of the amendment's passage. Still, some Democrats made clear their opposition. "The Almighty has fixed the distinction of the races; the Almighty has made the black man inferior, and, sir, by no legislation, by no partisan success, by no revolution, by no military power, can you wipe out this distinction," declared New York's Fernando Wood on the floor of the House of Representatives. "You may make the black man free, but when you have done that what have you done?" On January 31, the Thirteenth Amendment squeezed through the House by a narrow margin, secured in part due to the absence of key Democratic representatives. There also was good news elsewhere. In Maryland and Tennessee, voters ratified new state constitutions that abolished slavery, while in Missouri a state constitutional convention approved emancipation.

Another sign of Congress's concern for the fate of the freedpeople was its passage of a bill establishing the Bureau of Refugees, Freedmen, and Abandoned Lands, commonly known as the Freedmen's Bureau. For two years a bill establishing such an organization had been held up in Congress, as Republicans disagreed on whether to place it within the Treasury or War Department (the latter won out). The agency would supervise the transition from slavery to freedom throughout the South for blacks and whites alike. It would also provide for the leasing of forty acres of abandoned or confiscated Southern land to blacks and white Unionists with the opportunity to acquire outright ownership three years later—if the United States government could indeed transfer title. Finally, the agency would provide relief for the destitute—white and black—in the war-torn region and assist efforts to open public schools for the freedpeople.

Even as Lincoln and Congress moved to complete the work of emancipation, the president sought ways to make it more acceptable to white Southerners in order to enhance the prospects for a peaceful postwar order. In February, along with Secretary of State William H. Seward, Lincoln journeyed to Hampton

Roads, offshore Fort Monroe, to meet with three Confederate commissioners led by Vice President Alexander H. Stephens. In response to the Rebels' queries about what form a peace settlement might take, Lincoln declared that although he would insist upon reunion and emancipation, he was willing to negotiate other questions, including what form emancipation would take. With the Thirteenth Amendment in hand, the president informed the delegation that some arrangement might be worked out whereby he would compensate white Southerners for the loss of their slaves if the Confederacy immediately gave up their quest for independence and ratified the proposed amendment. Holding out for independence, Jefferson Davis rejected Lincoln's offer; Lincoln's cabinet assailed the compensation proposal until the president finally abandoned the notion for the last time.

At the end of February, under the pretense of a meeting to discuss the exchange of prisoners of war, James Longstreet and Union general Edward O. C. Ord, Butler's replacement as commander of the Army of the James, conjured up a plan whereby they could engineer a meeting between Grant and Lee, ostensibly on the topic of prisoner exchanges but with the underlying hope that the discussions might evolve into a peace negotiation. Unsure about his authority to go beyond accepting a Confederate surrender, Grant notified Washington of the offer on the eve of Lincoln's second inauguration. Back came the answer, composed by Lincoln but sent out under Stanton's signature, instructing Grant not to meet with Lee unless it was to discuss terms of surrender: "You are not to decide, discuss or confer upon any political question."

The next day, March 4, marked the beginning of Lincoln's second term. Crowds surrounded the capital, its completed dome testifying to the determination to see the nation reunited. Only one discordant note marred the proceedings. Vice President-elect Andrew Johnson had arrived at Washington in ill health. In order to steady his nerves, he consumed some alcohol, with the result that by the time he walked into the Senate Chamber to take the oath of office as vice president he was decidedly intoxicated. He proceeded to embarrass everyone present by delivering an off-the-cuff speech of his own composition, which served only to raise doubts about his qualifications for the office he was assuming. With this escapade brought to a quick end, Lincoln walked to the east front of the capital, where Salmon P. Chase, resplendent in the robes of the Chief Justice (and perhaps harboring just a little envy that he was not on the other side of the Bible that he held forth), swore Lincoln into office.

In his second inaugural address, Lincoln outlined both his understanding of the war and his hopes for peace. "Both parties deprecated war," he recalled, "but one of them would *make* war rather than let the nation survive; and the other would *accept* war rather than let it perish. And the war came." Neither side expected what was to follow; both knew that slavery "was, somehow, the cause of the war." The conflict had escaped the boundaries intended for it by each side, suggesting to Lincoln that in this war, "The Almighty has His own purposes." As much as he hoped "that this mighty scourge of war may speedily pass away," he accepted that the war might well go on until due retribution for enslaving human beings had been paid in blood. Such unsettling notions turned a moment of celebration into one of contemplation, as Lincoln made clear that North as well as South bore responsibility for what had happened.

Having thus chastened Northern pride, the president changed his tone as he spoke of peace:

With malice toward none; with charity for all; with firmness in the right, as God gives us to see the right, let us strive on to finish the work we are in; to bind up the nation's wounds; to care for him who shall have borne the battle, and for his widow, and his orphan—to do all which may achieve and cherish a just, and a lasting peace, among ourselves, and with all nations.

As he watched Lincoln from behind and above, a member of the audience had something different in mind. Later he shared his thoughts with others. "What an excellent chance I had to kill the President," boasted John Wilkes Booth.

From Richmond to Appomattox

With the approach of spring, Grant launched several thrusts into the Confederate interior. As his armies kept careful watch on Lee's soldiers, elsewhere blue-clad columns continued to penetrate what remained of the Confederacy. Attracting the most attention were Sherman and his veterans, who entered North Carolina as March began. Desperately hoping to hold Sherman in check, Jefferson Davis, acceding to the demands of Robert E. Lee, returned Joseph Johnston to command in the Carolinas. Johnston knew that his only chance for defeating Sherman lay in catching a portion of his army off guard and defeating it before it linked up with the Union forces at Wilmington, now under the command of John M. Schofield. An effort to turn back the lead elements of Schofield's column failed after three days of battle at Kingston, so Johnston decided to confront Sherman before the two invading columns joined forces. Before long, he detected an opportunity to strike a telling blow. On March 19, at Bentonville, his army fell upon a portion of Sherman's force, but after achieving initial success, the Rebels encountered Yankee reinforcements. After three days of fighting, Johnston ordered a withdrawal. "Sherman's course cannot be hindered by the small force I have," he told Lee. "I can do little more than annoy him." Days later Sherman's men linked up with Schofield's command. "Deal as moderately and fairly by North Carolinians as possible," Sherman, aware of the sentiment for peace among Tar Heels, instructed his subordinates. Terror broke the will of South Carolina; lenity would woo North Carolinians back into the fold.

Elsewhere Union forces sliced through the Confederate interior. James H. Wilson led a column of well-armed horsemen toward Selma, Alabama, while to the south Edward R. S. Canby laid siege to Mobile. A cavalry raid made its way from East Tennessee through southwest Virginia toward Sherman's army in North Carolina. Grant had pushed for these expeditions to get under way for some time; in later years, he reflected that the delay had rendered them ineffectual in closing out the war: the lives taken and the property destroyed by them had been for naught.

Grant's impatience reflected his own concern about Lee. For months he had found it difficult to wedge the Confederate out of his lines in Virginia. Bad weather had turned the roads to mud, and Lee's defenses remained strong. Meanwhile Sheridan's cavalry had not yet returned from the Shenandoah, although it no longer served a useful purpose there, for Sheridan kept dragging his heels in responding to Grant's instructions to destroy the Virginia Central Railroad, preferring instead to burn out the area in which John S. Mosby's partisan rangers still roamed. With the advent of spring, Grant feared that Lee might well seek to elude the Yankees and join forces with Johnston in North Carolina.

Lee had indeed been contemplating such a movement for some time. His supply situation was perilous. "We have been impressing food and all the necessaries of life from women and children, and have been the means of driving thousands from their homes in destitute condition," he acknowledged. With the surrounding countryside swept clean, the Confederates had to rely upon their rail links to the south, and by the beginning of March it was evident that Grant would sever this last lifeline as soon as he could. It was time to leave the trenches to avoid being trapped in them. To keep Grant off balance, Lee decided to strike the Union fortifications near Grant's headquarters, hoping to force his opponent to call back units from his left flank, thus enhancing Lee's ability to slide around that flank and march south to join Johnston. In the early hours of March 25, John B. Gordon led an assault column against the Union line at Fort Stedman. At first the assault overwhelmed the fort's defenders, but Gordon's efforts to widen the breach proved unsuccessful, and before long the attack stalled as the Rebels were caught in a crossfire of cannon shell and bullets. As the Confederates withdrew, Grant counterpunched on his left, tightening his hold on Lee's extreme right. Lincoln, at Grant's headquarters at the general's invitation, reported that there had been "a little rumpus up the line this morning, ending about where it began." Later the president visited the battlefield, coming away with a strong reminder that even a "little rumpus" had its cost.

Indeed, it was with the images of the battlefield still vivid in his mind that Lincoln met with Grant and Sherman aboard the *River Queen*, anchored off City Point, on March 27 and 28. Sherman wanted to huddle with Grant one more time to decide how best to close out the war; Lincoln wanted to know if that could be achieved without another large battle. The answer to that question rested in part with the Confederates; more interesting, at least to Sherman, were Lincoln's sentiments about the peace to follow. Lincoln, in line with his call for a peace "with malice toward none and charity for all," made clear his desire for a just settlement, with the victors displaying lenity toward the defeated. Civil governments would be reestablished in the South, although exactly how remained unclear. Lincoln expressed the hope that Jefferson Davis would somehow escape and flee the country, thus avoiding the need to put him on trial for treason. Animated, Sherman kept peppering the president with questions and laughed at his stories, while Grant quietly listened, taking in all the conversation.

Sherman returned to North Carolina. Grant, declaring, "I mean to end the business here," set out to do just that. His target this time was the South Side Railroad, the last major supply link between Lee's army and the Confederate interior. If Union forces captured the railway, Lee would have to abandon the Confederate capital or watch helplessly as his army starved. Three divisions of Ord's Army of the James moved into position on the southern end of the Union line, while Sheridan led his troopers and an infantry corps on the final flanking attack in the Petersburg campaign. In response Lee stretched his already thin lines to the breaking point in an effort to gather enough men to hold off Grant one more time. He could not do it. After two days of sharp battles, on April 1 Sheridan pulverized four butternut brigades under George Pickett at Five Forks, a critical road junction. Ahead lay the South Side Railroad. Richmond was doomed.

Sheridan's victory at Five Forks forced Lee's hand. At best he could delay Grant another day, for when the Union commander heard of Sheridan's success he immediately ordered an assault along the entire line. On April 2 the first Union soldiers made their way up to Petersburg; that night, the Confederates abandoned their lines, set fire to anything of military value in Richmond (resulting in a conflagration that exceeded the postevacuation infernos in Columbia or Atlanta), and marched west. The first Federal soldiers to march down the streets of the Confederate capital on the morning of April 3 were African Americans, members of the Twenty-fifth Corps, composed entirely of black regiments. Before long the flag of the United States flew over Richmond; that accomplished, the Union soldiers began to put out the fires still burning in the city. The next day another curious visitor arrived. As Abraham Lincoln rode into the city, blacks cheered the man they recognized as their liberator. He sat in Jefferson Davis's study and visited Libby Prison, once a less than comfortable home to many a captured Yankee officer.

As Lincoln toured the captured city, Lee gathered his scattered command at Amelia Court House. Initially he sought to join Johnston in North Carolina. But the Army of Northern Virginia did not move with its accustomed verve, and the Confederate commissary bungled its efforts to keep the Rebel soldiers supplied. As a result, Lee lost precious time trying to gather what supplies he could before setting off. Meanwhile, Grant's men, sensing victory, marched as they never had before, first cutting off Lee's southward escape routes and then smashing his rear guard on April 6 at Saylor's Creek. As the Rebel soldiers broke, a horrified Lee exclaimed: "My God! Has the army been dissolved?" Blocked from joining Johnston, Lee then turned westward toward the Blue Ridge Mountains. Perhaps there his men could rally and take advantage of the rugged terrain to frustrate their pursuers. Well aware of this possibility, Grant urged his commanders to concentrate on moving ahead of Lee's columns to cut them off. "If the thing is pressed," Sheridan assured Grant, "I think Lee will surrender." Back at City Point, Lincoln read Sheridan's missive and telegraphed Grant, "Let the thing be pressed." It was.

As the armies of the Potomac and the James marched to head off their Confederate counterparts, Grant, pointing out "the hopelessness of further resistance," asked Lee to surrender. At first Lee did not agree with Grant's diagnosis and refused to come forth. Then he tried once more to wangle the offer of a peace conference out of his opponent. Meanwhile he ordered his men on to Appomattox Court House, where trains filled with fresh supplies for his army awaited at a nearby railroad depot. From there it would be on westward to Lynchburg, followed by the foothills of the Blue Ridge. If the Army of Northern Virginia could reach its destination, the war would go on.

On April 9, Palm Sunday, the Confederates approached Appomattox Court House, only a few miles away from the train station. In front of them was a thin line of dismounted Union cavalrymen. The Confederate force surged forward; the troopers scattered. But just as Lee's men prepared to celebrate yet another victory, they looked up to see Union infantrymen, several lines deep, astride the road in front of them. It was over. Lee dismissed the entreaties of several of his officers who advised that the army be immediately disbanded and dispersed to carry on the war as guerrillas. Such a step, Lee knew, would simply prolong hostilities at great cost; it could not secure independence. Further attempts to evade pursuit were useless. "There is nothing left to do but go and meet General Grant," he sighed, "and I would rather die a thousand deaths."

Grant and Lee met in the living room of Wilmer McLean's home by the courthouse. The terms Grant proposed were generous. The Confederates could take home their farm animals for spring plowing; officers would keep their sidearms, avoiding the humiliation of having to surrender them to their conquerors. Most important, however, for establishing the foundations of peace was Grant's assurance that "each officer and man will be allowed to return to their homes not to be disturbed by United States authority so long as they observe their paroles and the laws in force where they may reside." This sentence put an end to the prospect of treason trials for Lee and his men, and in establishing the foundation for a lasting peace, Grant showed himself as much a statesman as a warrior. Lee, relieved, remarked, "This will have a very happy effect on my army."

After the two commanders made arrangements to feed Lee's army with the rations captured by Sheridan, the conference ended. Lee slowly rode back to his army. Choked with tears, he told the men who crowded around him of the surrender. Grant returned to headquarters. An aide had to remind him to telegraph the news to Washington. Hearing the cheers of his soldiers and the booming of cannon saluting the victory, he ordered an end to the celebration, remarking, "The Rebels are our countrymen again."

As news of Lee's surrender spread throughout the South, many Southerners realized that it sounded the death knell of the Confederacy. Lee himself knew it was all over. "A partisan war may be continued, and hostilities protracted, causing individual suffering and the devastation of the country," he told Davis, "but I see no prospect by that means of achieving a separate independence." It was time to end the bloodshed. One Union soldier in occupied Richmond put it best. Writing on stationery captured from the Confederate quartermaster general's office, he told his old college professor, "I so rejoice to think that our killing is ended; that we have no more hospital scenes; that snips of arms and legs and trenches of dead bodies, shall not be dug again. I have seen enough of war. Its pomp and circumstances do not move me [any] more. Let me go home."

Foundations for Peace

Even as Grant's columns caught up with Lee's army, Lincoln availed himself of every chance for a quick end to the war. He considered letting members of the Virginia legislature meet to take the Old Dominion out of the war, but he abandoned this notion after several cabinet members stridently objected—and, as even Lincoln had to admit, Lee's surrender to Grant had already effectively removed Virginia from the war. As lenient as he might want to be toward Southern whites, however, the president also wanted to secure the position of the freedpeople in the postwar South. On April 11, he outlined his thoughts to a crowd assembled at the White House. Reconstruction was "fraught with great difficulty"; not only were Southerners "disorganized and discordant," but even Northerners differed "as to the mode, manner, and means of reconstruction." He defended his policy in Louisiana, although he added that he was willing to abandon it should it falter. As to black suffrage, he now publicly indicated his preference that at least those blacks who were literate or had served in the military should be allowed to vote. Finally, he acknowledged that with peace would come new challenges and new approaches to Reconstruction, although he refused to outline any specifics. Three days later, at a cabinet meeting, the president commenced discussions about the appropriate policy to pursue.

But Abraham Lincoln never had the chance to define and implement a postwar Reconstruction policy. On April 14, 1865, a Confederate sympathizer, the actor John Wilkes Booth, entered the president's box at Ford's Theater during a performance of the comedy *Our American Cousin*. In one hand was a derringer; in the other, a knife. Booth levelled the handgun at the back of Lincoln's head, and, with an actor's sense of timing, squeezed the trigger as the audience laughed at the play. Some thought that the man who leapt from the box and crossed the stage was part of the performance until they heard Mary Todd Lincoln's piercing wail. The mortally wounded president was carried across the street to a boarding house. After an all-night vigil, Abraham Lincoln died at 7:22 AM on April 15.

The impact of Booth's bullet upon American history has long stirred controversy. It remains unclear exactly what Lincoln would have done during Reconstruction: the president himself had not been sure. That he was willing to do something to promote the future welfare of the former slaves is clear, although he had yet to frame a policy on that matter. Whether he could have formulated an approach that would have joined together the advancement of the freed blacks and reconciliation between North and South, or whether he could have secured the cooperation of Congress and other participants, including Southern whites, in implementing such a process remains an open question. Nevertheless, he would have had to exercise his political skill in a vastly different institutional environment, for with the end of hostilities he could no longer cite the war powers of his office as justification for his acts. Moreover, Lincoln's death, tragic as it was, in itself did not determine the course of events over the next several years: much of what happened was due to the beliefs and behavior of his successor. Perhaps the true tragedy of Lincoln's assassination was that it made Andrew Johnson the seventeenth president of the United States.

The new president wasted no time in setting forth his views. His pledge to remind Americans that "treason is a crime and traitors must be impoverished" rallied Radicals intent on placing extensive demands on the former Confederate states. "Johnson, we have faith in you," exclaimed Senator Benjamin F. Wade. "By the gods, there will be no trouble now in running the government." The days of "malice toward none" and "charity for all" seemed to have given way to a commitment to punish the transgression of secession. Within days the administration had a chance to demonstrate its new firmness. For several days Sherman and Johnston, their armies deployed around Raleigh and Durham, North Carolina, had been discussing the conditions under which Johnston would surrender his army. In informing Grant of the talks, Sherman promised his chief that he would "be careful not to complicate any points of civil policy." But the news of Lincoln's assassination changed all that. Johnston, believing the war over, offered to arrange terms providing for the surrender of all remaining Confederate forces; Sherman, afraid that Johnston's army would disintegrate into guerrilla bands if he did not settle things quickly, assented to an agreement that exceeded in scope Grant's terms to Lee. Confederate forces would return to their state capitals, where they would deposit their weapons, the federal government would recognize existing state governments as legitimate authorities, and a general pardon would be extended to all Southerners. Sherman dispatched an aide north with the proposal to obtain the approval of the authorities in Washington.

Approval was not forthcoming. The Sherman-Johnston agreement was silent on the question of slavery, and it promised an all-too-quick restoration of prewar conditions. Grant, who first read the terms, knew they were unacceptable; at a cabinet meeting on April 21, President Johnson and his advisers rejected them, with Stanton proclaiming Sherman a traitor. Only the interposition of Grant and other cooler heads avoided further repercussions. Hoping to avert hard feelings on both sides, Grant travelled to Sherman's headquarters to notify his old friend of the fate of his agreement and to supervise the negotiation of a new surrender based on the Appomattox terms. Johnston accepted these on April 26.

Johnson moved to punish the president's assassin and his allies, one of whom, Lewis Paine, had attacked and wounded the bedridden Seward on the night Booth murdered Lincoln. Within days Paine, George Atzerodt, Michael O'Laughlin, Ed Spangler, Samuel Arnold, and Mary Surratt were rounded up and imprisoned, all accused of participation in the assassination. Another man implicated in the conspiracy, Mary's son John, fled the country. But Booth eluded capture. Accompanied by accomplice David Herold, he had made his way south through Maryland and into eastern Virginia, hobbled by a broken leg, the result of his leap to the stage of Ford's Theater from the president's box. On April 26 a cavalry detachment tracked down the assassin in a barn south of the Rappahannock River. Although Herold surrendered, Booth defied his captors, who set fire to the barn in which he held out. Then a cavalryman, peering through the flames, shot him. Dragged out of the barn, Booth died on a farmhouse porch. Stories that Jefferson Davis had authorized the assassination resulted in the government offering a reward for his capture as a coconspirator—although as time passed efforts to implicate the Confederate president dwindled. Eventually eight people—Paine, Herold, Atzerodt, O'Laughlin, Spangler, Arnold, Mary Surratt, and Dr. Samuel A. Mudd, who had set Booth's broken leg—were tried by a military commission. All eight were judged guilty on June 30; on July 7, Paine, Atzerodt, Herold, and Mary Surratt were executed, while the other four were imprisoned at Fort Jefferson at Dry Tortugas, Florida. Mary Surratt's execution proved controversial, and before long it became evident that Mudd was innocent of participation in the conspiracy. O'Laughlin died in 1867. Mudd was pardoned in 1868. Spangler and Arnold were pardoned in 1869.

Jefferson Davis did not long evade capture. Union cavalry under the command of James H. Wilson cornered Davis and seized him on May 10 at Irwinville, Georgia. The Confederate president was imprisoned at Fort Monroe, Virginia, for two years while federal authorities debated whether to try him for treason. While Andrew Johnson craved to see Davis hoisted by a hangman's noose, others doubted that a jury trial, in which the jurors would be drawn from Virginia's population, would convict him. Several prominent Northerners, led by Horace Greeley, posted bail for Davis, and he was released from imprisonment in 1867, with the government deciding not to prosecute him.

Robert E. Lee also escaped prosecution. In May 1865, Lee sought presidential pardon, adding that he believed that the terms Grant offered at Appomattox protected him from prosecution for treason. Grant strongly endorsed this interpretation, but Johnson, toying with the idea of allowing Lee to be tried and convicted before pardoning him, raised no objection when a Norfolk grand jury indicted Lee and other prominent Confederates on charges of treason. Grant intervened, telling Johnson that if the prosecution of Lee persisted, he would resign his commission. The president backed down.

By the end of spring, the Confederacy had ceased to exist. On May 4, Richard Taylor, commanding what Confederate forces remained east of the Mississippi, surrendered; Edmund Kirby Smith, whose command in Texas and Louisiana, having been cut off from the rest of the Confederacy, approached an independent country by 1865, capitulated by month's end. On April 2, 1866, one year to the day of Petersburg's fall, President Johnson declared the rebellion at an end except in Texas; the following August 20 he added Texas to the list. By that time, of course, the nation was embroiled in a controversy over the terms of the peace settlement, commonly called Reconstruction, a process that did much to determine exactly what America's Civil War had determined. Nevertheless, the Union had been preserved and slavery had been abolished—and Americans moved forward knowing that their lives would never be the same again.

CONCLUSION

Why the Union Won

Explaining why the Union triumphed over the Confederacy has become a full-time occupation for some people. There are those who assert that the Union had been bound to win due to its superior resources and manpower. For Americans who live in the shadow of the Vietnam conflict, however, it should be evident that such conditions do not automatically or inevitably assure military victory. Taking as their inspiration the triumph of American independence during the Revolution, Confederates sought to repeat that feat, making clear the connection when they placed George Washington on the seal of their new nation. Proponents of the inevitability thesis also do no credit to the intelligence of either side, for if the war was destined to end in a Yankee triumph, one must wonder why both sides were unable to see then what now appears so clear in hindsight.

The Confederacy could have secured its independence. At several moments in the war it seemed as if it just might do so. Perhaps its best opportunity to achieve a battlefield triumph outright was in the late summer and fall of 1862, although one may place too much importance on Lee's invasion of Maryland as a possible turning point. The Army of Northern Virginia could not take advantage of what it had gained from June to August precisely because of the cost it had paid in blood on the battlefield. The same could be said to a lesser extent about the Gettysburg campaign, although here the performance of generals and soldiers on both sides proved critical to the war's outcome. Lee's gambles, daring as they were, had not paid off: he came up one card short. Union victories in 1863 at Vicksburg, Gettysburg, and Chattanooga meant that the best chance for Confederate independence from that point on rested explicitly on what had always been implicit: it depended upon the breaking of the Northern public's will to fight and to persevere to victory. This came close to happening in 1864.

Why, then, did the Union win? It did so because its leadership, civil and military, proved better equipped to meet the challenges of the war it waged. Abraham Lincoln managed to maintain sufficient unity and cooperation to sustain the Union through difficult times. Understanding the progressive nature of warfare, Ulysses S. Grant emerged as the military leader able to devise a strategy that mobilized the Union's resources and applied them in a coordinated fashion against Rebel resources to force the Confederacy to crack in time to secure Lincoln a second term. Each man proved as indispensable as anyone could be to the triumph of Union arms. Grant had already done much to set the stage for the situation he encountered as general-in-chief in 1864, for his victories at Fort Donelson, Shiloh, Vicksburg, and Chattanooga contributed greatly to the securing of the Mississippi Valley and paving the way for William T. Sherman's Atlanta campaign. Grant cashed in on his successes, while Lee's victories came at so dear a cost that he was unable to capitalize upon them.

The best chance for Confederate victory had come in 1864. Confederate generals could have won the war if they could have prevented their Union counterparts from scoring triumphs significant enough to ensure Lincoln's reelection. Grant knew that if he could win victories that would sustain Northern will, Lincoln would win, and Confederate will would crumble. Here his skill at conducting war on a grand scale paid huge dividends. He neutralized Lee's ability to seize the initiative, effectively preventing the Confederate commander from winning another attention-grabbing victory. Sherman and Philip H. Sheridan completed the work by winning sensational victories that inspired the Northern public, assuring Lincoln four more years. In turn, these triumphs eroded Confederate resources across the board—manpower, matériel, food, transportation—and chipped away at Confederate will.

The availability of resources and the willingness to persist are intertwined. One needs both to win a war. Resources without the will to use them effectively are wasted; will, without the resources to sustain it and achieve one's objectives, cannot triumph on its own. Lincoln, Grant, and Sherman devised ways to apply Union resources to strike at Confederate resources and will, in the process achieving triumphs that would sustain the will of the Northern public to keep on fighting. Union leadership proved equal to the challenges it faced, challenges that proved as demanding in their way as did the challenges confronting Confederate leadership. Although Confederate leaders worked hard and long, they could never forge solutions to the problems of will and resources that they faced.

The Confederacy also confronted a dilemma that its leaders never resolved completely. To achieve victory in the face of pre-existing Union advantages, it would have to mobilize its resources far more efficiently and effectively; to a surprising extent, it did so—especially in light of the fact that such mobilization required Confederate leaders to set aside cherished beliefs about localism and a limited federal government. Nevertheless, this very success also created great stress between the ideals of the Confederacy and the actions of its government. Conscription, impressment, and taxation all ran against the grain of the Southern mind and soul. Once the war actually began, Confederate policy tended to divide Confederate civilians; the acts of the type of national government that the conduct of the war had shaped made it more difficult to forge a sense of nationhood. Moreover, the success of Union strategy in depriving the Confederacy of much-needed resources through conquest and destruction further complicated the government's ability to serve the needs of its people. By 1865, when the Confederate Congress approved the enlistment of slaves as soldiers, the contradictions in the Confederate experiment were all too apparent. Confederate government policies had eaten away at the incipient nation's raison d' être; then the willingness of the victors to offer lenient terms made it easier for many Southern whites to venture back to the fold, although the exact terms of that return remained to be worked out.

Slavery both reflected and had much to do with these developments. Slaves formed a valuable resource for the Confederacy, allowing a much larger proportion of the white male population to be mobilized for combat. But slavery, the cornerstone of the Confederacy, proved vulnerable to the friction of war. The progress of Union armies southward, even before the Emancipation Proclamation had been issued, loosened the chains of slavery for many blacks, creating opportunities for escape. In seizing those opportunities, blacks helped press the issue of emancipation as policy, forcing Union policy makers to confront an issue a good number had hoped to avoid. As Lincoln and Grant both noted, emancipation and black enlistment augmented Federal resources as it ate away at Confederate strength. The increasing presence of blacks in the Union army in 1864—at a time when attrition in various forms was wearing away at the number of white soldiers—went far to maintain the margin of manpower Grant needed to persist in his strategy. On the other side, slaves proved less reliable as workers, quietly sabotaging the Confederate war effort, just as they had once silently subverted their masters, and causing alarm among those who wondered what might happen in the future. Confederate policy toward slavery, as reflected in conscription and impressment, divided Southern whites in multiple ways; the ultimate decision to enlist blacks in the Rebel ranks went against the fundamental reason the Confederacy existed in the first place— to protect a way of life based upon slavery.

In short, it was the interplay of Union military strategy as developed and executed by Grant and Sherman, utilizing available resources to achieve victory that would sustain Northern will while striking at Confederate resources and will, and the failure of Confederate policy to fashion constructive responses to the dilemmas it faced that led to Union victory. To highlight one without the other ultimately distorts our understanding of the process of events and distracts us from the real reasons for Union victory and Confederate defeat.

Union victory settled several issues. The viability of secession had been tested and crushed. The threat of disunion faded away from American political discourse. Although politicians would still talk about the importance of states rights and federalism, the permanence of the American nation was now assumed. That today people take this for granted should not diminish its importance; rather, it is testimony to the definitive nature of the Civil War's verdict. There is something to the notion that the most important constitutional decision in American history was handed down at Appomattox Court House. In time even most Southern whites came to accept that in the end the defeat of the Confederacy was best for all concerned. Few doubt that had the result been different, the course of subsequent history—both for the combatants and for the world—would have been significantly affected.

The conflict had also brought an end to slavery, the single most dangerous threat to the perpetuation of the Union. Although in years to come many people would claim that the demise of the peculiar institution was inevitable, one must recognize that these arguments were framed with the benefit of hindsight and with an awareness of the death and destruction wrought by the Civil War. There was no sign in 1860 that American slavery was in any danger—except, according to secessionists, from Lincoln's accession to the presidency and the prospect of Republican rule down the road. No one has yet offered an alternative scenario leading to the peaceful abolition of slavery that resides within the realm of the historically possible and plausible. In that sense, perhaps John Brown was more astute than his critics when he insisted that slavery would "never be purged away; but with Blood."

If slavery had much to do with the coming of the war—although exactly how remains a complicated story—the course of the war made emancipation possible. It was a result that few people had initially sought in going to war, although there were some people—Grant among them—who predicted that slavery would force the conflict. Blacks escaping to Union lines and a committed group of abolitionists and Radical Republicans did much to place pressure on the Lincoln administration's original disinclination to interfere with slavery, but what rendered emancipation inevitable, ironically, were Confederate military successes in the East and the checking of Union offensives in the West. The failure of the Union to secure victory and peace through waging a limited war while seeking to reconcile white Southerners left Lincoln no choice but to escalate the conflict in order to win it. George McClellan never won his climactic battle; the Union high command failed to press its early advantages in Tennessee and the Mississippi River valley; the long-awaited resurgence of Southern unionism never materialized; and secessionist support proved more durable than anticipated. It was Confederate persistence that forced the Union to broaden the aims of the war and to intensify its effort to win.

Yet it was not clear what victory meant. No one knew what the newly freed people could expect, and it was unclear exactly how the former Confederate states would regain full and equal membership in the Union. How much more change would occur? How much of the hard-won change would not last? For the next dozen or so years, Americans, white and black, struggled with these issues even as they turned renewed attention to other concerns such as westward expansion and economic development. Notions of restoration and reconciliation tended to blunt the revolutionary edge of the postwar change, as did persistent racism and the desire to move on to other matters. In this struggle the will of Southern white supremacists to regain control of their states proved superior to a faltering Northern will to protect all

U.S. citizens, black and white, as equal under law. Critics of Republican Reconstruction have been harsh in their condemnation of its failure to do more than it did, but that generation had already done a great deal, far more than many of those that followed, to rectify past wrongs and set a course for the future. Perhaps we should not be too demanding of that generation unless we are willing to demand as much of ourselves.

In some ways America's civil war has yet to end. Its major figures—Lincoln, Grant, and Lee—live on in myth and lore as well as in history. Americans debate the war's meaning with passion, shaping and reshaping their understanding of the conflict and its importance to comport with their own beliefs. If the war became a crucible of national identity, the exact nature and meaning of that identity remains contested. Nevertheless, the Civil War remains the central event of American history, in large part because it did give a reunited nation, at great and painful cost, "a new birth of freedom."

BIBLIOGRAPHICAL ESSAY

There are so many books about the American Civil War that one is pressed even to offer a selection of the best books about it. What follows is a discussion of titles for readers who want to learn more about the whole conflict; in turn these recommendations will serve as good introductions for those people who want to read in depth about certain topics or individuals.

General Overviews

At present the premier textbook that covers the period 1848 to 1877 in some detail is James M. McPherson, *Ordeal By Fire: The Civil War and Reconstruction* (1992). Among numerous briefer studies the best are William R. Brock, *Conflict and Transformation* (1973); David H. Donald, *Liberty and Union* (1978); Richard H. Sewell, *A House Divided: Sectionalism and Civil War, 1848–1865* (1988); and David M. Potter, *Division and the Stresses of Reunion, 1845–1876* (1973). James M. McPherson's *Battle Cry of Freedom: The Civil War Era* (1988) is a remarkable interpretive synthesis of the war (as well as of the coming of the war); Peter J. Parish's thoughtful *The American Civil War* (1975) remains provocative. For a briefer account see Bruce Catton, *This Hallowed Ground* (1956). Three multivolume histories stand out: Allan Nevins, *The War for the Union* (4 vols.: 1959–71); Bruce Catton's trilogy, *The Coming Fury* (1961), *Terrible Swift Sword* (1963), and *Never Call Retreat* (1965); and Shelby Foote, *The Civil War: A Narrative* (3 vols.:1958–74). In *An American Iliad: The Story of the Civil War* (1991), Charles P. Roland presents an insightful summary of much of the recent scholarship about the military history of the war. Brief but sprightly is Frank Vandiver, *Blood Brothers: A Short History of the Civil War* (1992). Another vivid narrative is offered by Allen C. Guelzo in *The Crisis of the American Republic* (1995). Two wonderfully illustrated histories are Richard M. Ketchum, ed., *The American Heritage Picture History of the Civil War* (1960), with text by Bruce Catton; and Geoffrey C. Ward with Ric Burns and Ken Burns, *The Civil War: An Illustrated History* (1990). Especially helpful for factual material are E. B. Long with Barbara Long, *The Civil War Day by Day: An Almanac* (1971); Mark M. Boatner III, *The Civil War Dictionary* (1959); and Ezra Warner, *Generals in Gray* (1959) and *Generals in Blue* (1964).

Two collections of essays offer interesting discussions of Union victory and Confederate defeat: David Donald, ed., *Why the North Won the Civil War* (1960), includes classic essays by Richard N. Current, T. Harry Williams, Norman A. Graebner, David Donald, and David M. Potter; Gabor S. Boritt, ed., *Why the Confederacy Lost* (1992) contains five essays (by James M. McPherson, Archer Jones, Gary W. Gallagher, Reid Mitchell, and Joseph T. Glatthaar) that hew more closely to military explanations of the war's outcome. Most provocative is *Why the South Lost the Civil War* (1986) by Richard E. Beringer, Herman Hattaway, Archer Jones, and William N. Still, Jr.: its central argument—that the Confederacy lost because its citizens lacked the will to persist—remains controversial, although it has the merit of linking the battlefront and the home front in seeking an integrated explanation of why the Union won. A searching and extensive reconsideration of Union and Confederate strategy, *How the North Won: A Military History of the Civil War* (1983), by Herman Hattaway and Archer Jones focuses on the importance of logistics and command.

Several overviews of the Union and the Confederacy present stimulating introductions to how both sides waged war and how war affected both sides. Phillip Shaw Paludan's *"A People's Contest": The Union and Civil War, 1861–1865* (1988) provides a masterful exploration of the North, while J. Matthew Gallman's *The North Fights the Civil War: The Home Front* (1994) argues that the war's impact upon Northern society should not be overestimated. For the Confederacy, Emory M. Thomas's *The Confederate Nation, 1861–1865* (1979) is an excellent point of departure, while his *The Confederacy as a Revolutionary Experience* (1971) argues that the process of war revealed contradictions between Confederate principle and practice—and casts doubt on interpretations that stress the triumph of Union innovation over a tradition-bound South. In *The Confederate Republic: A Revolution Against Politics* (1994), George C. Rable highlights the tensions in what Confederates wanted their new republic to represent. Drew Gilpin Faust's *The Creation of Confederate Nationalism: Ideology and Identity in the Civil War South* (1988) offers additional evidence of how the war changed conceptions of the Confederacy. The essays in Harry P. Owens and James J. Cooke, eds., *The Old South in the Crucible of War* (1983) suggest how the impact of war affected the South. In *Yankee Leviathan: The Origins of Central State Authority in America, 1859–1879* (1990), Richard F. Benzel argues that Confederate centralization exceeded that of the Union.

For compelling discussions of what the war meant, see Robert Penn Warren, *The Legacy of the Civil War* (1961) and William L. Barney, *Flawed Victory* (1975). Daniel Aaron's *The Unwritten War: American Writers and the Civil War* (1973) and Edmund Wilson's *Patriotic Gore: Studies in the Literature of the American Civil War* (1962) reveal how people struggled to set down their experiences on paper. The greatest success at that endeavor remains Ulysses S. Grant, *Personal Memoirs*, 2 vols. (1885–86).

Politics

In *The Road to Secession: A New Perspective on the Old South* (1972) and *The Secessionist Impulse: Alabama and Mississippi in 1860* (1974), William L. Barney presents two important perspectives on secession. Other state studies, offering different explanations, include Steven A. Channing, *Crisis of Fear: Secession in South Carolina* (1970); Michael P. Johnson, *Toward a Patriarchal Republic: The Secession of Georgia* (1977); and Marc W. Kruman, *Parties and Politics in North Carolina, 1836–1865* (1983). Daniel W. Crofts's *Reluctant Confederates: Upper South Unionists in the Secession Crisis* (1989) looks at the different course of events outside the Deep South. Three books explore how the North reacted to the secession crisis and the series of events that led to the confrontation at Fort Sumter: David M. Potter, *Lincoln and His Party in the Secession Crisis* (1942); Kenneth M. Stampp, *And the War Came* (1950); and Richard N. Current, *Lincoln and the First Shot* (1963).

For Abraham Lincoln, two excellent points of departure are James M. McPherson, *Abraham Lincoln and the Second American Revolution* (1991), and Richard N. Current, *The Lincoln Nobody Knows* (1958). The best single-volume biography is David Donald, *Lincoln* (1995), while Phillip Shaw Paludan's *The Presidency of Abraham Lincoln* (1994) is a rich and provocative study of Lincoln as president. David Donald's *Lincoln Reconsidered: Essays on the Civil War Era* (1956) contains several valuable pieces. In *Lincoln at Gettysburg: The Words that Remade America* (1992), Garry Wills presents a rather controversial interpretation of Lincoln's purpose at Gettysburg, which overshadows much else of worth in the study. Lincoln's chief cabinet ministers receive their due in Glyndon G. Van Deusen, *William Henry Seward* (1967); Benjamin P. Thomas and Harold Hyman, *Stanton: Lincoln's Secretary of War* (1962); and in two biographies by John Niven, *Gideon Welles: Lincoln's Secretary of the Navy* (1973) and *Salmon P. Chase* (1995).

Hans L. Trefousse's *Benjamin Franklin Wade: Radical Republican from Ohio* (1963), David Donald's *Charles Sumner and the Rights of Man* (1974), and Fawn Brodie's *Thaddeus Stevens: Scourge of the South* (1959), look at the leading Radicals in Congress. T. Harry Williams, in *Lincoln and the Radicals* (1941), emphasizes the conflict between the president and one wing of the Republican Party, while Hans L. Trefousse, in *The Radical Republicans: Lincoln's Vanguard for Racial Justice* (1969), perhaps went too far in defining their common ground. Two books by Allan G. Bogue, *The Earnest Men: The Republicans of the Civil War Senate* (1981) and *The Congressman's Civil War* (1989), offer a sophisticated understanding of how Congress went about its business. Leonard P. Curry's *Blueprint for Modern America: Nonmilitary Legislation of the First Civil War Congress* (1968) outlines the content of the Republican legislative agenda. James A. Rawley's *The Politics of Union: Northern Politics during the Civil War* (1980) presents a lucid overview of various issues. The Democrats receive their due in Joel H. Silbey's *A Respectable Minority: The Democratic Party in the Civil War Era, 1860–1868* (1977) and Frank L. Klement's *The Copperheads in the Middle West* (1960) and *The Limits of Dissent: Clement L. Vallandigham and the Civil War* (1970). David W. Blight's *Frederick Douglass's Civil War: Keeping Faith in Jubilee* (1989) explores how the black leader used the opportunity of war to advance the cause of his people, while Stephen B. Oates's *A Woman of Valor: Clara Barton and the Civil War* (1994) is a lively recounting of Barton's life.

Several fine biographies of Confederate civil leaders help readers understand the difficulties that those men faced as they tried to forge a new nation. William C. Davis's *Jefferson Davis: The Man and His Hour* (1991) stands as the standard single-volume study. In *After Secession: Jefferson Davis and the Failure of Confederate Nationalism* (1978), Paul D. Escott faults the Confederate government and its leader for failing to devise policies to bolster morale at home. The best biography of Davis's vice president is Thomas E. Schott, *Alexander H. Stephens of Georgia: A*

Biography (1988). Eli Evans's *Judah Benjamin: The Jewish Confederate* (1988) and Joseph T. Durkin's *Stephen R. Mallory* (1938) look at two important Confederate cabinet ministers. Joseph H. Parks's *Joseph E. Brown of Georgia* (1977) and Richard Yates's *The Confederacy and Zeb Vance* (1958) recount the efforts of two of Davis's antagonists. The Confederate Congress has not received the attention of its Union counterpart. Still, W. B. Yearns, in *The Confederate Congress* (1960), and Thomas B. Alexander and Richard Beringer, in *The Anatomy of the Confederate Congress* (1972), say much about who served and the issues that they confronted.

David P. Crook's *The North, The South, and the Powers, 1861–1865* (1974) surveys the diplomacy of the two sides. Brian A. Jenkins's *Britain and the War for the Union* (2 vols.: 1974, 1980) looks at British policy, while Lynn M. Case's and William F. Spencer's *The United States and France: Civil War Diplomacy* (1970) explores that tense relationship. Two books by Norman B. Ferris, *Desperate Diplomacy: William Henry Seward's Foreign Policy, 1861* (1977) and *The Trent Affair* (1975), examine the chaotic first year of Seward's tenure as secretary of state. Frank L. Owlsey's *King Cotton Diplomacy: Foreign Relations of the Confederate States of America* (1931) remains the best survey of Confederate diplomacy. Howard Jones, in *Union in Peril: The Crisis over British Intervention in the Civil War* (1992), offers a provocative reassessment of the impact of the Emancipation Proclamation upon British deliberations.

Armies, Battles, Leaders, and Soldiers

Bruce Catton's trilogy on the Army of the Potomac—*Mr. Lincoln's Army* (1951), *Glory Road* (1952), and *A Stillness at Appomattox* (1953)—remains unequaled. Oddly enough, neither the Army of the Tennessee nor the Army of the Cumberland has received like attention, despite their key contributions to ultimate Union victory. In *Lincoln and His Generals* (1952), T. Harry Williams offers what has long stood as the classic examination of the Union president as commander-in-chief, although more recent literature suggests major modifications of its arguments. Kenneth P. Williams's *Lincoln Finds a General*, 5 vols. (1949–59), is an extensive study of the evolution of Union commanders through September 1863.

Several books explore how the Confederacy waged war. Steven Woodworth's *Jefferson Davis and His Generals* (1990) covers the western theater, while his *Lee and Davis at War* (1995) looks at the East. Archer Jones, *Confederate Strategy from Shiloh to Vicksburg* (1961); Thomas L. Connelly and Archer Jones, *The Politics of Command: Factions and Ideas in Confederate Strategy* (1973); and Frank E. Vandiver, *Rebel Brass: The Confederate Command System* (1956) discuss the Confederate approach to the war. The best history of the Army of Northern Virginia is Douglas Southall Freeman, *Lee's Lieutenants*, 3 vols. (1942–44). Thomas L. Connelly's *Army of the Heartland: The Army of Tennessee, 1861–1862* (1967) and *Autumn of Glory: The Army of Tennessee, 1862–1865* (1971) look at the main Confederate army in the West. Richard McMurry's *Two Great Rebel Armies: An Essay in Confederate Military History* (1989) compares the Army of Northern Virginia with the Army of Tennessee.

Several books examine the art of war on both sides. Grady McWhiney and Perry D. Jamieson, in *Attack and Die: Civil War Military Tactics and the Southern Heritage* (1982), suggest that Confederates had a cultural propensity to the attack; Paddy Griffith's *Battle Tactics of the Civil War* (1987) is a controversial and not altogether persuasive argument reasserting the traditional nature of Civil War battles. Edward Hagerman's *The American Civil War and the Origins of Modern Warfare* (1988) emphasizes the importance of logistics; while Charles Royster's *The Destructive War* (1991) argues that civilians outstripped generals in the desire to escalate the conflict.

On Ulysses S. Grant see Bruce Catton, *Grant Moves South* (1960) and *Grant Takes Command* (1969); J. F. C. Fuller, *The Generalship of Ulysses S. Grant* (1929); and Brooks D. Simpson, *Let Us Have Peace: Ulysses S. Grant and the Politics of War and Reconstruction* (1991). William S. McFeely's *Grant: A Biography* (1981) is a flawed work that must be used with care. Three biographies—John F. Marszalek, *Sherman: A Soldier's Passion for Order* (1993), Lloyd Lewis, *Sherman: Fighting Prophet* (1932), and Michael Fellman, *Citizen Sherman* (1995)—chronicle the life of Grant's chief lieutenant. Stephen W. Sears's *George B. McClellan: The Young Napoleon* (1988) and William W. Hassler's *General George B. McClellan: Shield of the Union* (1957) offer distinctly different visions of this controversial commander. For Sheridan, see Roy Morris, Jr.'s *Sheridan: The Life and Wars of General Phil Sheridan* (1992); for George H. Thomas, see Freeman Cleaves's *Rock of Chickamauga: The Life of General George H. Thomas* (1948) and Francis B. McKinney's *Education in Violence: The Life of George H. Thomas and the Army of the Cumberland* (1961); for Meade, see Cleaves's *Meade of Gettysburg* (1960).

For life studies of the Confederacy's foremost general see Douglas Southall Freeman, *R. E. Lee* (4 vols.: 1934–35); Emory Thomas, *Robert E. Lee: A Biography* (1995); Thomas Connelly, *The Marble Man: Robert E. Lee and His Image in American Society* (1975); and Alan Nolan's controversial *Lee Considered* (1991). Biographies of other prominent Confederate commanders include Frank E. Vandiver, *Mighty Stonewall* (1957); William G. Piston, *Lee's Tarnished Lieutenant: James Longstreet and His Place in Southern History* (1987); Jeffry D. Wert, *General James Longstreet* (1993); Craig L. Symonds, *Joseph E. Johnston* (1992); Emory Thomas, *Bold Dragoon: The Life of J. E. B. Stuart* (1986); T. Harry Williams, *P. G. T. Beauregard: Napoleon in Gray* (1955); Charles P. Roland, *Albert Sidney Johnston: Soldier of Three Republics* (1964); Richard McMurry, *John Bell Hood and the War for Southern Independence* (1982); and the two-volume biography of *Braxton Bragg and Confederate Defeat* by Grady McWhiney (Vol. I, 1969) and Judith Lee Hallock (Vol. II, 1991).

There are literally hundreds of books about Civil War battles and campaigns. Among those studies most worth consulting for battles in the eastern theater are Stephen W. Sears, *Landscape Turned Red: The Battle of Antietam* (1983); John J. Hennessy, *Return to Bull Run: The Campaign and Battle of Second Manassas* (1993); Edwin B. Coddington, *The Gettysburg*

Campaign: A Study in Command (1968); and Gordon H. Rhea, *The Battle of the Wilderness, May 5–6, 1864* (1994). Among the best studies of the war in the western theater are Wiley Sword, *Shiloh: Bloody April* (1974); Glenn Tucker, *Chickamauga: Bloody Battle in the West* (1961); Peter Cozzens, *The Shipwreck of Their Hopes: The Battles for Chattanooga* (1994); and Albert Castel, *Decision in the West: The Atlanta Campaign of 1864* (1992). We still lack definitive studies of the Vicksburg campaign and the various phases of Grant's campaign against Lee in 1864–1865, especially the siege of Petersburg and the Appomattox campaign. Students looking to explore the operations in the Trans-Mississippi West should start with Alvin Josephy, *The Civil War in the American West* (1991).

For the war on the water, see Virgil Carrington Jones, *The Civil War at Sea* (3 vols.: 1960–62); James M. Merrill, *Battle Flags South: The Story of the Civil War Navies Down the Mississippi* (1970); William N. Still, Jr., *Iron Afloat: The Story of the Confederate Armorclads* (1971); Stephen R. Wise, *Lifeline of the Confederacy: Blockade-Running During the Civil War* (1988); William C. Davis, *Duel Between the First Ironclads* (1975); and Rowena Reed, *Combined Operations in the Civil War* (1978).

Bell Wiley's two studies, *The Life of Johnny Reb* (1943) and *The Life of Billy Yank* (1952), were the first serious examinations of the life of the common soldier. Two books by Reid Mitchell, *Civil War Soldiers* (1988) and *The Vacant Chair: The Northern Soldier Leaves Home* (1993), are very suggestive about how the war shaped soldiers' lives, as is Gerald F. Linderman's *Embattled Courage: The Experience of Combat in the Civil War* (1987). Joseph T. Glatthaar's *The March to the Sea and Beyond: Sherman's Troops in the Savannah and Carolina Campaigns* (1985) and Lee Kennett's *Marching Through Georgia: The Story of Soldiers and Civilians During Sherman's Campaign* (1994) offer readers a closer look at how soldiers behaved toward civilians. James M. McPherson's *What They Fought For, 1861–1865* (1994) is richly suggestive about soldiers' motivations for fighting. On the experience of African Americans in uniform, one should consult Dudley Taylor Cornish, *The Sable Arm: Negro Troops in the Union Army, 1861–1865* (1956); and Joseph T. Glatthaar, *Forged in Battle: The Civil War Alliance of Black Soldiers and White Officers* (1990).

Civilians

Anne C. Rose's *Victorian America and the Civil War* (1992) and Louise L. Stevenson's *The Victorian Homefront: American Thought and Culture, 1860–1880* (1991) offer overviews of Civil War society. Mary E. Massey's *Bonnet Brigades* (1966) and Catherine Clinton and Nina Silber, eds., *Divided Houses: Gender and the Civil War* (1992) contain valuable information on women and the war. Grace Palladino's *Another Civil War: Labor, Capitol, and the State in the Anthracite Regions of Pennsylvania, 1840–1868* (1990) and J. Matthew Gallman's *Mastering Wartime: A Social History of Philadelphia during the Civil War* (1990) present two perspectives on the war in the Keystone State. For resistance to the draft see Adrian Cook, *The Armies of the Streets: The New York City Draft Riots of 1863* (1974), and Iver Bernstein, *The New York City Draft Riots: Their Significance for American Society and Politics in the Age of the Civil War* (1990). Stanton Garner's *The Civil War World of Herman Melville* (1993) is a panoramic view of Northern society.

Several works explore key aspects of the North and the war. Mark Neely, in *The Fate of Liberty: Abraham Lincoln and Civil Liberties* (1991), persuasively argues that previous images of the repressive policies of the Lincoln administration are much exaggerated. Harold M. Hyman's *A More Perfect Union: The Impact of the Civil War and Reconstruction on the Constitution* (1973) demonstrates the conflict's impact on concepts of governance and law. Phillip S. Paludan's *A Covenant with Death: The Constitution, Law, and Equality in the Civil War Era* (1975) and George Frederickson's *The Inner Civil War: Northern Intellectuals and the Crisis of Disunion* (1965) demonstrate the ambivalence of many Northern whites to the change wrought by the conflict, while *Economic Change in the Civil War Era* (1965), David T.

Gilchrist and William D. Lewis, eds., collects several of the most important essays on this question.

Among the leading works that look at how Southern civilians experienced the war are Charles W. Ramsdell, *Behind the Lines in the Southern Confederacy* (1944); Bell I. Wiley, *The Plain People of the Confederacy* (1943); George C. Rable, *Civil Wars: Women and the Crisis of Southern Nationalism* (1991); Bell I. Wiley, *Confederate Women* (1975); and Mary Elizabeth Massey, *Refugee Life in the Confederacy* (1964). Wayne K. Durrill, *War of Another Kind: A Southern Community in the Great Rebellion* (1990); John Cimprich, *Slavery's End in Tennessee, 1861–1865* (1985); Clarence L. Mohr, *On the Threshold of Freedom: Masters and Slaves in Civil War Georgia* (1986); and Stephen V. Ash, *Middle Tennessee Society Transformed, 1860–1870* (1988), trace how the war reshaped Southern society. Michael Fellman's *Inside War: The Guerrilla Conflict in Missouri during the American Civil War* (1989) and Richard McCaslin's *Tainted Breeze* (1994) suggest how fierce internal conflict could become.

Emancipation and Reconstruction

James M. McPherson's *The Struggle for Equality: Abolitionists and the Negro in the Civil War and Reconstruction* (1964) traces how abolitionists pushed for their long-sought goal of emancipation. Benjamin Quarles's *The Negro in the Civil War* (1953) looks at blacks in the North as well as the South, while Bell I. Wiley, *Southern Negroes, 1861–1865* (1938); C. Peter Ripley, *Slaves and Freedmen in Civil War Louisiana* (1976); and Willie Lee Rose, *Rehearsal for Reconstruction: The Port Royal Experiment* (1964) suggest the complex meanings of slavery and emancipation. The border states provide a different perspective on the process of emancipation; see Barbara Jeanne Fields, *Slavery and Freedom on the Middle Ground: Maryland during the Nineteenth Century* (1985); Charles L. Wagandt, *The Mighty Revolution: Negro Emancipation in Maryland, 1862–1864* (1964); and Victor B. Howard, *Black Liberation in Kentucky: Emancipation and Freedom, 1862–1884* (1983). Peter Maslowski's *Treason Must Be Made Odious: Military Occupation and Wartime Reconstruction in Nashville, Tennessee, 1862–1865* (1978) and Louis S. Gerteis's *From Contraband to Freedman: Federal Policy Toward Southern Blacks, 1861–1865* (1973) examine how the Union military handled issues connected to wartime reconstruction.

John Hope Franklin's *The Emancipation Proclamation* (1963, 1995) remains the best study of the events leading to the issuance of Lincoln's war measure. Herman Belz's *Reconstructing the Union: Theory and Policy During the Civil War* (1969) traces the debate over Reconstruction in Congress. In *Lincoln's Plan of Reconstruction* (1960), William B. Hesseltine suggests that Lincoln considered several approaches, never settling upon any one. LaWanda Cox's *Lincoln and Black Freedom: A Study in Presidential Leadership* (1981) emphasizes the limits politics placed upon Lincoln's actions, making pragmatism and moderation essential. Peyton McCrary's *Abraham Lincoln and Reconstruction: The Louisiana Experiment* (1978) may push its case for Lincoln's radicalism a bit too far. Finally, Robert F. Durden, *The Gray and the Black: The Confederate Debate on Emancipation* (1972) recounts the course of that controversial decision.

INDEX

America's Civil War

Copyeditor: Andrew J. Davidson
Production editor: Lucy Herz
Typesetter: City Desktop
Cartographer: James Bier
Printer: Versa Press

About the author: Brooks D. Simpson, associate professor of history at Arizona State University, received his B.A. from the University of Virginia and his M.A. and Ph.D. from the University of Wisconsin–Madison. His other books include *The Political Education of Henry Adams, Advice after Appomattox,* and *Let Us Have Peace: Ulysses S. Grant and the Politics of War and Reconstruction, 1861–1868,* a History Book Club selection.